The Protected Vista

The Protected Vista draws a historical lineage from the eighteenth-century picturesque to present-day planning policy, highlighting how the values embedded within familiar views have developed over time through appropriation by diverse groups for cultural and political purposes.

The book examines the intellectual construction of the protected vista, questioning the values entrenched within the view, by whom, and how they are observed and disseminated, to reveal how these views have been, and continue to be, part of a changing historical and political narrative. With a deeper knowledge and understanding of the shifting values in urban views, we will be better equipped to make decisions surrounding their protection in our urban centres. The book identifies the origins of current view protection policy in the aesthetic convention of the picturesque, drawing on a range of illustrated examples in the UK, the US, Australia, Canada and South Africa, to serve as a useful reference for students, researchers and academics in architecture, architectural conservation, landscape and urban planning.

Tom Brigden is Leverhulme Early Career Research Fellow at Newcastle University, UK, and Associate at Purcell, the UK's leading conservation specialist. His heritage consultancy work has included compiling view assessments for significant historic buildings, from London to Melbourne, Australia.

Routledge Research in Architectural Conservation and Historic Preservation
Series Editor: Wen-Shao Chang

The Routledge Research in Architectural Conservation and Historic Preservation series provides the reader with the latest scholarship in the field of building conservation. The series publishes research from across the globe and covers areas as diverse as restoration techniques, preservation theory, technology, digital reconstruction, structures, materials, details, case studies and much more. By making these studies available to the worldwide academic community, the series aims to promote quality architectural preservation research.

Architectural Conservation and Restoration in Norway and Russia
Edited by Evgeny Khodakovsky and Siri Skjold Lexau

Reconstructing Historic Landmarks
Fabrication, Negotiation, and the Past
Wayde Brown

Equity in Heritage Conservation
The Case of Ahmedabad, India
Jigna Desai

The Protected Vista
An Intellectual and Cultural History
Tom Brigden

www.routledge.com/architecture/series/RRACHP

The Protected Vista
An Intellectual and Cultural History

Tom Brigden

LONDON AND NEW YORK

First published 2019 by Routledge

2 Park Square, Milton Park, Abingdon, Oxon, OX14 4RN
605 Third Avenue, New York, NY 10017

Routledge is an imprint of the Taylor & Francis Group, an informa business

First issued in paperback 2020

Copyright © 2019 Tom Brigden

The right of Tom Brigden to be identified as author of this work has been asserted by him in accordance with sections 77 and 78 of the Copyright, Designs and Patents Act 1988.

All rights reserved. No part of this book may be reprinted or reproduced or utilised in any form or by any electronic, mechanical, or other means, now known or hereafter invented, including photocopying and recording, or in any information storage or retrieval system, without permission in writing from the publishers.

Notice:
Product or corporate names may be trademarks or registered trademarks, and are used only for identification and explanation without intent to infringe.

British Library Cataloguing-in-Publication Data
A catalogue record for this book is available from the British Library

Library of Congress Cataloging-in-Publication Data
A catalog record for this book has been requested

ISBN: 978-1-138-50264-2 (hbk)
ISBN: 978-0-367-72928-8 (pbk)

Typeset in Sabon
by Apex CoVantage, LLC

To Mum
A constant source of enthusiasm and encouragement, and an enduring inspiration.

Contents

Introduction   1

PART 1
The origins of the protected view: the view from Richmond Hill   7

1   Introduction   9
 Early history 9
 Royal retreat 10
 Richmond Hill: the oblique aerial view 11
 Terrace Walk 15
 'Scopic regimes' and 'Cartesian perspectivalism' 17
 Prince Henry, Solomon de Caus and the Renaissance gardens of Richmond-upon-Thames 19
 Perspective and the theatre: Richmond Hill theatre 22
 Theatre of human interaction: Richmond Hill pleasure garden 23
 Richmond Hill villas 26
 Alexander Pope and the naturalistic garden 28
 Kent, Burlington and the influence of the Italian landscape 33
 Richmond's poetic landscape 35
 Theorising a picturesque convention 38
 Gothic's absorption of the picturesque 44
 Centring the imperial landscape in Richmond 47
 The railway, suburbia and the persistence of the picturesque 49
 'Indignation': what man owns the glory that Turner painted? 61
 Concluding remarks 70

PART 2
Translating images of Richmond   81

2   Introduction   83

3   Two American Richmonds: 'Richmond Hill', New York, and Richmond, Virginia   87
    'Richmond Hill', Manhattan Island, New York 88
    Richmond, Virginia 91
    The view as symbol of American nationalism: Church Hill, Richmond, Virginia 95
    The view, and its manipulation, in the work of Benjamin Henry Latrobe 98
    Latrobe and the picturesque 100
    Latrobe's Virginia villas 101
    Thomas Jefferson in Richmond 103
    Libby Hill's Greek Revival villas: Richmond as classic city 106
    The literary portrayal of Libby Hill and the visual construction of the 'South' 108
    Photography and the city 110
    Monumentalising the view: Libby Hill as memorial to the Confederate cause 113
    Windsor Farms: suburban projections of 'Old England' 115
    William Lawrence Bottomley: re-imagining 'colonial' Richmond 120
    The enduring re-inscription of Richmond's romantic image 122
    Cinematic itineraries in the nostalgic picturesque: Colonial Parkway 124
    The moving image: parkways and cinema 126
    Scenic byways: projecting the romantic vision 127
    Interstate image corridors: the persistence of parkway vision 131
    Concluding remarks 134

4   Richmond, NSW   141
    The Hawkesbury River 141
    'Discovery' 142
    The picturesque and the panoramic 143
    Three 'Richmond Hills' 145
    Developing the Hawkesbury landscape: Governors Grose and Macquarie 147

The Frontier Wars 151
Depicting the Hawkesbury 152
The persistence of the Hawkesbury picturesque 159
'No trucks through historic square!' 160
Concluding remarks 162

5 **Richmond Hill, Port Elizabeth, South Africa**   167
Strangers' Location 168
Richmond Hill 173
Richmond Hill as emblematic gentrification 176
Policing Richmond Hill: vision, surveillance and the SRA 183
Concluding observations 187

Conclusion   192
A sense of nostalgia 193
The aesthetic convention of the picturesque 195
Regional, cultural or national identity 196
The power of the gaze 198
The question of authenticity 199
Concluding observations 203

Bibliography   206
Index   213

Introduction

It is a common view among academics that the visual sense has been privileged in Western thought, from Plato and Aristotle's association of vision with reason to the structure of European languages where "to see is to believe" and to "shine a light" on something is to uncover its "truth". Dubbed 'ocularcentrism' by Marshall McLuhan, Martin Jay and others, such a privileging of the visual sense may be observed in the everyday material products of culture, from painting to literature, advertising, branding and visual merchandising. At the same time, there is a theme in Western scholarship that the visual sense has been inseparably bound up with notions of power and control, from the military function of the sightline through to the psychological effect of the gaze as deployed in nineteenth-century prison design and the continuing expansion of contemporary digital surveillance technologies.

Despite these well-established themes, little research has been conducted into the phenomena of the 'protected view' in contemporary planning policy, by which I mean the propensity for cities, World Heritage Sites and cultural landscapes to impose rigid systems of control over the visual impact of new development. The City of London is a powerful example: its skyline is determined by "protected vistas" – lines of sight from Primrose Hill, Hampstead Heath, Richmond Park and other famous prospects, as described by planning policy guidance, including the mayor of London's *View Management Framework* (2007). The City of London now recognises 26 protected vistas and 52 designated viewing points. London's sightlines determine the profile and location of many of the city's buildings, exerting power over the economic value of real estate and the sites of commerce. These vistas act to shape the city aesthetically, by preserving and enforcing particularly admired visual compositions, as well as historically and politically, by promoting certain landmarks and associated narratives. Where development has been perceived as 'damaging' to views deemed to be of cultural and/or historical value, controversy has followed. London has been a hotbed of such controversy, from UNESCO's threats to remove the Tower of London from its list of World Heritage Sites – a reaction to surrounding commercial developments – to criticism over the effect of

Renzo Piano's 'Shard' upon views of St Paul's Cathedral. In each case, development has been perceived to 'damage' vistas, visual environments or settings invested with values beyond the purely intrinsic.

Such systems often rely upon an understanding of cities and sites as a series of fixed visual compositions, to be perceived at eye level from static viewpoints, and determined by the scientific apparatus of vectors, planes and coordinates. In this sense, one could view the phenomenon of the protected view – as exemplified by London's *View Management Framework* – as a natural extension of Western ocularcentrism, a typical example of the privileging of the visual over other sensual perceptions of cities, and a demonstration of the use of vision in patterns of control.

As cities such as London continue to grow in population, and to increase density through developing upwards, the impact of tall buildings upon significant urban views is likely to be increasingly contentious. Issues of view protection in the development of contemporary cities are often financially and politically risky for developers, architects, planners and politicians alike. It is likely, therefore, that policies of view protection will become an ever greater consideration in the management of our historic environment and yet there is little understanding of the ideas that underpin such policies.

The aim of this book is to investigate the intellectual construction of the protected vista – namely, *what values* are associated with particular vistas, *by whom*, and *how* are they observed and interpreted? What does the act of view protection say about the society that enforces it, both at home and abroad, and how is this message disseminated? In short, I will illustrate how the protected vista is loaded with shifting historical and political narratives, which can be 'read' by the observer.

In order to narrow the search for embedded values, the first part of this book will focus on one particular viewpoint, the view of London from Richmond Hill, Surrey, UK, demonstrating how, within this particular view-shed, a remarkable proliferation of writers, poets, artists, architects and landscape architects developed a theory of the picturesque from the early eighteenth century onwards. The focus is the picturesque view from Richmond Hill, which was celebrated by leading artists and writers in the eighteenth and nineteenth centuries and is the earliest vista to have been afforded statutory protection as we now understand it.[1] It is argued here that the values informing global view protection policies remain, in no small part, the values of the eighteenth- and nineteenth-century English landscape movement as produced by, and which contributed to the production of, the view from Richmond Hill. It is important to understand the historical development of this specific vista in order to appreciate how protected view policies continue to overlay eighteenth-century picturesque values onto contemporary world cities.

The second part of the book will follow the famed view from Richmond Hill, which, transmitted via the prolific distribution of mass-produced prints, photographs and other media, would go on to etch its likeness in the architectural and urban form of towns and cities across the former British colonies. It is the first attempt to connect the histories of four 'other' Richmonds – Richmond Hill, Manhattan, New York (USA); Richmond, Virginia (USA); Richmond, New South Wales (Australia); and Richmond Hill, Port Elizabeth (South Africa) – with the intellectual history of the picturesque in landscape design and the 'English landscape movement'. It is also the first substantial account of how contemporary view protection policies remain saturated with the values of the picturesque. In doing so it will demonstrate, via the view's transposition onto 'other' landscapes of former British colonies, how the simple composition of a river's bend, glimpsed obliquely from a wooded hilltop, has come to symbolise a complex, apparently contradictory and shifting series of historical and political narratives. Visions of Richmond Hill, both real and imagined, have played a part in determining the architectural and cultural development of former colonies, and in the cases discussed in this book have seemingly been complicit in the power relationships of exclusion and displacement. By following the evolution of these narratives and emergent preservation movements, I suggest that the very act of a vista's protection serves to reinforce particular dominant interpretations of cities and landscapes, both defining identities and excluding others. At the same time, the intellectual and cultural history of the view from Richmond Hill has shifted in parallel with increasingly kinetic and systematised understandings of the view, as seen from the camera's viewfinder, the train window and the car windscreen and on the cinema screen.

The study of this small selection of international 'Richmonds' is an important and inseparable component of the intellectual history of the view from Richmond Hill, revealing how values laid down in eighteenth-century Richmond-upon-Thames were overlaid upon new contexts, recycled and reinterpreted over the course of centuries. It seems that the well-known view and the values it represented repeatedly resurface in unexpected locations. In eighteenth-century Manhattan, connotations of the view played a part in the power relations between empire and colonial subject, serving as the backdrop to the domestic lives of influential political figures, and oscillating between American and British ownership. At around the same time, Richmond, Virginia, explored in Chapter 3, was being developed almost as a reinterpretation of Richmond-upon-Thames, influencing the architecture of American and British immigrant architects alike. The works of these architects were part of a broader cultural movement which set the city on a path towards its identification with the great classical cities of the past, and which would later boil over in the ideological gulf between North and South which precipitated the American Civil War. Meanwhile, in New South Wales, Australia, explored in Chapter 4, the anticipated discovery of new 'Richmond Hills' fuelled exploration and domestication of the supposedly 'empty' antipodean landscape, appropriating indigenous lands for both British aesthetic consumption and commercial profit. Such a story is echoed in the displacement of indigenous communities from the landscape of Richmond Hill, Port Elizabeth, South Africa, explored in Chapter 5, and in the continued enforcement of a romantic colonial gaze via the city's regeneration initiatives and regimes of surveillance. As such, the values embedded within the view from Richmond Hill recur in distinctive and yet surprisingly consistent ways, revealing the power of the view, and its perceptions, to shape both physical and political terrains across the world.

For its sources this book relies heavily on 'material culture', drawing upon a wide variety of media, from fine art and literature to postcards, posters, advertisements, novels and newspaper articles. This range of sources demonstrates the widespread and ongoing reproduction of picturesque images of Richmond Hill, and illustrates the addressing of this imagery to multiple and diverse audiences. The intellectual histories of each Richmond given here are necessarily detailed, as it is only through tracing the recurring details of imagery and language that the recycling, absorption and development of specific values may be highlighted. From its development in the mid-eighteenth century, the image of Richmond has been transposed through shifting media technologies, while its continued reproduction has rendered it familiar – capable even of self-perpetuation without acknowledgement of its presence or influence. Thus, images of Richmond Hill cease to function simply as pictorial representations of a physical location but, via our saturation in a 'mediascape' composed of thousands of images, have become symbols of a landscape paradigm, a model that may be translated from any one landscape or location to any other.

This book will argue that the origins of view protection lie in the emergence of picturesque visual conventions. At Richmond-upon-Thames, the coincidence of these ideas may be seen as both temporal, developing from the early eighteenth century onwards, and geographical: the Richmond landscape served as both model and test-bed for a fledgling picturesque movement and fittingly became home to Britain's first statutorily protected vista. The campaign to protect this view, deemed to be a component of Britain's shared national and cultural heritage, may also be viewed in relation to this particular landscape's role in the development of a national trope: the idea of the 'English landscape'. If views of Richmond have, since at least the early eighteenth century, been increasingly layered with such cultural meanings, their subsequent protection may be interpreted as the reinforcement of embedded narratives. Thus, despite common perceptions of the picturesque as "a synonym for aesthetic failure, trivial cultural products and naïve tastes",[2] one could argue that contemporary view protection policy continues to be informed by the picturesque, inscribing visual traditions, and their associated discourses, into the urban and architectural form of contemporary cities across the globe.

Notes

1 Certainly, it was the first view to be afforded statutory protection for public benefit within the Anglo-American context, though private views protected by legal covenants may be traced to earlier periods.
2 J. Macarthur, *The Picturesque: Architecture, Disgust and Other Irregularities* (London: Routledge, 2007), p. 1.

Part 1
The origins of the protected view
The view from Richmond Hill

1 Introduction

The aim of Part 1 of this book is to outline the complex history of London's original protected vista, that of the River Thames viewed from the terrace atop Richmond Hill, Richmond-upon-Thames. The idea of that view is produced by a series of narratives encoded within the Richmond landscape, which repeatedly resurface in accounts of the view during the course of centuries. These narratives are decisive to any appreciation of the view, and – as the original protected vista, in the sense that it is now understood – they are decisive in the conception of the idea of the protected view more broadly. This chapter will argue that the origin of the protected vista reflects a desire to reinforce particular cultural and intellectual values within the representation of landscape and, subsequently, cityscape.

The structure of this chapter is chronological, beginning with a historical survey of the Thames landscape between Hampton and Kew. The intention of this is to set the Richmond Hill vista within its wider geographical, cultural and intellectual contexts. As we shall see, this landscape has for centuries been perceived as more than its physical topography, as the setting for Caesar's crossing of the Thames and the crowning place of Saxon kings, a history certainly not lost upon subsequent monarchs who located their courts here, each generation positioning themselves symbolically within a romanticised and apparently seamless historical lineage. This chapter will outline the evolution and development of this landscape and account for the ideas which form its cultural topography.

Early history

The Thames between Hampton and Kew suddenly enters written history with Caesar's account of the conquest of Britain.[1] At this time, the river acted as a natural boundary between a complex system of tribal territories. The region stretching from the northern bank of the Thames as far north as East Anglia was ruled over by Cassivellaunus, king of the Celtic tribe known as the Catuvellauni.[2] According to some scholars, it is from the Celtic period that we inherit the word 'Thames', interpreted as 'dark one'.[3] Brentford also claims to have been the crossing point of Caesar's invasion force in

54 BC, as geographically it was the simplest and lowest place to ford the tidal river. Remains of sharpened stakes defending the crossing point, as mentioned in Caesar's accounts, have been discovered on the edge of the Duke of Northumberland's Syon estate.

After the collapse of Roman order in the fifth century AD, the area north of the Thames was gradually settled by Saxon farmers. Situated between the East and West Saxon regions, this stretch of the Thames was identified as the 'Middle Saxon' region, reflected today in the name of Middlesex County. Many of the area's place names are inherited from the Saxons – for example, the 'hamms' or meanders of the river at Twickenham ('Twicca's hamm') and Petersham ('Peohtric's hamm').[4] Early in its history, this was a royal landscape, the town of 'Kingston' taking its name from the council held there by King Egbert of the kingdom of Wessex in the ninth century.[5] The kings of Wessex continued to hold their coronations there until the Danish king Canute defeated Edward Ironside in 1016, bringing to an end the West Saxon dynasty.

Royal retreat

What's important to note for the purposes of this book is that royal associations were deeply rooted in historical narratives of the Thames landscape at Richmond, stretching back in a supposedly seamless lineage to Saxon, Roman and Celtic kings. It is perhaps no coincidence then that royalty returned to the area in 1299 when, as a refuge from the insanitary conditions of the City of London, Edward I relocated his court to the manor house at 'Shene' (Richmond).[6] Despite Edward III's demolition of the palace in 1394, monarchs did return some 20 years later; Henry V and then Henry VI rebuilt the palace at Shene, only for it to be destroyed again by fire in 1497.[7]

Despite demolition, abandonment, rebuilding and fire, the palace rose again during Henry VII's prosperous and peaceful reign, acquiring its famed silhouette of towers, pinnacles and heraldry. At this time, the palace was renamed after Henry's favourite earldom of Richmond, North Yorkshire. It has been argued that the chivalric devices, turrets and dramatic skyline seen in Anton van den Wyngaerde's sketches of the palace (1561–62) are a romantic reference to Henry's Norman castle at Richmond, North Yorkshire, itself similarly sited on a hill commanding extensive views over a bend in a river.[8] Whatever truth there is in this, the palace was clearly intended to leave an impression on the visitor approaching from the river. Henry VIII was frequently in residence at his father's Richmond Palace in his early years, and it was later Elizabeth I's favoured winter refuge and the place of her death in 1603.[9] Beyond the palace of Richmond, huge areas of land were appropriated by royalty for the pursuit of pleasures such as hunting, and to feed the enormous retinues of the royal court. Charles I found James I's former deer park so inadequate that in 1637 he enclosed 2,500 acres of heath land on Richmond Hill with an 8-mile-long brick wall, thus creating Richmond Park.[10]

Gradually, the old palace of Richmond fell out of favour in preference for the more comfortable Hampton Court upstream near Kingston, acquired by Henry VIII from the unfortunate Cardinal Wolsey. When fire ripped through Whitehall Palace in 1698, Hampton Court was established as the primary royal residence and subsequently greatly remodelled by William III, involving the demolition of Henry VIII's private apartments and the erection of a new baroque palace by Christopher Wren.

Royal patronage brought many of the great names of art, architecture and landscape architecture to the Thames between Hampton and Kew. Prince Henry, James I's son, had planned a Renaissance court at Richmond laid out with magnificent gardens designed by hydraulic engineer Solomon de Caus and architect Inigo Jones. Unfortunately, this scheme, which included an enormous Italianate giant and grotto located on an island in the Thames, was abandoned upon Henry's death.[11]

Wren's remodelling of Hampton Court complemented Charles II's earlier gardens, laid out by André and Gabriel Mollet, and an elaborate parterre by Daniel Marot (1689). The three radiating avenues of Hampton Court, the 'patte d'oie' or goose-foot laid out by Charles II,[12] were originally aligned on 'eye-catchers' positioned across the river, with the northern avenue terminating in the spire of All Saint's church, Kingston, and the southern avenue planned to terminate in a trianon designed by William Talman in 1699 (unexecuted).[13] These early landscape schemes are notable partly because they provide the context in which the early picturesque movement evolved. Prince Henry's Pratolino giant in the Thames and Charles II's vistas indicate a developing appreciation of the naturalistic river landscape of the Thames, which would later prove to be of immense influence upon artists, architects and landscape architects.

Richmond Hill: the oblique aerial view

The extraordinary wealth of aristocratic seats and gardens developed along this stretch of the Thames is evidence that landscape views of the river have long been admired. A clue to the popularity of this particular landscape can be gleaned from a consideration of its many representations. Upon inspection, one finds that many early depictions of the Thames between Hampton and Kew adopt an oblique aerial point of view in which the eye is directed both downwards and laterally. The oblique aerial view is most commonly recognised from the summit of a hill, the 'prospect', meaning "an extensive or commanding sight or view".[14] The geological forces which shaped the terraces above the Thames floodplain created ideal vantage points from which to view the landscape in this manner, but the popularity of the oblique view also points to a distinctive perception of correct, authentic vision and landscape. The particular authority accorded to the oblique aerial view is important in appreciating the potency and longevity of the Richmond Hill vista.

Comparisons could be made, for example, between Richmond Hill's elevated prospect and the practice of cartography, where the map-maker takes up an imaginary raised position, thus acquiring the power to create boundaries and divide up the land as seen from a heavenly viewpoint, wielding a godlike mastery over the landscape. The cartographical use of an imagined aerial vantage point is demonstrated by the depiction of partial elevations of buildings in early maps, as if the map-maker really could view the city in its entirety from a nearby hilltop. For example, engraver Franz Hogenberg's bird's-eye plan of London published in Georg Braun's *Civitates Orbis Terrarum* (1572) illustrates the city as though it were observed from the summit of a hill by four foreground figures. Braun and Hogenberg's collection of prospect views and city plans was published in tandem with *Theatrum Orbis Terrarum*, which, as a systematic collection of maps in uniform style, was perhaps the first true atlas.[15] It has been suggested that the simultaneous publication of these two works reflects two distinct audiences. Where the latter work was produced for serious geographers, the former was intended for wider distribution as a form of travel literature. This intention is highlighted by the former's additions of foreground figures in local costume, depicted as if observing the idealised view from a real hilltop. Thus, one could argue that the *Civitates Orbis Terrarum* provided the observer with a visual experience of the city akin to the hilltop prospect, whereas the *Theatrum Orbis Terrarum* presented only an abstract planimetric projection.[16]

Samuel Edgerton has seen the development of the orthographically projected plan as a solution to the problem of the limited boundaries of the visual field as observed obliquely from a single point. Even the orthographic projection, in an age before true aerial imagery became technologically achievable, was surveyed from an oblique position using a staff and ranging rod.[17] If the oblique view focused reflected rays of light from the observed object into a single point, the orthographic projection relocated the conceptual viewpoint to an infinite height, so that the rays become parallel to one another. This scientific conceptualisation of an infinitely high viewpoint, from where the whole structure of the world may be observed and understood, recalls Leon Battista Alberti's use of the winged eye as his crest, reflecting his opinion that an understanding of the laws of vision could allow one to approach God's view of the world.[18] It could be argued, therefore, that the oblique aerial view of the Thames landscape, as observed from the raised vantage point of Richmond Hill, afforded the viewer a palpable sense of power and mastery over the landscape.

This may explain the construction of a huge earthen mound on the crest of Richmond Hill, thought to have originated as a prehistoric burial mound. This mound, known as King Henry's Mound, is popularly believed to have later served a function associated with hunting in the royal park, the raised view serving as strategic lookout or as a place from which to observe the spectacle. Indeed, there were structures serving this function associated with the royal palaces: Greenwich, Richmond, Whitehall and Hampton Court all possessed tiltyards with raised terraces, mounts and towers designed to accommodate spectators of military-style jousting tournaments.[19]

The mount didn't always serve a military or sporting purpose, but is often associated with garden design from the medieval period right through to the nineteenth century.[20] Henry VIII commissioned an elaborate mount garden at Hampton Court in 1533, reputedly utilising over 256,000 bricks and "12,000 quicksets (hawthorns) to hold the soil".[21] The enormous two-storey banqueting house crowning its summit – long since demolished – presented the diner with an expansive oblique aerial view of the river, reinforcing a sense of empowerment over the landscape. The prospect was also a source of aesthetic delight, where the activity of boats on the river provided an ever-changing backdrop to court festivities.

Other Thames-side gardens also conspicuously featured mounts. Elizabethan master-mason Robert Smythson recorded the mount garden of Twickenham Park in a plan of c. 1609, indicating four circular mounts raised at the corners of a square formal garden. Roy Strong has suggested that from these points the observer could contemplate the plan of the garden, which, with its six concentric rings of trees, can be interpreted as a microcosm and diagram of the pre-Copernican universe.[22] By taking up a raised viewpoint and looking down upon the garden, the observer is raised to the all-seeing and all-powerful position of the creator – creator of the garden as allegorical universe. One could argue that this oblique aerial view, a common feature of seventeenth-century Mannerist garden design achieved with mounts, earthworks and terraces, may have influenced the way in which artists chose to depict landscapes, reflected in their adoption of an imagined bird's-eye viewpoint.

Later, the aerial viewpoint would be adopted by military surveys, which, in a similar way to depictions of gardens, may be associated with notions of power, control and the appropriation of landscapes. For example, the artist Paul Sandby, well known for his aerial views of eighteenth-century aristocratic gardens, had originally been employed as chief draughtsman on the military survey of North Britain in 1747–52.[23] These military surveys of cities, landscapes and coastlines would later become the working drawings for the popular panoramas of the mid-eighteenth century,[24] which popularised the idea of the prospect and made it accessible to the general public.

Given the extent to which images of Richmond, exported across the world, were complicit in forging ideas of imperial and national identity (explored in Chapters 2–5), it is important to note that in the proliferation of the panorama the reverse was also true: images of Britain's far-flung colonies displayed in London also fed the imperial gaze, appropriating distant locales in the process (e.g., the Panorama of Sydney, Australia, exhibited in London's Leicester Square, 1829).[25] For the price of a ticket, the population of Britain's industrialising cities could experience travelling exhibits of 360-degree views, representing cities, landscapes, battles and historical events, both at home and abroad. Competing promoters profited from the popularity of such spectacles, demonstrating the willingness with which individuals paid for the privilege of viewing a prospect.[26]

The commercial potential of the prospect, harnessed by the panorama, is also reflected at this time in the auction notices of contemporary London; descriptions of 'genteel' or 'enchanting' prospects command a value as objects of sales inventories. In *The London Town Garden*, Todd Longstaffe-Gowan suggests that, in many cases, the amenity of a prospect was sufficient to overcome the lack of any real access to a garden.[27] This ownership of a prospect, administrated through complex rights and building covenants, reflects the "proprietorial gaze"[28] of the observer and the objectification of landscapes caught within this gaze. The prospect raised the status of the observer and at the same time "marked the estrangement of an observer who stood outside of the landscape and looked in".[29] According to eighteenth-century landscape designer Stephen Switzer, this division allowed the observer to "see the busie [*sic*] World acting their several Parts of their Labour and Toil below, [which] fills the Mind with immense Idea's [*sic*], and makes the World below us *as our own*".[30] Switzer's comment highlights the superior status of the observer, positioned outside of and above the landscape, over the rural peasant toiling *in* the landscape *below*.

One could argue that this visual opposition between landscape and observer was accentuated by a physical separation in the architecture of the landowning elite. For example, Wyngaerde's sketches of Richmond Palace show a raised gallery surrounding the Privy Garden from where the king could survey the intricate symbolism of the knot gardens below without having to venture outside. Likewise, Malcolm Andrews has discussed the use of the *piano nobile*,[31] or raised principal storey, in the country houses of the seventeenth and eighteenth centuries,[32] from where the observer could gaze obliquely across the landscape but had little physical connection with it. This vantage point also makes sense of the highly geometric parterre gardens of this period, whose intricate patterns, like embroidered textile, could be properly appreciated only from above.

In *The Theory and Practice of Gardening* (1712),[33] John James refers to the parterres at James Johnston's riverside garden of Orleans House, Twickenham, part of which still stands. Here,

> A Parterre is the first Thing that should present itself to sight [. . .]; as well on Account of the Opening it affords the Building, as for the Beauty and Splendour wherewith it constantly entertains the Eye, when seen from every Window of the House.

James then goes on to state how regard should be given to the wider landscape, where, if the

> Prospect [. . .] be agreeable; [. . .] the sides of the Parterres should be kept entirely open [. . .] to make best of our View, and taking Care not to shut it up with Groves, unless they are planted with Quincunce [sic] [. . .] which hinder not the Eye from [. . .] discovering the Beauties of the Prospect on every Side.[34]

James's comments are indicative of this period in which large glazed sash windows with evermore refined frames introduced the landscape into the house, as if it were a series of landscape paintings hung on the walls of the grand reception rooms.

What is important to understand here is that the landscape of Richmond-upon-Thames illustrates the emergence of, and gave rise to, a series of tropes which later came to characterise the picturesque: the oblique aerial view; the raised viewpoint; the elevated status of the observer; the idea of the subjectivity of the viewer as the centre of his or her own universe; the emphasis, and creation, of curated opportunities for viewing the landscape and architectural objects within it; and, indeed, the emerging objectification of landscape and architecture itself through the located, perspectivised age of the gaze.

Terrace Walk

The view from Richmond Hill, like other elevated views, might be said to elevate the status of the observer through its oblique aerial vantage point over the landscape. Relationships of power in landscape vistas have also been accentuated through the use of perspective techniques to reinforce the separation between observer and object, as demonstrated by Renaissance axial garden design and in contemporary representations of landscape. The view from Richmond Hill, later famous for its naturalistic prospect, did not escape the influence of the Renaissance garden, having been accentuated with the addition of a perspectival 'Terrace Walk' sometime in the late 1690s. In *The Renaissance Garden in England*, Strong has argued that axial perspective acted as a culturally mediated frame through which to view the landscape beyond.[35] Thus, one could argue that the development of Richmond Hill's Terrace Walk marks the first concrete expression of the landscape as a cultural object to be viewed. In this way, the following section will develop in the context of Richmond Strong's argument that perspective introduced to garden design the concept of pictorial space.[36]

Not unlike the Long Galleries of the great Elizabethan prodigy houses, the Terrace Walk atop Richmond Hill remains a linear space defined by movement. What little furniture there is is pushed to one side, allowing the visitor to stride unencumbered from end to end. Benches are positioned to take in sweeping views of the gardens below and to act as intermediate pausing stations: locations for informal discussion and brief respite. Memorial plaques indicate the favoured vantage points of revered ancestors, mirrored by the gaze of ancestral portraits lining the Long Gallery. Where the enclosed space of the gallery allowed for the enjoyment of nature despite a physical separation from it, so too Richmond Hill's Terrace, embowered by its shady oaken canopy, protects the visitor from inclement weather while simultaneously framing the brilliantly lit landscape beyond.

If the Terrace acts as a viewing gallery for the landscape beyond, one could also argue that the landscape was viewed as a series of pictures on the gallery's walls. Dutch landscape artist Leonard Knyff painted two views of Richmond Hill in c. 1700–20, one looking upstream from a point in Richmond itself, the other downstream from a point near the entrance to Richmond Park. Knyff's depictions, from an artificially high viewpoint, illustrate how the hill was, by this time, already a favoured vantage point from which to admire the river landscape, experienced through movement along the promenade from the town to the royal park. Knyff's paintings also include the earliest known views of the Terrace Walk itself, a double row of pleached trees positioned to divide the landscape view into frames observed from the windows of a grand new terrace opposite.

The construction of this terrace of grand homes (now demolished) demonstrates a period of speculative property development taking place within Richmond from around the 1690s.[37] A major impetus for this period of prosperity appears to have been an influx of London merchants seeking country retreats away from the city. As John Cloake has demonstrated in *Richmond Past*, these merchants might rent property, then purchase it, remodel it, or even replace it for profit. Typical of the kind of merchant who arrived in Richmond at this time, John Knapp, a member of the "Company of Merchant Adventurers Trading in the North West Part of America" first rented a property, before buying, demolishing and replacing it with a fashionable new villa, 'Marshgate House', in 1699.[38] This lucrative and expanding market for property development was soon discovered by the 'Master Builders' of Richmond, originally tradesmen specialising in bricklaying or carpentry who were often referred to with the new description 'architect'. New construction was often self-financed by these developers, many of whom appear in manor rolls with a new description: 'architect'. One such amateur developer/'architect', Michael Pew, purchased a row of cottages on Richmond Hill in the late 1690s and replaced them with the three large houses appearing to the right of Knyff's downstream painting. Cloake has suggested that the construction of the Terrace Walk immediately opposite, and at around the same time, may indicate that Pew was involved in either its commission and/or design.[39]

If indeed, the Terrace Walk did form part of a single development with Pew's homes opposite, the role of the terrace in framing the landscape view from the windows of Pew's homes is implicit. Certainly, any act deemed to 'spoil' the view was met with outrage, as demonstrated by a 1717 statement that "the Hill common was full of great holes, and that the big houses discharged their filth on it. Also that the foregoing people were planting trees without permission, which might at some future time obstruct the view".[40] Despite the use of the hill common as a dumping ground, and the scars left by gravel extraction, these comments prove that the parish vestry was determined to protect the amenity of the view by forbidding tenants to plant trees which might obstruct it. This was probably influenced by the growing popularity of the hilltop for leisurely walks, celebrated in contemporary poetry, such as Tom D'Urfey's *Ode to Cynthia Walking on Richmond Hill* (c. 1692):

On the brow of Richmond Hill,
Which Europe scarce can parallel,
Ev'ry eye such wonders fill
To view the prospect round;
Where the silver Thames does glide,
And stately courts are edified,
Meadows deck'd in summer's pride,
With verdant beauties crown'd.[41]

That D'Urfey's romantic description of walking on Richmond Hill was set to music by popular composer Henry Purcell points to the general familiarity of the locality among public audiences at this time as a prospect and as a destination for summer promenades.[42]

The suggestion that Terrace Walk may have been conceived as a single development associated with the construction of a row of grand homes may, it could be argued, place it within an established history of seventeenth-century aristocratic garden design; it is as if the terrace walk is a detached fragment of the grand axial allées of the roughly contemporary gardens at Ham House, completed in 1671. In the following section, we shall see how the design of axial gardens along this stretch of the Thames reveals a change in optical principles which overtook early Stuart England. The compact, enclosed and symbolic Renaissance garden gradually evolved into what Strong has called "a sequence of interconnecting spaces whose vital link is the vista" and whose organisational strategy is perspectival.[43]

'Scopic regimes' and 'Cartesian perspectivalism'

Dubbed 'scopic regimes' after Christian Metz's *The Imaginary Signifier: Psychoanalysis and the Cinema*, Martin Jay defined pre-Renaissance two-dimensional and Renaissance perspectival vision as differing visual frameworks "designed to construct the gaze and control the consciousness".[44] Strong has compared the aesthetic of the pre-perspective age to the work of the court miniaturist Nicholas Hilliard: "his is a flat, two-dimensional world lit by an even, brilliant light".[45] Hilliard's picture surfaces are not presented as "separate, enclosed worlds governed by their own optical principles"; instead, "everywhere there is pattern [. . .] and this pattern was created by the embroiderer".[46] This reference to the embroiderer's pattern-work alludes to the 'knot' gardens of the late medieval age. Incorporating emblematic, chivalric and allegorical symbols, knot gardens were designed to be 'read' from an oblique aerial viewpoint. Already going out of fashion by 1625, Francis Bacon remarked in his essay 'Of Gardens', "As for the making of knots or figures [. . .] they be but toys; you may see as good sights many times in tarts".[47] One could argue that Bacon's comments highlight a contemporary upheaval in the visual perception of the natural world, a gradual scepticism towards the symbolic and allegorical in favour of an increasingly subject-centred scientific approach to vision. Strong writes that "a magical age of alchemy and occult symbolism had given way to the age of experiment and the Royal Society".[48] Strong's conception of a changing visual perception is mirrored by Svetlana Alpers's description of the differences between Hilliard's aesthetic, what she calls the 'art of describing', and what Martin Jay calls 'Cartesian perspectivalism'. Alpers states,

> [Hilliard deals with] the surface of objects, their colours and textures, [. . .] rather than their placement in legible space; an unframed image versus one that is clearly framed; one with no clearly situated viewer compared to one with such a viewer.[49]

This tide-change began in fifteenth-century Italy, where the great Renaissance polymaths[50] had 'rediscovered' the science of perspective first observed by Lucretius in the first century BC.[51] These polymaths, models of the Renaissance 'universal man', including Leonardo and Brunelleschi, were architects, artists and sculptors but also inventors of machines and scientific optical instruments. Brunelleschi is widely credited with the rediscovery of one-point perspective with his optical experiments conducted around 1415.[52] In one such experiment, the viewer peered through a small hole in the back of a painting, of Florence's baptistery, observing the painting's reflection in a mirror opposite. This image could then be directly overlaid upon the real view of the baptistery as observed from the door of the cathedral.[53] By positioning the viewing hole at the point of perspective convergence, Brunelleschi had introduced the vanishing point to art, and had placed the eye, and the perceiving subject, at the centre of the visual world.[54]

It has been argued that Brunelleschi's mode of vision reorganised the world in relation to the eye. As John Berger has written, linear "perspective makes the single eye the centre of the visible world".[55] Moreover, this single eye was "understood to be static, unblinking, and fixated, rather than dynamic".[56] In Norman Bryson's terms, it followed the logic of the "Gaze rather than the Glance, thus producing a visual take that was eternalized, reduced to one 'point of view' and disembodied".[57] Bryson's use of the term 'disembodied' reflects Cartesian perspectivalism's distancing of the subject from the object, and the subject's assumption of a 'godlike' distanced gaze, which persists as the observational basis of modern Western science.[58] John Berger has suggested that this detachment of the observer from the object, achieved via the Renaissance rediscovery of Cartesian perspective, is mirrored by the contemporary proliferation of mobile canvas or board paintings, detached from the visual field and circulated for consumption.[59]

Leon Battista Alberti, perhaps Cartesian perspectivalism's first theorist, believed in the Renaissance polymath's powers to uncover order and rule in nature. According to Alberti, a proper understanding of the mathematical science of perspective was a critical attribute of the 'universal man'.[60] Piero della Francesca's paintings arguably demonstrate an obsession with Alberti's science of perspective, used in the construction of virtual architectural space.[61] In Francesca's *Ideal City* (c. 1470), each plane of virtual buildings remains in sharp focus while receding into the distance.[62] Piero's paintings are also devoid of movement and human presence. As Bernard Berenson has written, Piero della Francesca "did not always avail himself of his highest gifts. At times you feel him to have been dogged by his science".[63]

It is this dogged determination to prioritise the science and geometry of perspective which has been most routinely criticised by theorists, from Erwin Panofsky's criticism of perspective as convention or "symbolic form"[64] to Martin Heidegger's suggestion of its complicity with "a subject willed to mastery".[65] Following Panofsky's argument, Jay has written that the disembodiment and 'de-textualization' of Cartesian perspectivalism led to "abstract, quantitatively conceptualised space [becoming] more interesting to the artist than the qualitatively differentiated subjects painted within it" and thus "the rendering of the scene became an end in itself".[66] Following Heidegger, Cartesian perspectivalism has been criticised as a scopic regime "complicitous with a certain notion of an isolated bourgeois subject",[67] a subject who viewed the structure of the world from a detached 'godlike' position, thus failing to "recognise [his or her] corporeality, intersubjectivity and embeddedness in the flesh of the world".[68]

Prince Henry, Solomon de Caus and the Renaissance gardens of Richmond-upon-Thames

In architectural and landscape design, the scientific and mathematical precision demanded by the study of perspective ensured its association with straight axes and vistas which came to define the dominion of the viewer over his or her surroundings. In seventeenth-century Richmond, the Huguenot 'engineer' Solomon de Caus, in many ways himself a model of the Renaissance 'universal man', was employed as tutor of perspective to the young Henry, Prince of Wales. Henry, himself an artist, was also a collector and enthusiast for Italian Renaissance art. In fact, Henry wanted more than to collect Italian Renaissance art – he wanted to transform his palace at Richmond into a model Italianate court with the help of architects Inigo Jones and Constantino dei Servi. Henry's palace was to be set within an elaborate garden influenced by the Mannerist gardens of Pratolino, Tuscany, and the French court.[69] De Caus's work alongside Jones, an architect and theatre-set designer, highlights the apparent connection between the science of perspective and the theatre. For example, Jones's contemporary set design for Ben Johnson's *The Fortunate Isles and Their Union* (1625) depicts a deep perspective view of grotto-like arcades – easily interpreted as a Mannerist garden scene – such as De Caus may have intended for Richmond Palace. As Strong has pointed out, surely it can be no coincidence "that radiating walks and vistas begin to appear at the same time as single point perspective on the stage".[70] Indeed, some have argued that the absorption by garden and theatre design of optical techniques of perspective demonstrates a general enthusiasm for illusion at this time. For example, Paul Virilio has spoken of the 'dematerialisation' of the world, a new condition in which "the image prevails over the object present",[71] where the virtual prevails over the real, while Gina McPhee states, "[P]erhaps not surprisingly, the dissemination of perspectivalism in the Renaissance and Baroque was accompanied by a renewal of interest in *trompe-l'oeil*, anamorphosis, the distorting effect of mirrors, and the *camera obscura*".[72]

The change undergoing scopic regimes from the Renaissance onwards is also evident in the development of landscape garden. For example, architect Robert Smythson's collection of house and garden plans (c. 1609)[73] shows the clumsy relationship between early seventeenth-century houses and their gardens – the result of topographical convenience, or for functional access from the kitchens. In stark contrast, Smythson's later garden plans demonstrate their integration with the figurative plan of the house. For example, Smythson's plan of Ham House, Petersham, shows the house and gardens laid symmetrically about a determining central axis, which Strong argues "can only have been designed to be a perspective effect".[74] Via this optical device, the wider landscape is manipulated in reference to the house; a long avenue "invades and takes possession of the landscape",[75] tying the village of Ham to the house, funnelling the ideal urban formality of Albertian perspective from village through house to garden and into the landscape beyond.

At Ham, the architectural formality of the house was extended beyond into the landscape, but this force could also operate in reverse, enforcing the formality of the garden upon an earlier house. An example of this may be observed in Wren's 1689 remodelling of Hampton Court, where Wren took the opportunity to realign Henry VIII's palace with the axial symmetry of André Mollet's 'patte d'oie'[76] of 1662, itself largely determined by visual connections to the neighbouring urban centres of Kingston and Hampton. This ebb and flow of influence reminds John Jackson "of the close collaboration which once existed between urban design and what we now call landscape architecture".[77]

It should be clarified that the urban quality of seventeenth-century axial garden design was far from the lived experience of the majority of contemporary British towns. Rather, the garden's urban quality was that of the *idealised* city expressed by Renaissance artists such as Piero della Francesca.[78] The image of the idealised city constructed around perspective vistas is strikingly illustrated by Wren's plan to rebuild London after the Great Fire of 1666. Wren proposed a city of axial thoroughfares, in contrast to the preceding tangle of medieval alleys as depicted in van den Wyngaerde's oblique aerial views. In Wren's ideal London, the city would be shaped around a number of vistas terminated by monuments and grand buildings – although Wren's plans remained largely unexecuted because issues of land ownership and hasty construction returned the city to much of its medieval layout.[79]

Perspective's manipulation of the viewer suggests that the perspectival garden possessed a controlling dimension. The great avenues of the seventeenth-century garden take possession of the wider landscape and pronounce the visual, if not physical, dominion of the spectator. Johannes Kip's 1708 engraving of New Park (built 1683), on the edge of Richmond's royal park, illustrates the extent to which a network of vistas could take possession of the landscape (Figure 1.1). Control and possession are articulated on the ground by this vast network of vistas, while Kip's oblique aerial viewpoint connotes the power of New Park's owner, the Earl of Rochester. Samuel Molyneux wrote of a visit to New Park that it was "interspers'd with Vistos [sic] & innumerable private dark walks thro' every part of it [. . .] with unconfin'd [sic] prospects [. . .] every now and then of the [. . .] Country and River beyond".[80]

The avenues depicted in Kip's engraving appear to extend to infinity, drawing the gaze through deep space. As Robin Evans has remarked, "[W]hen any vista cuts through the lives of others it is a political instrument of a certain complexion. And when architecture petrifies its passage and forces movement and vision into the same privileged paths, even more so is architecture politicised".[81] Evans's remark suggests that the optical principles of the axial garden may have been developed in association with the increasing visibility of the political power wielded by the landed gentry from the latter seventeenth century onwards,[82] and as exemplified by the Earl of Rochester's gardens of New Park.

22 The origins of the protected view

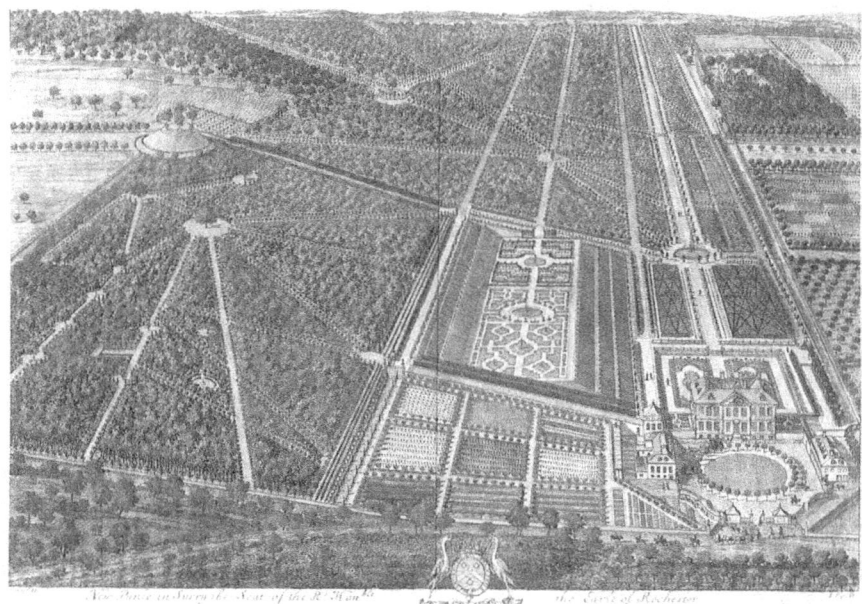

Figure 1.1 'New Parke', Petersham, as depicted by Johannes Kip in 1708. Some features of the gardens may also be discerned in John Rocque's later Survey of London. Richmond Hill and the commons are beyond the frame to the bottom left, while King Henry's Mound and the avenue of trees framing St Paul's appear as extensions to the perspectival garden at the top left.

Perspective and the theatre: Richmond Hill theatre

The aforementioned link between theatrical architecture and axial landscape design is demonstrated by the siting of Richmond's first theatre on Richmond Hill, housed in a barn opposite Terrace Walk in the summer of 1714.[83] In 1725, the theatre finally moved to a purpose-built structure on Richmond Hill (on the site of 10–12 The Terrace).[84] On performance days, Terrace Walk was, no doubt, buzzing with theatre-goers taking the air between acts, or refreshing themselves in the neighbouring Roebeck Inn, one of a serious of taverns which contributed to the hilltop's reputation as a popular leisure district. Indeed, Terrace Walk and the Richmond Hill view may well have formed the painted backdrops to such performances, as idyllic landscapes as well as local and garden scenes were the popular subjects of set-designers. This might be supported by an interior sketch of the later Richmond Theatre (relocated to Richmond Green) by F. Cornman of 1896, which, with a little imagination, could be interpreted as the view from Richmond Hill.[85]

The elaboration of theatrical scenery highlights a new priority given to the visual sense over the practical. Previously, very little scenery was utilised apart from the common background of the theatre building itself and its various entry and exit points; the eye was focused upon the activity of the actors. With the introduction of complex scenery, greater emphasis was placed upon the experience of setting and atmosphere. The perspectival 'picture frame' stage drew the eye into this setting, constructing another virtual world through perspective, into which the viewer peered. This had also been mirrored in Mannerist garden design, which had moved away from the medieval model of the garden, displaying plants of a medicinal and practical utility,[86] to a purely visual appreciation of the garden. As John Jackson has written, garden design "became the art of views and perspectives", "the design of the landscape as background for the theatre of human interaction".[87]

Theatre of human interaction: Richmond Hill pleasure garden

The overlaying of a theatrical urban axiality onto the seventeenth-century garden has been observed by several writers. John Dixon Hunt suggests that "the French [. . .] were more inclined towards the city and took it with them into their gardens, which were decorative and ornamental",[88] while Jackson argues that "Regardless of its location, the ornamental or pleasure garden [. . .] belongs to the city. It is an expression of urban values and of an urban way of life".[89] The urbanity of the axial perspective garden is reflected by the popularity of formal pleasure gardens established across London during the seventeenth century. These gardens, part landscape, part theatre, were open to paying guests who could take tea in garden pavilions, visit inns, attend balls and watch open-air performances or firework illuminations. Of the famous pleasure gardens at Vauxhall (begun 1661), *The London Magazine* wrote,

> Thy bowers, O Vaux-Hall then shall rise,
> In all the gay pride of the field;
> Thy musick, shall sweetly surprise;
> To thee fam'd *Elysium* shall yield.[90]

The theatrical splendour of Vauxhall pleasure gardens is illustrated by an engraving by B. Cole (1751–86), which shows the receding perspective of a shady avenue, framed by what could be the proscenium arch of a stage.

The discovery of a spring below Richmond Hill in the 1670s, marketed as medicinal, further attracted visitors to a burgeoning leisure district which included the royal park, promenade, view, hilltop inns and theatre.[91] By 1696, the area immediately adjacent to Terrace Walk had been developed as a popular pleasure garden, on the model of Vauxhall, known as 'Richmond Wells', complete with a pump room, assembly hall and gaming rooms. The health benefits afforded by taking the waters at Richmond, followed by a stroll through the pleasing river landscape, were extolled by contemporary writers. For example, traveller Charles Moritz wrote in 1782,

> [From Richmond] you enter immediately into a most charming valley, that winds all along the banks of the Thames. It was evening. The

sun was just shedding her last parting rays on the valley; but such an evening, and such a valley! The terrace at Richmond does assuredly afford one of the finest prospects in the world. Whatever is charming in nature, or pleasing in art, is to be seen here.[92]

According to Cloake, daily concerts and weekly balls became a regular feature of Richmond's pleasure gardens, attracting not only local visitors but also Londoners, arriving by river boat or by carriages, housed in an extensive mews.[93] Surviving contemporary paintings, such as Knyff's views, show only the scantest positioning of buildings, rendering it difficult to appreciate the scale of the gardens or their design. However, it is clear that the area had developed into a popular resort, ranked alongside London's other pleasure garden resorts of Islington, White Conduit House and Windsor in Reverend C. Jenner's *Town Eclogues* (1772):

> Time was, when satin waistcoats and scratch wigs,
> Enough distinguish'd all the city prigs,
> Whilst every sunshine Sunday saw them run
> To club their sixpences, at *Islington*;
> When graver citizens, in suits of brown,
> Lin'd ev'ry dusty avenue to town,
> Or led the children and the loving spouse,
> To spend two shillings at *White Conduit House.*
> But now, the prentices in suits of green,
> At *Richmond* and *Windsor* may be seen;
> There in mad parties they run down to dine,
> To play at gentlefolks, and drink bad wine:
> Whilst neat post-chariots roll their masters down
> To some snug box, a dozen miles from town.[94]

As this poem demonstrates, the pleasure gardens of Richmond, and no doubt the neighbouring Terrace Walk, had begun to attract the "prentices" or *nouveau riche*. The theatricality of the pleasure garden allowed the middle class to "play" at being aristocracy, indulging in extravagant parties in the grand illusory landscape setting of a stately home. The pleasure garden, which had once attracted the wealthy at Islington, and the poor at White Conduit House, now catered for a society of suburban villa owners, dwelling in their "snug box[es], a dozen miles from town", who aspired to the grand estates of the landed gentry.

Richmond Wells' cultivation of drunkenness and debauchery gradually eroded its popularity locally as well as among the fashionable elite. Finally, in 1763, Susanna Houblon, living almost opposite, bought up the pleasure gardens and promptly closed them to the public, demolishing its buildings.[95] Despite the closure of the gardens, the Terrace Walk, theatre and inns continued to draw visitors to the hill, immortalised by the song 'The Lass of Richmond Hill', first sung at Vauxhall pleasure gardens in 1789.[96]

Introduction 25

Remaining popular well into the nineteenth century, contemporary song sheets typically juxtapose a view of the Thames from Terrace Walk with the accompanying lyrics (Figure 1.2).

As this chapter has argued, Richmond Hill's Terrace Walk conformed to the seventeenth-century fashion for axial perspectivalism in landscape

Figure 1.2 Nineteenth-century song sheet for 'The Lass of Richmond Hill' (left), first sung at Vauxhall gardens in 1789, and illustrating the by now familiar view of the Thames.

design, likened to the extension of country house architecture to the garden or to the overlaying of urban axiality upon the natural landscape. Terrace Walk, as an example of this integration of architecture and landscape, was a designed space for the appreciation of the landscape view and the act of the promenade, similar to the Long Galleries of Elizabethan houses. The avenue of trees served as a frame through which the landscape was to be viewed either from the promenade, from the passing carriage or from the windows of the grand houses opposite. Knyff's downstream painting contrasts the sinuous curve of the river prospect with the hard-line geometry of this constructed perspective. The prospect itself appears flattened against the perspective spatiality of the foreground, creating a foil between the viewer and the view beyond, like the proscenium arch of contemporary theatres – a perspective construction of space separating the landscape out as an object *observed* from the *outside* by the viewer peering *into* the image. If, following Strong's argument, perspective had introduced to garden design the *concept of pictorial space*, in the following section we will see how eighteenth-century landscape architects would 'leap the fence' of the seventeenth-century axial garden and, in doing so, step into the image itself.

Richmond Hill villas

Where, in the seventeenth century, the landscape was to be seen from the house via the perspective techniques of axial garden design, during the eighteenth century a shift occurred in which the house itself was seen as integral to landscape views. This chapter will explore the property boom which overtook eighteenth-century Richmond-upon-Thames and demonstrate how local intellectual circles began to look to natural views of the Thames for inspiration in contemporary literature, architecture and landscape design.

Stepping down from the shady promenade of Terrace Walk into the gardens below, one crosses from public property to what had once been a series of privately owned riverside estates, most of which have been swept away in the course of the last century. From the early 1700s, a wealthy elite began building elegant villas along the banks of the Thames at Richmond. The resulting profusion of riverside estates is demonstrated by Augustin Heckel's engraving *Cholmondeley Walk* (1749) and Samuel Leigh's later *Panorama of the Thames from London to Richmond* (c. 1830). Writing in 1724, Daniel Defoe described the scene: "From Richmond to London, the River sides are full of Villages, those villages so full of Beautiful Buildings, Charming Gardens, and Rich Habitations of Gentlemen of Quality, that nothing in the World can imitate it".[97] By the 1770s, several impressive villas had grown up around Terrace Walk, notably No. 3 The Terrace, rebuilt by architect Sir Robert Taylor in 1769; Downe House, completed in 1771; Ancaster House, commissioned by the Duke of Ancaster in 1772; and Wick House, built for the Royal Academy's first president, Sir Joshua Reynolds, by architect Sir William Chambers.[98] These grand villas were positioned to take advantage of unrivalled river prospects from their hilltop locations. Morritz even remarked that "I never saw a palace which, if I were the owner of it, I would not give for any of the houses I now saw on Richmond Terrace".[99]

Villa builders and developers alike had been drawn to Richmond Hill by its profitability, the result of a favourable combination of distance from the city of London, river views, theatre, inns and pleasure garden. Reynolds was himself clearly drawn to the view from Terrace Walk, painting a romanticised version of it in 1788, one of the portraitist's few landscapes (Figure 1.3).[100]

The site neighbouring Reynolds's Wick House, formerly a collection of cottages composing the Bull's Head Tavern, was purchased by Lady St Aubyn in 1774, and developed by architect Robert Mylne as an elegant classical villa named The Wick.[101] Mylne's redevelopment allowed for an extension of Terrace Walk up to the Star and Garter Inn opposite the entrance to Richmond Park, seen in a watercolour by J. I. Richards of c. 1800 and in George Hilditch's *The Terrace, Richmond Hill* of 1837.[102]

Lower down the hill, brewer Edward Collins built a comfortable villa which appears to the left of *A View from Richmond, Looking towards Twickenham* by William Marlow, 1776.[103] This villa was replaced with

Figure 1.3 A highly romanticised view of The Thames from Richmond Hill, a painting by Sir Joshua Reynolds, 1788.

Source: © Tate, London 2018.

a considerably larger house in 1796 – latterly known as Lownsdowne House – and was successively host to such illustrious residents as Charles William Molyneux, Duke of Molyneux and Earl of Sefton (1770s), Lady Di Beauclerk, George Townshend, Earl of Leicester and second Marquis of Townshend (1790s), the Marquess of Stafford, the Marquess Wellesley (1811), the Earl of Lansdowne (1830) and the Prince de Joinville.[104]

A further mansion, also designed by architect Robert Mylne, was constructed in 1791–93 on the site of part of Richmond Wells, roughly in the position of the buildings which appear to the right of Marlow's painting. This was to be known as Cardigan House, the country retreat of the Duke of Clarence and subsequently the Earls of Cardigan.[105] Despite their demolition in 1875 and 1970 respectively, images of Lansdowne House and Cardigan House survive in late nineteenth-century sale catalogues, which show them to have been substantial villas set within landscaped grounds, with projecting bay windows and verandas taking maximum advantage of fine river views.[106]

At the foot of Richmond Hill, a sign proclaims a section of the hill as Buccleuch Gardens. The name originates in the Duchess of Buccleuch, daughter of the Earl of Cardigan, later Duke of Montagu, who built a mansion here in 1761–63. Decades of clay extraction at the foot of the hill resulted in a steep, pockmarked landscape deemed useless for the grazing of cattle. The Vestry of Richmond therefore decided to grant the land to the Duke of Montagu, who created, at great cost, extensive landscape gardens on either side of Petersham Road, linked by a subterranean grotto which survives to this day.[107] Twickenham resident Horace Walpole said of a visit to the gardens in 1790 that "it is perfectly screened from human eyes, tho' in the bosom of so populous a village: and you climb til at last, treading the houses under feet, you recover the Thames and all the world at a little distance".[108] The spectacular setting of the Duke of Montagu's gardens played host to a number of lavish garden fêtes entertaining, among others, King Leopold of Belgium, the Duke of Wellington, Lord Melbourne and the sultan of Turkey.[109] One such occasion is recorded in an engraving by T. A. Prior, depicting the fête held at Buccleuch House in honour of Queen Victoria's visit in 1842.

Alexander Pope and the naturalistic garden

In order to understand why Richmond had become such a favoured site for the villa estates of the gentry, it is important to understand how the landscape had entered the fashionable psyche, via whose agency, and through what imagery. Approaching the crumbling stone vaults of the Duke of Montagu's subterranean grotto at Buccleuch Gardens, one is struck by the sudden reappearance of the Thames, framed by arches of rusticated rubble. The duke and his landscape architects were no doubt familiar with the same effect at poet Alexander Pope's grotto, across the river at Cross

Deep, Twickenham. What little remains of Pope's grotto today allows an insight into Pope's innovative experimentation in landscape architecture and the flowering of a genteel villa society on the banks of the Thames.

Alexander Pope (1688–1744) had suffered from a crippling bone disease as a child which had stunted his growth, leaving him with a hunchback and rendering him unable to walk without the aid of a stick.[110] As Mavis Batey has pointed out, Pope's preoccupation with the reading and translation of works of classical literature may have acted as a release from "the many restrictions his deformity and frailty imposed upon his activities".[111] Pope's poetry in particular was inspired by the works of Horace and Virgil,[112] whose renderings of idyllic landscapes – lawns, shady bowers, glittering streams and the simple and innocent lives of the comfortable rural farmer – reminded Pope of the Thames-side meadows. Pope transferred this classical vision to the Thames, stating that on his journeys through the country he had seen "no scenes of paradise, no happy bowers, equal to those on the banks of the Thames".[113] Pope's transferral of an Italianate classical vision onto the Thames landscape is illustrated by his pastoral 'Spring', which quotes from Virgil in the first sentence:

> First in these fields I try the Sylvan strains,
> Nor blush to sport on Windsor's blissful plains:
> Fair Thames, flow gently from this sacred spring.
> While on thy banks Sicilian Muses sing.
> ...
> Blest Thames's shores the brightest beauties yield,
> Feed here, my lambs, I'll seek no distant field.[114]

Pope's idyllic imagery continues in 'Summer' with an allusion to the simple and contented life of the shepherd, who is himself a component of the landscape presented as an earthly paradise:

> A Shepherd's boy (he seeks no better name)
> Led forth his flocks along the silver Thame,
> Where dancing sunbeams on the water play'd,
> And verdant alders form'd a quivering shade.
> ...
> See what delights in sylvan scenes appear,
> Descending gods have found Elysium here.[115]

Pope's literary successes enabled him to lease a small house at Cross Deep, Twickenham, in 1719, and to substantially rebuild it as a classical villa. Pope wrote of his move, "The Gods and fate have fix'd me on the borders of the Thames, in the Districts of Richmond and Twickenham", and frequently referred to his villa as his "Tusculum" after Cicero's rural retreat outside Rome.[116] His conspicuous presence in Twickenham, and the work he completed there, including his translation of Homer's *Iliad* (begun in 1715 but not completed until 1720), earned it the popular eighteenth-century title of the 'classic village'.

Pope was not alone in Twickenham, but at the heart of a literary circle which included satirist Jonathan Swift and poet John Gay. The Duchess of Queensberry even gifted the latter with a riverside summer house in which to compose his works. Pope's influential friends also included George II's mistress Henrietta Howard, at Marble Hill House, Twickenham, and Lord Burlington downriver at Chiswick. Thus, the banks of the Thames between Hampton and Chiswick were developing as a community of wealthy, fashionable and influential individuals, well connected by established networks of societal propriety and patronage of the arts.

The Twickenham villa which Pope had built in 1719 was separated from the river by a public road, so he leased a plot of land on the opposite side of the road in which to extend his garden. These two plots were linked by a subterranean grotto, directly inspired by classical precedent, particularly the grotto of the nymph Egeria,[117] outside Rome, a popular stop on the Grand Tour of the time. Pope, in a letter to his friend Edward Blount, remarked, "Were it to have nymphs as well – it would be complete in everything".[118] In the tradition of the eighteenth-century 'cabinet of curiosities', the interior of Pope's grotto was decorated with alabaster, marbles, ores and crystals, while a 'camera obscura' projected an inverted moving image of the Thames onto the grotto's walls. The projection of the dappled light of the river into the darkened grotto, and its numerous reflections in crystal and mirror, is hinted at in Pope's description:

> Thou who shalt stop, where Thames' translucent wave
> Shines a broad Mirror thro' the shadowy Cave;
> Where ling'ring drops from min'ral Roofs distill,
> And pointed Crystals break the sparkling Rill,
> Unpolish'd Gems no ray on Pride bestow,
> And latent Metals innocently glow.
> ...
> Approach; but awful! Lo! Th'Egerian Grot,
> Where, nobly-pensive, St. John sate [sic] and thought;[119]

For architectural advice, Pope turned to architect William Kent on the recommendation of his friend, Lord Burlington, himself an amateur architect and collector of Italian paintings and classical sculpture. Kent, at that time working on Burlington's house and grounds at Chiswick, designed additions to Pope's garden, such as the Shell Temple, appearing in a sketch by Kent of 1725–30. With a fiery altar at its centre, a bronze tripod in the foreground, and the distant river and boatman, perhaps an allegory of the River Styx, the observer is clearly invited to read Pope's garden as a classical scene. On the riverside, Kent was also engaged in the design of a portico, added to the front of the villa in 1732 (Figure 1.4).

Figure 1.4 Comparison with Peter Tilleman's depiction of Pope's villa (Fig. 4.49) shows the addition of the classical portico by architect William Kent in 1732. Engraving by unknown artist.
Source: © The British Library Board.

John Serle's *A Plan of Mr. Pope's Garden as It Was Left at His Death* (1745) shows that traces of the geometry of the formal perspective garden, of Ham House's *grand allées* and Terrace Walk's promenade, remained in the planning of Pope's garden, though plantings were not to be carefully clipped but left to take their natural shapes.[120] As Batey et al. have commented, Pope thought "Nature was to be dressed, but not overdressed", a theme which came from the writings of Horace and the idea of *simplex munditiis*, translated by John Milton as "plain in its neatness".[121] These ideas come across in Pope's *An Essay on Criticism* (1711), in which he writes,

> First follow NATURE, and your Judgment frame
> By her just Standard, which is still the same:
> ...
> Life, Force, and Beauty, must to all impart,
> At once the Source, and End, and Test of Art
> Art from that Fund each just Supply provides,
> Works without Show, and without Pomp presides.[122]

Later, in his *Epistle to Lord Burlington* (1731), Pope makes a specific reference which ties this idea of *simplex munditiis* to the act of landscape design, remarking,

> In all, let Nature never be forgot.
> But treat the Goddess like a modest fair
> Nor over-dress, nor leave her wholly bare.[123]

Between 1711 and 1731 then, Pope had linked the idea of Horace's simple rusticity to landscape architecture. The connection may well have been made at Princess Caroline's conference on gardening, held at the Prince and Princess of Wales's new home of Richmond Lodge in 1719, to which Pope, Burlington and Kent were invited.[124]

Also developing at this time was a sense that gardens could be designed as painted scenes, perhaps an inheritance of the theatrical stage-set design of the perspectival garden. Indeed, William Kent, as Inigo Jones before him, had been a stage-set designer, working primarily in scenic sketches rather than in plan. There was a benefit to designing Pope's garden as a series of scenes – Pope's garden was small and therefore could not take advantage of the grand optical effects of perspective and a broad prospect. In effect, Pope's garden had to be arranged with respect to pictorial composition. Dixon Hunt states that where Pope did make use of perspective he distorted it "in the same manner as they do in painting",[125] by narrowing the planting of trees and creating areas of shade to enhance the illusion of depth. These optical illusions allowed Pope to create a series of idealised 'scenes' in a compact space, revealed in visual sequence rather than in the single distanced gaze of the axial garden. This principle is revealed in Pope's *Epistle* to Lord Burlington of 1731:

> Let not each beauty ev'ry where be spy'd,
> Where half the skill is decently to hide.
> He gains all points, who pleasingly confounds
> Suprizes, varies and conceals the Bounds.[126]

Garden commentator Joseph Spence wrote in the 1750s that Kent and Pope had been the first that "practiced painting in gardening",[127] supported by Pope's comment that "All gardening is landscape painting. Just like a landscape hung up".[128] Kent's method of scenic design was no doubt informed by his personal collection of Italian landscape paintings, and the landscapes he had witnessed on the Grand Tour, incidentally where he had first become acquainted with Lord Burlington. Arguably Kent's most important work with regards to the development of the picturesque movement was his role in co-designing the villa and gardens of Chiswick House with Burlington himself.

Kent, Burlington and the influence of the Italian landscape

Kent and Burlington's design shares a formal relationship with Andrea Palladio's villas, such as those lining the River Brenta outside Venice, a popular stop on the Grand Tour of the time. Significantly, the villa was intended as an art gallery to house Burlington's large collection of landscape paintings acquired during his extensive travels. Works by artists such as Gaspar Poussin and Claude Lorrain were sought after and acted as ideal models for landscape improvements. Just as owning such a work was desirable, so too a landscape, modelled in their image, would become a status symbol.[129] As Gina Crandell has written, "the landscape spectators of the eighteenth century had so thoroughly incorporated the ideas of form from painters that the actual landscape they saw could not be separated from the formal painting conventions".[130]

Princess Caroline's 1719 gardening conference coincided with Kent and Burlington's return from the Grand Tour, and no doubt they returned brimming with an enthusiasm for classical scenes. This is demonstrated by Burlington's commission of a graphical reconstruction of Pliny's *Tusculum*, Robert Castell's *Villas of the Ancients Illustrated* (1728), in which both villa and garden landscape were re-imagined from Pliny's description. Surely Pliny's comment that the villa gardens were "a landscape painting drawn with all the beauties imaginable"[131] did not escape the attention of Pope, Kent and Burlington. Royal Gardener Charles Bridgeman was also present at the conference and, following their introduction, Pope and Bridgeman collaborated in the design of Henrietta Howard's garden at Marble Hill, Twickenham. Batey et al. have demonstrated how a contemporary plan of Marble Hill bears many similarities with Robert Castell's work, including a semi-circular 'hippodrome' lawn and irregular wilderness garden.[132]

Designed by architect Colen Campbell, and carried out by Roger Morris between 1724 and 1729, the architecture of Marble Hill too was an essay in the idea of the Palladian villa, a simple, compact cube inspired by Palladio's River Brenta villas. As Julius Bryant has written, "Marble Hill House [. . .] has long held a recognized position [. . .] as a perfect example of an English Palladian villa",[133] with the influence of what John Summerson has referred to as an "epoch-making model".[134] Marble Hill's influence can be attributed to its publication in the third volume of Colen Campbell's *Vitruvius Britannicus* (1725), as well as its visibility from the public thoroughfare of the Thames. The conspicuous nature of the house, along with the dramatic stage-set frame of Pope and Bridgeman's gardens, led to its popular depiction by travelling artists, mass-produced in prints and engravings. The influence of the house certainly also impressed upon its many guests, some of whom would go on to build their own essays in Anglo-Palladianism. For example, Lord Islay, Duke of Argyll, was probably influenced in the design of Whitton Park, Twickenham, built in 1730,[135]

34 *The origins of the protected view*

Figure 1.5 Architect Roger Morris's White Lodge, Richmond Park, with its flanking wings, added in 1754.

Source: Drawing by J. Gandon and engraved by T. Miller, as illustrated in Volume VI of Colen Campbell's Vitruvius Britannicus (1767).

possibly to designs by Roger Morris.[136] A 1794 engraving of Whitton Park shows it to have been a Palladian cube with flanking pavilion wings, while a plan of the park (1766) shows it to have been in the manner of Marble Hill, with formal plantings and hippodrome-shaped pools, giving way to an irregular wilderness garden.

The extent of Marble Hill's influence is illustrated by architect Roger Morris's involvement in the design of a third Palladian villa, this time for a royal patron: White Lodge in Richmond Park, published in the fourth volume of Colen Campbell's *Vitruvius Britannicus* (1767) (Figure 1.5). Begun by George I sometime after 1727 and completed by George II, the villa was a favourite retreat of Princess Caroline. The elegant simplicity of the Palladian villa, advocated by Pope, Burlington and Kent, perfectly befitted the lodge's use as a simple rural retreat, set within a largely naturalistic park designed for the rustic sport of hunting.

In the same year that work had begun on White Lodge, Bridgeman and Kent were in the process of laying out the royal gardens at Richmond Lodge (now Kew Gardens), Caroline and the Prince of Wales's personal Thames-side retreat. The combined influences of these figures helped to produce at Richmond a transitional garden, combining elements of the old perspective tradition with the scenographic and naturalistic qualities of an emerging picturesque taste. This combination of perspective geometry and aesthetic scenery is demonstrated by the way in which the gardens were recorded, drawn as geometric plans surrounded by scenic vignettes – for example, in John Rocque's *An Exact Plan of the Royal Palace Gardens and Park at Richmond* (1754) (Figure 1.6). Despite the Prince of Wales's initial comment that his wife should be "abused for such childish silly stuff",[137] Royal patronage had secured the longevity of naturalistic gardening and thus placed Richmond at the forefront of a fledging picturesque movement.

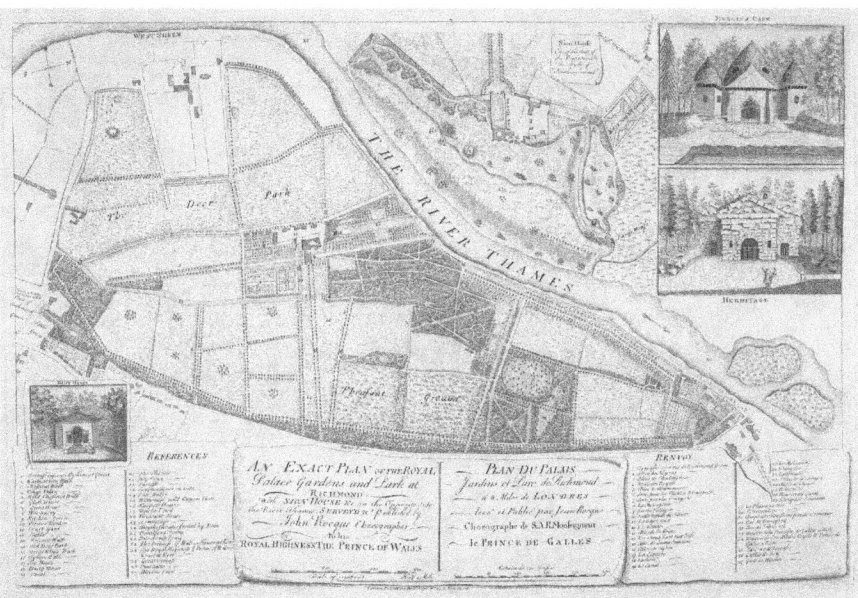

Figure 1.6 John Rocque's *An Exact Plan of the Royal Palace Gardens and Park at Richmond* (1754), showing Charles Bridgeman's landscape plan, inset with vignettes of William Kent's garden *fabriques*.

Source: © The British Library Board.

Richmond's poetic landscape

Returning to Richmond Hill's Terrace Gardens, one may now appreciate that the wealth of villas, constructed from the mid-eighteenth to the nineteenth centuries, not only was the result of economic pragmatics but also was influenced by a local though nationally renowned and fashionable elite, which included royalty and members of the court, poets, artists, architects and landscape architects. This circle popularised the notion of the simple pastoral retreat, and the appreciation of landscapes composed as a series of naturalistic or 'picturesque' scenes. The mass production and circulation of architectural designs, as well as of prints of garden views, greatly increased the accessibility and dissemination of the new fashion, which would be further bolstered in the writings of the nineteenth century. The potency of this imagery in the contemporary perception of the Richmond Hill view is best summed up by poet James Thompson's frequently quoted passage in *The Seasons* (1727), in which the landscape is described almost as a canvas, over which the eye must roam (Figure 1.7):

> To where the silver Thames first rural grows,
> There let the feasted eye unwearied stray:

36 *The origins of the protected view*

Figure 1.7 William Kent's frontispiece to 'Spring' in James Thompson's The Seasons (1730 edition).
Source: Public Domain.

    Luxurious, there, rove through the pendant woods,
    That nodding hang o'er Harrington's retreat
    And stooping thence to Ham's embowering walks,
    Hence let us trace the matchless vale of Thames;
    Far-winding up to where the muses haunt

> To Twit'nam's bowers
> ...
> Heavens! What a goodly prospect spreads around,
> Of hills and dales, and woods, and lawns, and spires,
> And glitt'ring towns, and gilded streams, till all
> The stretching landscape into smoke decays.[138]

Thompson's works, alongside those of Pope, Swift and others, secured the classical and romantic literary images of the Thames landscape. William Wordsworth, arguably Britain's most influential poet, championed as a figurehead of patriotism, would later write of the Thames at Richmond (1790),

> Glide gently, thus forever glide
> O Thames! That other bards may see,
> As lovely visions by your side
> As now, fair river! Come to me.
> ...
> That in thy waters may be seen
> The image of a poet's heart,
> How bright, how solemn, how serene!
> Such heart did once the poet bless,
> Who, pouring here a later ditty,
> Could find no refuge from distress,
> But in the milder grief of pity.[139]

The poet to whom Wordsworth refers is William Collins, whose *Ode Occasion'd by the Death of Mr. Thomson* (1749) was published in his lifetime.[140] Collins's poem paints Thompson's life as simple and rural, referring to him in suitably romantic fashion as a 'druid'; he writes,

> The genial meads, assign'd to bless
> Thy life, shall mourn thy early doom;
> Their hinds and shepherd-girls shall dress,
> With simple hands, thy rural tomb.
>
> Long, long thy stone and pointed clay
> Shall melt the musing Briton's eyes;
> O! vales and wild woods, shall he say
> In yonder grave your Druid lies![141]

Wordsworth's reference to Collins thus also references Thompson, perpetuating a mythic and nostalgic view of the Thames, learned via the writing styles of his predecessors.

What is important to note here is that the nostalgic and romantic vision of an Arcadian landscape, attributed by Pope to the Thames first in literature

38 *The origins of the protected view*

and then in the physical realities of his architectural innovations, became deeply engrained. In promoting such a vision, Pope, Burlington, Howard, Thompson, Wordsworth and others explicitly linked the Thames to the landscapes of a classical 'golden age', suggesting that eighteenth-century Britain was, or could be, a glorious new Augustan age. At a time of increasing mass production of prints and literary works, the view from Richmond Hill became a recognisable and distributable model of this Arcadia, in whose image new architectural and landscape set-pieces could be designed.

Theorising a picturesque convention

Where the previous sections have followed the emergence of picturesque landscape design and literature along the Richmond stretch of the Thames, the following sections will chart the apogee of its theoretical expression. From the mid-eighteenth to mid-nineteenth centuries, the appreciation of the picturesque was hotly debated in the writings of Uvedale Price and Richard Payne Knight, whose works remain subjects of academic debate to this day.[142]

Central to the theorisation of a picturesque convention at this time had been the works of Lancelot 'Capability' Brown, which were initially praised for sweeping away the rigid formality of the seventeenth-century garden, and later criticised for their blandness. Perhaps Brown's single greatest contribution was the interaction between undulating lawns and graceful lakes. For example, descending through the Duke of Montagu's subterranean grotto at the foot of Terrace Gardens, Richmond-upon-Thames, one emerges onto a verdant lawn stretching seamlessly to the lapping water at the river's edge. Such an effortless meeting of lawn and water might seem natural enough, but it is in fact a man-made landscape intervention, a feature of Buccleuch's eighteenth-century gardens. A striking illustration of the eighteenth-century introduction of this feature appears in John Rocque's *An Exact Plan of the Royal Palace Gardens and Park at Richmond* (1754) (Figure 1.5). In this image, Rocque juxtaposes the residual geometry of Charles Bridgeman's 1718 Richmond Lodge gardens with the recent re-landscaping of Syon Park, on the opposite bank, by Brown. Rocque's plan illustrates how Bridgeman's gardens had been walled in and screened by dense plantings of trees along the riverbank, with but a few openings providing for key vistas from the house. The innovation which allowed for such a breaking down of physical boundaries is clearly depicted in Rocque's plan; a serpentine line snaking across the parkland indicates the introduction of a 'ha-ha', confining the cattle to the riverside meadows without interrupting views to, or from, the house.

Brown's work at Syon, commissioned by the Duke of Northumberland, was probably begun in 1753.[143] By this time Brown had already served as head gardener at Stowe for over ten years in collaboration with Kent.

Brown's work, particularly the 'Grecian Vale' at Stowe, began to show a preoccupation with serpentine forms and an emphasis on the manipulation of landscape forms, rather than the playful scattering of architectural follies exercised by Kent. Weekly newspaper *The World* noted William Hogarth's contemporary advocation of the 'serpentine line of beauty', as detected in works of art and the human form. In one anecdote, the editor of *The World* was shocked to find "a young lady of the most graceful figure" in the act of being corseted into the most fashionable flattened shape of the time:

> I protest, when I saw the beautiful figure that was to be so deformed by the stay maker, I was as much shocked, as if I had been told that she was come to deliver up those animated *knowls* of beauty to the surgeon – I borrow my terms from gardening. . . . Let us suppose that Mr Brown should, in any one of the many Elysiums he has made, see the old terraces rise again and mask his undulating knowls, or straight rows of trees obscure his noblest configurations of scenery.[144]

In this passage, supposedly 'unspoilt' and natural garden design is equated with innocent, youthful femininity. Perhaps not coincidentally, in the year Brown began his work at Syon Park, local man Hogarth (like Brown, a fellow resident of Hammersmith and close friend of Twickenham's Horace Walpole) published his *Analysis of Beauty* (1753), complete with diagrams to illustrate the superior beauty of the serpentine line.

In 1764, Brown returned to work at Richmond Lodge under the patronage of George III, where he began the transformation of the garden through 'sweeping away' the formality of Bridgman and Kent's design.[145] The high fences, terrace walk and plantations bordering the Thames were removed to create a continuity with Syon's graceful riverside meadows opposite. United in a single naturalistic landscape composition, Brown's redesign appears in Richard Wilson's *The Thames at Syon* (1760s) (Figure 1.8) and was described at the time by Arthur Young:

> Richmond Gardens have been lately altered: the terrass [sic] and the grounds about it, are now converted into waving lawn that hangs to the river in a most beautiful manner: the old avenue is broken, and the whole clumped in some places with groves; in others with knots of trees, and a very judicious use is made of single ones: . . . The lawn waves in a very agreeable manner, the wood is so well managed, that the views of the river vary every moment. A gravel walk winds through it, which commands the most pleasing scenes . . . a flock of sheep scattered about the slopes, add uncommonly to the beauty of the scene.[146]

Brown's graceful vision of undulating lawns melting into shimmering bodies of water would inspire many imitators. Indeed, the Brownian style would soon become conflated with patriotic notions of an idealised English

Figure 1.8 *The Thames at Syon* by Richard Wilson (c. 1760s), demonstrating 'Capability' Brown's seemingly effortless merging of the Kew and Syon estates into one picturesque landscape composition.

Source: Public Domain.

landscape. This is suggested by Princess Augusta's[147] commissioning of Brown in the design of a park near Brunswick, Germany, in 1767, to be "laid out in the English Tast [sic]".[148] It would appear that even by this date, the Brownian picturesque had come to be associated with an idealised vision of Richmond, demonstrated by Augusta's naming of her German estate 'Richmond' due to the topographical and compositional similarities of its sloping site, overlooking the River Oker. David Watkin has suggested that the elegant house at Richmond, Brunswick, was also designed with reference to the royal gardens at Richmond, in a Palladian style which recalled aspects of William Chambers's work.[149] If Brown's remodelling of the Richmond Lodge estate inspired imitation, Lord Montagu also certainly sought to emulate it in his re-landscaping of the Buccleuch riverbank, seeking the effect of Brown's "waving lawn that hangs to the river".[150]

Satisfied with our stroll along the sweeping lawns of the Buccleuch riverbank, we now recross Petersham Road, beginning the ascent back to our starting point on Richmond Hill's Terrace Walk. A serpentine path hugs the contours of the hill, weaving between groves of ornamental trees in a gentle ascent. As we have seen, the serpentine path had been a feature of Kent and Bridgeman's landscapes, though they were often combined with geometric avenues and vistas as at Richmond Lodge. Brown took the serpentine path and made it the dominant feature of his landscapes, as demonstrated by the circuitous carriage drive with which he encircled the Duke of Northumberland's estate at Syon Park. While only the largest estates could provide for such a carriage drive, even the smallest could incorporate a series of serpentine paths, guiding the visitor through successive garden scenes.

An example of the application of the serpentine picturesque to a small estate is the garden of actor David Garrick, a few miles upstream at Hampton. Garrick developed his riverside gardens soon after his purchase of a villa there in 1754.[151] As Batey et al. have pointed out, Garrick was a keen collector of Hogarth's paintings, even writing the epitaph for Hogarth's tomb in 1764. Garrick's close friendship with Hogarth no doubt informed the serpentine paths of his garden, one of which appears in *A View of the Seat of the Late David Garrick, Esq.* (1779). This path and a series of Brownian 'clumps' acted to break up the regular shape of the riverside lawn, which lay sandwiched between the river and parallel road, while directing the visitor's gaze to carefully composed scenes. These included views of Garrick's Temple to Shakespeare, constructed in 1755. Indeed, the Brownian nature of Garrick's garden, as observed in Johann Zoffany's *Mr and Mrs Garrick by the Shakespeare Temple at Hampton* (1762) and *A View in Hampton Garden with Mr and Mrs Garrick Taking Tea* (1762), may indicate Brown's contribution to its design. Certainly, Brown was consulted in 1756 over the construction of a grotto, similar to Alexander Pope's, which would link the house and riverside lawns.[152]

Hogarth and Brown were just two of Garrick's influential acquaintances and neighbours.[153] Garrick commissioned architect Robert Adam, who had been employed locally with the remodelling of the Duke of Northumberland's Syon Park in the 1760s, with rebuilding his own villa in 1775. Garrick also sought landscaping and design advice from his neighbours, antiquarian and politician Horace Walpole, of Strawberry Hill, Twickenham, and poet Richard Owen Cambridge of Cambridge Park, Twickenham. Walpole, Garrick and Cambridge all contributed to satirical observations on the new taste for serpentine landscapes, published in the weekly newspaper *The World*. Garrick's own play *The Clandestine Marriage* (1766) includes the line "Ay, here's none of your strait [sic] lines here – but all *taste* – zig-zag – crinkum-crankum – in and out – right and left – to and again – twisting and turning like a worm my Lord".[154] Despite their satirical witticisms, the taste for serpentine design extended to Walpole's and Cambridge's own Thames-side gardens. Certainly, the neighbours shared views on the picturesque in architecture, landscape and literature. Indeed, Walpole is said to have provided many of Garrick's trees from his own gardens at Strawberry Hill.[155]

Walpole set about developing his own gardens at Twickenham in 1747. By 1754 he had created a picturesque meadow, enclosed by a ha-ha, on which cattle grazed in view of the windows of the house. The aesthetic function of the cattle is suggested by Walpole's remark that they were "studied for their colours for becoming the view",[156] and indicates his familiarity with Philip Southcote's Woburn Farm, Addlestone.[157] Walpole's own garden was certainly influenced by Woburn's circuitous perimeter walk, which presented views of the farm as a series of scenes. This, Walpole imitated; the house and landscape at Strawberry Hill were framed in successive views, experienced in motion along a perimeter serpentine path. At points along the path, Walpole created a series of secluded nooks within his serpentine woodland path, including a gothic chapel and shell bench. These romantic spots, dripping with climbing flowers, had been inspired by the writings of poets, particularly Edmund Spenser's *Faerie Queene* (1596) and the works of William Mason, a frequent visitor to Strawberry Hill, and author of *The English Garden* (1772).

In particular, the visitor came to view a series of openings in Walpole's circuitous woodland path which directed the viewer to carefully composed scenes of the villa and picturesque Thames landscape beyond. A watercolour by Paul Sandby (1775) illustrates such a view towards Twickenham which "in the setting sun and the long autumnal shades" Walpole comments "enriched the landscape to Claude Lorrain".[158] Mason also makes explicit references to the Italianate landscape paintings of artist Claude Lorrain; in one such passage from *The English Garden* (1772) he writes,

> your eyes entranc'd,
> Shall catch those glowing scenes, that taught a CLAUDE
> To grace his canvas with Hesperian hues,
> And scenes like these, on Memory's tablet drawn,
> Bring back to Britain; there give local form
> To each Idea; and, if Nature lend
> Materials fit of torrent, rock and shade,
> Produce new TIVOLIS.[159]

In 1771, Walpole published *An Essay on Modern Gardening*, which re-emphasised both the contribution of poetical works such as Pope's and Mason's and the influence of classical sources of art and literature in modern movements in naturalistic landscape architecture.[160]

Along with the improvements Walpole made to his gardens at Strawberry Hill, dramatic alterations were made to the existing villa. Many of these alterations were intended to take advantage of the views, which Walpole commented were

> very different from every side, and almost from every chamber and makes a most agreeable contrast; the house being placed almost in an elbow of the Thames, which surrounds half, and consequently beautifies

three of the aspects. Then my little hill . . . gazes up to royal Richmond; and Twickenham on the left and Kingston Wick in the right, are seen across bends of the river, which on each hand appears like a Lilliputian seaport.[161]

Since Walpole's views differed "from every side", one could argue that the symmetrical placement of chambers in conventional Anglo-Palladian villa design could not maximise the site's scenic potential. Walpole's piecemeal additions took advantage of the contrasting aspects, while simultaneously creating a series of irregularly planned rooms, themselves an unfolding series of contrasting scenes. The picturesque irregularity of the interior is mirrored by the exterior, which appears ever-changing in the sequential views observed from Walpole's serpentine woodland path (Figure 1.9). As opposed to the relatively strict compositional rules of the Anglo-Palladian style, Walpole's fanciful gothic was freer and could be applied easily to

Figure 1.9 Walpole's fanciful Strawberry Hill Gothic revels in irregularity, allowing the adaptation of an older building and the adoption of a freer and irregular plan, in contrast to the rigid symmetry of Anglo-Palladian architecture. Sir Joshua Reynolds, among others, suggested that architects consider their buildings with a painterly eye, whereby interiors as well as exteriors become picturesque sequences of unfolding images.

irregular plans. Joshua Reynolds, a resident of Richmond Hill, was to write of irregular planning in 1786,

> It may not be amiss for the Architect to take advantage *sometimes* of that to which I am sure the Painter ought always have his eyes open, I mean the use of accidents; to follow where they may lead, and to improve them, rather than to trust to a regular plan. It often happens that additions have been made to houses at various times, for use or pleasure. As such buildings depart from regularity, they now and then acquire something of scenery by this accident. . . . Variety and intricacy is a beauty and excellence in every other of the arts which address the imagination; why not in Architecture?[162]

One could argue that William Chambers's curious design for Reynolds's Wick House, Richmond Hill (1772), torn between an asymmetrical plan which includes a corner stair tower and the symmetry of Chambers's classical façade, is a little more understandable in the light of Reynolds's endorsement of architectural irregularity.

Gothic's absorption of the picturesque

A comparison between six abortive plans for royal palaces at Richmond proposed between 1735 and 1828 gives a clear demonstration of the changing fashion, from severe Anglo-Palladianism to fanciful gothic. Kent had been involved in the design of a palace from 1735[163] and, though no drawings survive, an architectural model demonstrates the influence of Lord Burlington's Chiswick House, particularly the Italianate steps and Palladian windows Kent had provided there. Chambers's second plan (1765), intended to replace Richmond Lodge and to complement Brown's landscape, shows a neat 23-bay Anglo-Palladian edifice. George III's taste had, however, already begun to change. Chambers's subsequent five classical schemes were eventually dropped in favour of architect James Wyatt's scheme for a huge castellated palace on the banks of the Thames at Kew (Figure 1.10). Construction began on the palace in 1802, though by 1828 George IV, already weary of the gothic style, had begun construction of his oriental pavilion in Brighton, and promptly had it demolished.[164] Kew's castellated palace belongs to a series of early gothic designs, including Robert Adam's Culzean Castle (1777) and Roger Morris's Inverary Castle (1746), which retained Palladian symmetry while adopting gothic motifs. Nevertheless, a shift towards picturesque "variety and intricacy" in works of architecture had been initiated.

Upstream at Windsor in 1824, Wyatt's nephew Jeffry Wyatville was commissioned to remodel large portions of the medieval castle, increasingly in favour as a summer retreat from 1776.[165] In the late eighteenth century, Windsor Castle had been visible on the horizon in views from Richmond Hill (now obstructed by the terminal buildings of Heathrow Airport). The

Figure 1.10 'The Palace of His Majesty George the Third at Kew', in G. Cooke's *The Beauties of England and Wales* (1806). James Wyatt's castellated palace at Richmond was begun in 1802, and demolished by 1828 before it was even completed.

picturesque romanticism of Wyatville's neo-gothic 'restoration' successfully reconnected the Germanic royal family to a romanticised conception of English history and identity. Watkin has argued that this could be viewed as a potent visual statement in the wake of the French Revolution,[166] pointing out that Edmund Burke's *Reflections on the Revolution in France* (1790), admired by George III, drew political comparisons between the preservation of historic buildings and historic institutions, such as the monarchy.[167] Richmond itself had become a refuge of the French aristocracy, fleeing the violence on the continent for the 'old world' of the British monarchy; Walpole's letters are full of references to this immigrant community.[168] No doubt the nostalgic and patriotic overtones of gothic architecture, as opposed to continental classicism, soothed the nerves of a paranoid English aristocracy.

The gothic style had been promoted as nostalgic and patriotic since at least the early eighteenth century. Pope argued that Shakespeare's work resembled "an ancient majestic piece of *Gothick* [sic] Architecture, compar'd with a neat Modern building: The latter is more elegant and glaring, but the former is more strong and more solemn".[169] Pope's neighbour, garden commentator Batty Langley, even authored a book entitled *Ancient Architecture, Restored,* and *Improved [. . .] in the Gothic Mode for the Ornamenting of Buildings and Gardens* (1742), in which he promoted the style "as part of his patriotic campaign for English traditions, crafts and craftsmen".[170] While gothic was emerging as a suitably patriotic architecture, the picturesque English landscape style was being heralded as symbolic of English conservatism. In *Sketches and Hints on Landscape Gardening* (1795), landscape architect Humphrey Repton wrote,

> The neatness, simplicity, and elegence [sic] of English gardening, have acquired the approbation of the present century, as the happy medium betwixt the wildness of nature and the stiffness of art; in the same manner as the English constitution is the happy medium between the liberty of savages, and the restraint of despotic government; and so long as we enjoy the benefit of these middle degrees, between the extremes of each, let experiments of untried theoretical improvement be made in some other country.[171]

Repton's dedication of *Sketches and Hints* to George III likewise demonstrates it as a work of patriotism.

Familiar with Repton's famous 'Red Books', in which he presented fold-out watercolour sketches of proposals to clients, it was probably on George III's recommendation that Repton was commissioned to re-landscape the grounds surrounding Richmond Park's White Lodge for Prime Minister Henry Addington in 1805.[172] Repton shared the criticisms of the Brownian picturesque as set out in Uvedale Price's *Essay on the Picturesque* (1794) and Richard Payne Knight's *The Landscape* (1794), which they regarded as "bland and outdated".[173] Repton's surviving 'Red Book' watercolours illustrate the lodge in its Brownian state, with the house marooned in an ocean of lawn. Repton's proposed improvement, illustrated on a folding 'flap', was to introduce a simple floral arbour, mediating between the park and house, and framing strategic vistas. This enables a pair of figures to once again populate the garden, allowing for the rustic intellectual pursuits of gardening and botany. Here, again, is the English landscape's ability to mediate between the 'wildness of nature' and the 'stiffness of art'.

The patronage of the rustic gothic style by eminent figures such as Walpole encouraged a proliferation of new gothic 'castles' on the banks of the Thames. Richmond Hill's Terrace Gardens were bordered by several of these gothic villas. Gothic House on Petersham Road was constructed in about 1810, including the substantial remodelling of an earlier house, and was for a time the home of Madame de Stael, a member of Richmond's aforementioned French immigrant community. Though Gothic House and a neighbouring villa were demolished in 1938, a third gothic villa survives on Richmond Hill (now the Old Vicarage School). The applied stucco ornamentation, turrets and crenellations disguise a late seventeenth-century mansion, also completely remodelled in 1810.[174]

Centring the imperial landscape in Richmond

Along with gothic and Palladian schemes, Chambers experimented with oriental designs in his role as architect to Princess Augusta at Kew from 1757.[175] Born in Sweden to British parents, Chambers's employment in the Swedish East India Company had taken him to Bengal and China (1740–49), where he observed oriental buildings. Chambers created more than 25 structures at Kew, including typical features, such as classical temples and a Palladian bridge, along with the unconventional additions of a gothic 'cathedral', 'mosque', Moorish 'alhambra' and Chinese pagoda (1761) (Figure 1.11). According to Watkin,

> Chinese garden buildings were associated with the new appreciation of nature and the 'natural' style in gardening which also symbolised individual liberty and the politics of the country Whigs in opposition to Robert Walpole. For members of this 'Patriot Opposition' or country party, landscape design and the politics of 'retirement' into the countryside became a medium for the expression of patriotism.[176]

Nature and rustic simplicity could thus find expression in oriental as well as gothic styles, while the collection of structures at Kew demonstrated the nation's learned society and the extent of British political influence worldwide. At Kew, the English picturesque garden was presented as equivalent to any that the world could offer. The idea of the superiority

Figure 1.11 A View of the Wilderness with the Alhambra, the Pagoda and the Mosque. Engraving from Sir William Chambers's *Designs for Kew* (1763).

48   *The origins of the protected view*

of the English landscape over even the most famed of foreign landscapes is illustrated by a later verse from Alaric Watts's *Lyrics of the Heart* (1851):

> Let poets rave of Arno's stream
> And painters of the winding Rhine
> I will not ask a lovelier dream,
> A sweeter scene, fair Thames, than thine;
> An 'neath a summer's sun's decline
> Thou wanderest at thine own sweet will
> Reflecting from thy face divine
> The flower-wreathed brow of Richmond Hill.[177]

That one could interpret the garden buildings of Kew as a reflection of a society which viewed itself assuredly as the enlightened centre of the world is suggested by the incorporation of scientific instrumentation in the garden design. At Richmond, Chambers was responsible for the design of George III's personal observatory, constructed for the king's observation of the transit of Venus on 3 June 1769.[178] The interest in developing such an observatory was stimulated by a rivalry with other nations, particularly France, in viewing the transit.[179] Designing in collaboration with the king's astronomer, Stephen Demainbray, Chambers produced a plain Anglo-Palladian structure, a Thames-side villa in its own right, not unlike Sir Robert Taylor's neighbouring Asgill House, a few hundred metres upstream. As architectural historian James Early explains, the use of Anglo-Palladianism for scientific buildings was befitting of the contemporary "belief in a uniform standard of taste valid for all arts in all ages" and "is analogous to Newton's effort to comprehend all the diversity of the physical universe within a single system of mathematical laws".[180] Thus, the simplicity and logic of Palladian architecture conformed to the "close, naked, natural way of speaking [. . .] near [to . . .] mathematical plainness"[181] advocated by the scientists of the Royal Academy.

Richmond's gardens seemed to be at the epicentre of the scientific world at that time; with the construction of the Observatory, a new meridian was established at Richmond, marked by a series of obelisks positioned in the gardens. Though the Richmond meridian never succeeded in overtaking Greenwich's Prime Meridian, the idea was the same, that all timepieces should be adjusted in relation to the Royal Time at Richmond. The empire, and the world, thus looked to Richmond, and the king's Arcadian gardens would be at the spiritual and scientific centre of it all.

We have seen how the Thames landscape, and the visual conventions by which it was observed, evolved during the course of centuries, moving from the rigid axiality of the Renaissance garden to the informal naturalism of the picturesque. Each advance in fashion, taste and science is reflected in the architecture and landscape architecture along this stretch of the Thames. From the late eighteenth century, Richmond would undergo drastic economic and infrastructural changes, but as we shall see, the picturesque mode would continue to absorb these technological shifts, remaining relevant right up to the present day. As I will argue in the remaining sections of this chapter, only where development has challenged the picturesque quality of the view from Richmond Hill has controversy arisen. Thus, even the 'Indignation' campaigns of the early 1900s, which led to the preservation of the view from Richmond Hill, may be seen as a continuation of a culturally engrained picturesque mode of vision.

The railway, suburbia and the persistence of the picturesque

This section will chart the story of increasing suburban and infrastructural developments along this stretch of the Thames from steamboat to rail and the extension of the London Underground. It is remarkable that the picturesque mode of vision persisted, and indeed was reinforced in this process, not least by the advertising campaigns of transport companies. As the view from Richmond Hill became increasingly accessible to the wider general public, one could argue that its continuous reproduction in tourist literature also truly rendered it visual public property. Thus, one might suggest that this sense of public ownership over the view would inevitably lead to calls for its transfer into state protection, to be achieved under the *Richmond, Petersham and Ham Open Spaces Act* of 1902.

As we have seen, the second half of the eighteenth century saw a period of prosperity which encouraged a spate of development along the Thames. A rash of fashionable villas may be discerned in Samuel Leigh's *Panorama of the Thames from London to Richmond* (c. 1830). Along with this explosion in development, new infrastructure rapidly increased the number of visitors to the town for leisure purposes. Leigh's panorama, taken from a boat in the Thames, and designed to be shown to audiences in movement via its winding onto two rotating poles, reflects the popularity of excursions by public river steamers, introduced in 1816. Such steamers allowed all classes the opportunity to take a day trip to the country from London Bridge in affordable and relative comfort.[182] An 1825 newspaper correspondent gives an account of the journey which, along with Leigh's panorama, paints a vivid picture of the Thames landscape around Richmond at this time:

> The Aits, or Osier Islands, are picturesque interspersions on the Thames. Its banks are studded with neat cottages or elegant villas [. . .] the lawns come sweeping down like green velvet to the edge of its soft-flowing waters, and the scenery improves till we are borne into the full bosom of its beauty – the village of Richmond. On coming within the sight of this, the most delightful scene in our sea-girt isle, the band on board the steam boat plays "The Lass of Richmond Hill" while the vessel glides on translucent water.[183]

Many of the qualities which made steamboat travel so alluring are highlighted in this passage. In particular, the picturesque gardens and villas lining the Thames could, in many cases, be viewed only from the river. Moreover, the visual experience of 'gliding' through the unfolding scenery remained in stark contrast to the experience of contemporary road travel. The paucity of the road network is highlighted by the lack of a river crossing at Richmond until the construction of the first bridge, proposed in 1772.[184] The bridge proposal caused widespread controversy as it was feared it might damage the picturesque qualities of the Thames landscape. As such it represents perhaps the earliest expression of 'indignation' over the development of a landscape which was then already perceived to be of special historical, cultural and aesthetic value. A correspondent of *Lloyd's Evening Post* angrily remarked,

> It is to be a wooden bridge – what a cat-stick building this must be, to be executed in so short a time! Methinks I hear Old Thames groan, to be so vilely strode [. . .] If our view up and down that delightful River must be obstructed [. . .] let it be an elegant and free bridge.[185]

Succumbing to pressure, Parliament passed the *Richmond Bridge Act* (1772), selecting 90 commissioners to redesign the bridge, among whom were Brown, Walpole and Garrick. Architect James Paine, a noted designer of ornamental landscape garden bridges across the country,[186] was selected to design a Palladian crossing in white Portland stone, completed in 1777. Contemporary writers praised the new bridge for its scenic embellishment of the picturesque landscape; as an article in *The London Magazine* of 1779 stated, "[The bridge] presents the spectator with one of the richest landscapes nature and art ever produced by their joint efforts, and connoisseurs in painting will instantly be reminded of some of the best performances of Claude Lorrain".[187] Further promoting the Richmond landscape as if it were the picturesque garden of a gentleman's estate, Paine illustrated his bridge design in the second volume of his *Plans, Elevations, and Sections of Noblemen and Gentlemen's Houses* (1783). Paine's bridge is celebrated in Reverend Thomas Maurice's *Richmond Hill; A Descriptive and Historical Poem* (1807), which references Anglo-Palladianism ("no useless, glaring ornaments offend"), classical Greece ("Attic elegance") and the Thames landscape ("embowered in verdure heaped unbounded round"):

> Mark where yon beauteous Bridge with modest pride
> Throws its broad shadow o'er the subject tide –
> There Attic elegance and strength unite,
> And fair proportion's charms the eye delight;
> There, graceful while the spacious arches bend,
> No useless, glaring ornaments offend –
> Embowered in verdure heaped unbounded round
> Of every varied hue that shades the ground.

Its polished surface of unsullied white
With heightened lustre beams upon the sight.[188]

Maurice's poem was employed by the Thames steamboat companies, which added it to their posters in order to advertise their services. Prior to the construction of Paine's bridge, all traffic had to be ferried over the river. Up to this date, the river landscape of Richmond was, therefore, most commonly appreciated from the water, which afforded the traveller unrivalled views of the riverside villas and their gardens. This is demonstrated by an article from *The Builder*, which pointed out in 1890 that "thousands have scanned curiously from the deck of a river steamer"[189] the gardens of Marble Hill House. Their diligent search was for the fictional location of a scene from Walter Scott's popular novel *The Heart of Mid-Lothian* (1818), in which character Jeanie Deans pleads with Queen Caroline, in the company of Lady Suffolk, for her half-sister's life.[190] The contemporary reader was probably already familiar with the picturesque view from Richmond Hill via its many literary and pictorial reproductions, but Scott's historical novel reinforced its perception as an important historic landscape view, describing it as

> A commanding eminence . . . where the beauty of English landscape was displayed in its utmost luxuriance. . . . A huge sea of verdure, with crossing and intersecting promontories of massive and tufted groves, was tenanted by numberless flocks and herds, which seemed to wander unrestrained and unbounded through the rich pastures. The Thames, here turreted with villas, and there garlanded with forests, moved on slowly and placidly, like the mighty monarch of the scene, to whom all its other beauties were but accessories, and bore on its bosom an hundred barks and skiffs whose white sails, and gaily fluttering pennons, gave life to the whole.[191]

By 1840, there were three daily steamboats from London Bridge to Richmond, increasing to six daily by 1843. On the roads too, the number of users was booming; the combined users of public coaches and omnibuses (introduced from 1830) on the Richmond to London route in 1843 has been estimated at 1,180,000 passengers a year.[192] Railway promoters soon realised that the abundance of passengers was a potentially lucrative market, and hoped to tap some of the profit themselves.

The arrival of the London & South Western Railway in Richmond (1846) further increased the attraction of this stretch of the Thames for weekend retreats and leisure pursuits. The line's extension to Twickenham (1848) necessitated the crossing of the Thames with three 100-foot cast-iron spans. However modern the introduction of Joseph Locke's Twickenham railway bridge was, it was quickly absorbed into the picturesque landscape of the Thames and appropriated by artists for their own pictorial effects. This is demonstrated by artist George Hilditch's *Richmond from beneath the Railway Bridge* (c. 1849), which depicts Paine's Richmond road bridge, neatly framed by the brick vault of Locke's new railway. Hilditch, whose many works depicting the area[193] earned him the nickname of "the Richmond painter",[194] frames this picturesque landscape with what could be interpreted as the archaeological remains of some ancient Roman structure, though it is the land-arch of Locke's newly constructed railway bridge. The classical cornicing and rustic collection of loose stones to the foreground strengthen this allusion to the landscapes of classical antiquity.

Another local artist, J.M.W. Turner, had also experimented with the addition of classical antiquities to the Richmond landscape. In *Thomson's Aeolian Harp* (1809) (Figure 1.12), Turner introduced the shattered remains of the Egerian Grotto, a classical association with which we are already familiar from the writings of Pope. Pope is himself indirectly referenced in the painting by Turner's distortion of the landscape to include the Thames-side villas of Twickenham. In doing so, Turner connected the writings of Pope and Thomson, and the classical histories to which they referred, directly to the view from Richmond Hill.

A further demonstration of the reinforcement of eighteenth-century perceptions of the view is Turner's own poetry, which he modelled on that of Thomson. For example, *Thomson's Aeolian Harp* was accompanied by a poem in tribute to the two poets:

> On Thomson's tomb the dewy drops distil,
> Soft tears of pity shed for Pope's lost fane,
> To worth and verse adheres sad memory still,
> Scorning to wear ensnaring fashion's chain.

Figure 1.12 *Thompson's Aeolian Harp* by J.M.W. Turner (1809) distorts the view of the Thames to include a clear view of Twickenham and Pope's villa. Turner also freely adds a depiction of the Egerian grotto to the right of the scene, complete with classical dancers.

Source: Public Domain.

In silence go fair Thames for all is laid;
His pastoral reeds untied and harp unstrung,
Sunk is their harmony in Twickenham's glade.
While flows thy stream, unheed'd and unsung.[195]

Turner's poem conveys a melancholic vision of decay echoed in his contemporary painting *A View of Pope's Villa during Its Dilapidation* (1808). The ruinous villa in Turner's painting performs the same role as the classical ruin in an Arcadian landscape, drawing out nostalgic recollections of a former golden age. To accompany the painting, Turner wrote the following lines in despair:

O lost to honor and the sence [*sic*] of shame,
Can Britain so forget Pope's well earned fame,
To desolation doom the poet's fane,
The pride of Twickenham's bower and silver Thame,
...
Now to destruction doom'd thy peaceful grott,
Pope's willow bending to the earth forgot.[196]

Though Turner's poetry suggests his deep regret – his 'indignation' – at the loss of Pope's villa and gardens, representatives of a former golden age subjected to melancholic and ruinous decay, he did in fact continue to paint many aspects of the Thames landscape, reinforcing the notion of the landscape's national historic and cultural significance. Turner returned to Richmond Hill with *England: Richmond Hill, on the Prince Regent's Birthday* (1819) (Figure 1.13). The title of this work underscores the painting as a patriotic

Figure 1.13 England: Richmond Hill, on the Prince Regent's Birthday, by J.M.W. Turner (1819). In this work, the landscape of Richmond and the hill in particular are emphatically linked with the notion of Englishness.

Source: © Tate, London 2018.

work; the view from Richmond Hill comes to represent England itself, and the theme is a celebration of the British monarchy. The party, held in the open air on the terrace of Richmond Hill, recalls the rustic fêtes galantes of Queen Caroline's Augustan court at Richmond, a symbolic return to and celebration of nature and pastoral simplicity.

Turner himself practised this idealised dream of pastoral life, building himself a comfortable suburban villa on land adjacent to Marble Hill House, Twickenham, in 1807. 'Sandycombe Lodge' has survived, albeit in a much-altered state, hemmed in between ranks of Edwardian terraces. Though the villa is thought to be of his own design, it has been suggested that Turner's friend the architect John Soane may have provided advice.[197] The villa's generous gardens ran seamlessly into Twickenham Park in one direction, and Marble Hill's parkland in the other; thus, Turner benefitted from an unbroken view of the Thames and first-hand familiarity with the popular image of Richmond as a picturesque landscape of genteel villas.

The image of an affluent society of riverside villas within easy reach of the city, promoted by the work of artists and writers, began to attract scores of commuters after the arrival of the railway – Turner and Charles Dickens included – who set up their own comfortable villas and gardens in the vicinity of Richmond. As land prices continued to rise, the ample gardens of these villa estates came under increasing development pressure. An Ordnance Survey map of 1879 shows Turner's gardens largely as they were at the time of their sale in 1826, and illustrates the villa's location on a quiet country lane.[198] By 1913, however, Turner's garden and adjacent Twickenham Park had been subdivided into a number of villa plots, leading to Sandycombe Road's current appearance as a typical suburban street.[199]

As these expanding suburban developments encroached upon large areas of former landscape garden, they began to adopt many of the features associated with picturesque landscape design. An excellent example is the suburban estate of St Margaret's, Twickenham, developed in 1854 on a part of the grounds of Twickenham Park which had been severed from the house by the building of the railway (1848). This land was bought from the Earl of Kilmorey by the Conservative Land Association, who immediately began to develop the site as a residential estate for the professional middle classes. At the centre of the scheme, a large medieval fishpond was reworked into a more picturesque serpentine lake, set amid a series of pleasure gardens for the sole use of the occupants. To maintain the elegance of the buildings and grounds a trust was established and legal covenants produced, to prevent visual alterations to the estate. The topography of the site was used in the creation of separate grades for pedestrians and road traffic, linking three pleasure gardens and a riverside promenade with grotto-tunnels similar to those of Pope, Garrick and Lord Montagu. This move created an unbroken landscape setting for the suburban villas which lined the grounds, recreating elements of the picturesque landscape of Twickenham Park despite its redevelopment. The St Margaret's estate successfully played to the middle-class market, who dreamed of the perfect blend of privileged *rus-in-urbe*, provided by the estate's riverside location, aristocratic pleasure gardens and the adjacent mainline station with direct services to London Waterloo.

The absorption of the railway into the picturesque composition of St Margaret's is mirrored by the contemporary admiration of railway technology by artists. For example, in *Rain, Steam and Speed* (1844), Turner's novel depiction of a speeding locomotive seen through a haze of thundering rain is nevertheless set in a fairly conventional picturesque landscape; the view is of Isambard Kingdom Brunel's Great Western Railway Bridge at Maidenhead, with a bend of the Thames, complete with boatman, bridge and distant wooded hills, all conforming to conventions familiar to us from Richmond Hill's popular view.

Equally struck by the railways' picturesque potential, other artists, such as French Impressionist Camille Pissarro, were attracted to the new suburbs growing up around London. In 1892, Pissarro moved to 1 Gloucester Terrace, Kew, painting *Bank Holiday, Kew* and *Kew Green* from the windows of this house.[200] Pissarro's affinity with picturesque landscapes is demonstrated by his depiction of 'Capability' Brown's *Rhododendron Dell at Kew* (1892), which he described as "a dream. What trees, what lawns, what attractive and subtle undulations of the land!"[201] Pissarro's paintings, including *Upper Norwood in the Snow*, *The Avenue, Dulwich* and *Crystal Palace*, present London's growing suburbs as picturesque scenes. In particular, Pissarro's *Bath Road, Bedford Park* (1897) could be an image of an idyllic rural lane complete with cottages and smoking chimneys, but the subject is a new suburb of semi-detached homes; the artist's picturesque composition reflects the idyllic dreams of suburban commuters. Camille's son Lucien Pissarro had moved to a new home at 62 Bath Road, Bedford Park, Chiswick, in the 1890s. On a visit in 1897, Camille Pissarro made a series of seven paintings, all taken from the windows and roof terrace of the Bedford Park home. The role played by the railways in encouraging the development of the Bedford Park suburb is highlighted by Pissarro's paintings *Lordship Lane Station* and *The Train, Bedford Park* (c. 1870s), both of which seem to promote the railways as a means to tour the countryside – a continuation of the picturesque tourism advocated by Reverend William Gilpin and others. Pissarro's paintings are full of rural imagery, despite their depiction of suburban subjects; *The Footbridge at Bedford Park* (1897) and *Jubilee Fête at Bedford Park* (1897) are full of people enjoying country life amid open fields and verdant landscapes, and the railway's conspicuous presence is as the facilitator of this blissful suburban existence. Camille's son Lucien[202] would himself later go on to produce over 50 paintings of Chiswick, Kew Gardens and Richmond, where he came to live briefly in 1935, including *Richmond Bridge, View from My Window at Richmond* and *The Thames at Richmond* (all 1935).

The semi-rural imagery presented by the Pissarros' works is a feature of the design of Bedford Park itself, which has been described by John

Betjeman as "the most significant suburb built in the last century, probably in the western world".[203] Architect Richard Norman Shaw's designs had a profound effect upon

> The architectural character of Bedford Park, one which delighted and surprised visitors who, emerging from Turnham Green station, felt themselves to be in a village or small country town where nothing had happened for at least a hundred years. In fact none of the houses bore more than a superficial resemblance to anything built in the 17th or 18th centuries; their apparent artlessness concealed a great deal of sophistication.[204]

Shaw's architecture referred to the historic buildings of the surrounding towns of Chiswick, Kew and Richmond, with prominent gables, ornamental bargeboards and jettied overhangs. These touches, combined with an irregular street plan which took into account existing mature trees, made for a picturesque streetscape with a certain rural quality. A contemporary advertisement dubbed it "The Healthiest Place in the World"[205] due to its provision of private gardens to every home and the addition of a communal club and tennis courts. These attributes of villa life were in contrast to the dirty and cramped conditions of the city with which it was always meant to be compared. The Bedford Park architects took the idea of the country villa, popular since the eighteenth century, and condensed it onto a smaller plot, reproducing the idyllic dream of villa life but making it accessible to middle-class professionals. As Herman Muthesius has written, "It signifies neither more nor less than the starting point of the smaller modern house, which spread from there over the whole country".[206]

The function of the railway as a machine for viewing the landscape, suggested by the works of Turner and the Pissarros, is illustrated by a proliferation of contemporary railway posters advertising excursions to picturesque locations across the country. The ever-changing view from the carriage window was a popular subject, directly tying railway technology to the picturesque view – for example, in posters of *Knaresborough* (LNER, 1928) and *Felixstowe* (LNER, 1934). Later, the new technology of photography would reproduce this arrangement, proposing the railway carriage as an ideal location for capturing the landscape on film. As a popular destination of weekend sojourns, Richmond itself was a subject of several of these railway posters, designed to entice weary city dwellers to weekend retreats and, in the process, to make a profit for the railway companies – for example, Charles Sharland's *Valley of the Thames* (1908), which shows a view of Richmond Hill crowned by its villas from the riverbank. A subsequent poster by John Henry Lloyd entitled *Too Much of a Good Thing* (1910) (Figure 1.14) depicts Sharland's poster, along with a selection of other picturesque views, lining a subway tunnel, each calling

Figure 1.14 John Henry Lloyd's *Too Much of a Good Thing* (1910) showing Sharland's Valley of the Thames to the left, competing for the attention of the day tripper. The landscape poster acted as a window to eternal summer weekends on the walls of London's dingy underground tunnels.

Source: © TfL.

for the attention of the weekend traveller. The posters are themselves like windows on idyllic landscapes of eternal summer, viewed from the dimly lit grime of the tunnel, and promise respite from the realities of city life, an escape to Richmond's Arcadia.

This effect, where the landscape view is framed as through a window, is a recurrent theme of railway poster art depicting the Thames landscape at Richmond. Alfred France's *Richmond* and Thomas Robert Way's *The Silver Thames* (both 1910) are composed of a series of small windows, like photographic snapshots or William Gilpin's watercolour vignettes. Significantly, the Richmond Hill view is illustrated in the bottom left-hand scene of the latter work, and the title is a nostalgic reference to James Thomson's description of the view in *The Seasons* (1730). The Richmond Hill view also features in a 1908 poster entitled *Richmond for Walking . . . and Other Jollities*, accompanied by an extract from William Ernest Henley's *Ballade of Midsummer Days and Nights* (1897) (Figure 1.15).

It could be argued that the poetical references of these railway posters continue Turner's attachment of poetry to his scenes of Richmond, which itself continued an illustrious regional history of poetry from the seventeenth century onwards. Arthur G. Bell's 1913 poster *Richmond Park* is again accompanied by a poem (author unknown), which directly advocates a painterly vision of the Richmond landscape:

> Here as the green leaves fade, the gold leaves fall.
> A still enchantment widens over all,
> Painting the woods with vaguer autumnal dyes
> Like ancient tapestries.[207]

Later posters would return to idealised views of picturesque tranquillity, choosing to adopt scenes from eighteenth-century landscape gardens as representative of the whole Thames valley region – for example, in Trerick John Williams's depiction of Chambers's Temple of Bellona, Kew Gardens (1929), Vera Ross's *Chiswick House* (1937) and Alan Sorrell's view of Garrick's Temple to Shakespeare (1938).

Lured to Richmond by the imagery of London Underground posters, by the early twentieth-century visitors could take a piece of this imagery home, or send it on to family and friends, in the form of mass-produced photographic postcards. Originally blank, the first photographic postcards were introduced around 1895, though the image was usually small to allow the message to be written on the same side. By 1902, the Post Office allowed the picture to take over a full side, with message and address written on the reverse.[208] In doing so, the role of the postcard changed from a simple note to a souvenir of travel, leisure time and landscapes seen. The Richmond Hill view, familiar from the mass circulation of prints, was an obvious and popular subject for postcard views. Though photography had taken over from the work of the artist, a certain painterly quality remains as the result of the hand colouring of many of these images. A 1906 postcard *View from*

Figure 1.15 Richmond for Walking . . . and Other Jollities (1908), showing the view from Richmond Hill as a destination for "Sunday afternoons".

Source: © TfL.

60 *The origins of the protected view*

Figure 1.16 Postcard *View from the Terrace, Richmond* (1906).
Source: Image from author's personal collection.

the Terrace, Richmond prominently displays a foreground vacant bench (Figure 1.16), as does *View on the Terrace, Richmond* (1909), enticing the viewer to project his or her presence into the image. The latter image draws attention to the implied view, framed by an opening in the trees opposite. Interestingly, images of the Terrace itself are common, suggesting that the activities of walking and observing others were as important to the Edwardian visitor as the view itself.

The effect of these postcards and posters was to perpetuate the mythic landscape of Richmond Hill, recycling the associations placed upon it by eighteenth-century poets, architects and artists. When the Marble Hill estate, which lies at the centre of the famous view, was threatened by redevelopment in 1901, a local newspaper article recycled a quote from Jonathan Swift's *Pastoral Dialogue between Richmond Lodge and Marble Hill* (1727):

> Some South Sea broker from the City,
> Will purchase me, and more's the pity,
> Lay all my fine plantations waste
> To fit them to his vulgar taste.

The author went on to state that the contemporary threat was not this time from a South Sea broker but from "the demon builder who will in all probability destroy this historical demesne with his exhibition of latter-day villadom".[209] Swift's fear that the Marble Hill estate might be destroyed, as early as 1727, highlights a perceived vulnerability of Richmond Hill's prospect from at least the first few decades of the eighteenth century, and its reuse here demonstrates the propensity of campaigners to consistently apply eighteenth-century values to the view's present reality.

'Indignation': what man owns the glory that Turner painted?

'Indignation', the name given to a number of popular campaigns which have voiced concern over development within the Richmond Hill view, originated in the late nineteenth century. Perhaps the first move to protect the view was taken in 1886, when the Richmond Vestry, headed by one-time mayor of London Sir Whittaker Ellis, purchased the Lansdowne and Buccleuch estates to form Richmond Hill's Terrace Gardens. In celebration, the popular magazine *Punch* published a satirical cartoon showing the 'Lass of Richmond Hill' being saved from the 'Jerry-Builder' dragon, whose stucco and cast-iron tail and smoking chimneypot hat (Figure 1.17) threaten to destroy the view with the following line:

A finer spot for a Building Lot,
Mine eyes did never see.

Despite this early success, towards the end of the century the Richmond Corporation had grown increasingly nervous about the motives of Richmond landowners who might be tempted to redevelop their land for profit. In a letter dated 10 December 1892, Charles Burt, mayor of Richmond, wrote to the trustees of the Earl of Dysart's estate at Ham House to discuss concerns that the trustees intended to construct a new road along the riverbank at Ham, and the conjecture that this might be the first step of a larger redevelopment of the historic estate. The trustees' response reminded Burt of their rights over Petersham Common, stating that "the apple of the eye to the view" from Richmond Hill "could at once be made available for building . . . by putting roads through [. . .] which would give a ready access to Petersham and Kingston". The only prevention of such a drastic redevelopment of the critical focal point of the view from Richmond Hill would be Richmond Corporation's "recompense" to the trustees through their consent of development proposals elsewhere.[210] In effect, the Dysart trustees were pressing for the abolition of public access rights to its vast 'Lammas Lands',[211] freeing them up for profitable development.

In the meantime, a bill known as the *Petersham and Ham Lands and Footpath Bill* (1896) was being prepared for presentation to Parliament,

Figure 1.17 Cartoon from *Punch* magazine showing the 'Lass of Richmond Hill' being saved from 'Jerry-Builder Dragon', whose stucco, cast-iron railings and smoking chimneypot hat threaten to invade the landscape.

Source: Image from *Punch* (9 October 1886), p. 170.

the culmination of the work of a number of local 'amenity societies' which sought to preserve Richmond's open spaces for their aesthetic and recreational value. In fact, these groups had already appealed to Her Majesty's First Commissioner of Works to purchase Bute House, from the same Sir Whittaker Ellis, in order to preserve another portion of Richmond's view.[212] Alas, the proposed purchase of Bute House in 1894 came to nothing, while the bill's concession to the Dysart trustees in the abolition of certain Lammas rights was its eventual undoing. Opponents of the bill claimed that residents were pursued by Richmond Corporation to give up their rights in return for £15,000 towards the cost of a new school – an accusation tantamount to bribery. Defeated, Burt wrote to *The Times* in frustration that "The Corporation indignantly repudiate the suggestion that they were to receive money for the sacrifice of public rights", adding that "the saving of the view from Richmond-Terrace is what the Corporation and their constituents have been striving after for years; it is one of the great objects of their existence".[213] To Burt, these slanderous accusations would achieve nothing but the undermining of the bill under which "the view would be secured forever", adding that "by the rejection of the Bill [the view] is gravely imperilled".[214]

One year previous to the Lammas Lands controversy, another property with a direct impact on the view, a tiny island in the middle of the Thames known as Petersham Ait, was put up for sale by owner Joseph Glover. Ellis, the adjacent landowner, declined to purchase the island for a sum of £5,000, proposing that the Richmond Corporation buy it for the town. Burt's Amenities Committee considered the proposal, eventually concluding

> That while the Committee think it desirable that the Island should be acquired for the Corporation if it could be obtained at a reasonable price, they are of the opinion that in view of the sum now named, it would be useless to enter into any negotiation for its purchase.[215]

In the end, no suitable purchaser could be found for the island. Three years later, Glover put the island up for public auction, again offering it to the Richmond Corporation for a reduced price. To further motivate the Richmond Corporation, Glover publicly announced he was prepared to sell the island to an advertising company,[216] as the island's conspicuous nature, in terms of passing boat and road traffic as well as its prominence within the Richmond Hill prospect, had potential as a lucrative location for billboards.[217] Glover's sale cards noted that "It will be seen that 'Glover's Island' [. . .] is a most conspicuous object from Richmond Hill", while an auction notice stated it would make "a splendid site for the erection of a first class Club or Hotel, or for an electric storage station, Launch Works, or as an advertising medium" (Figure 1.18). Somewhat

64 *The origins of the protected view*

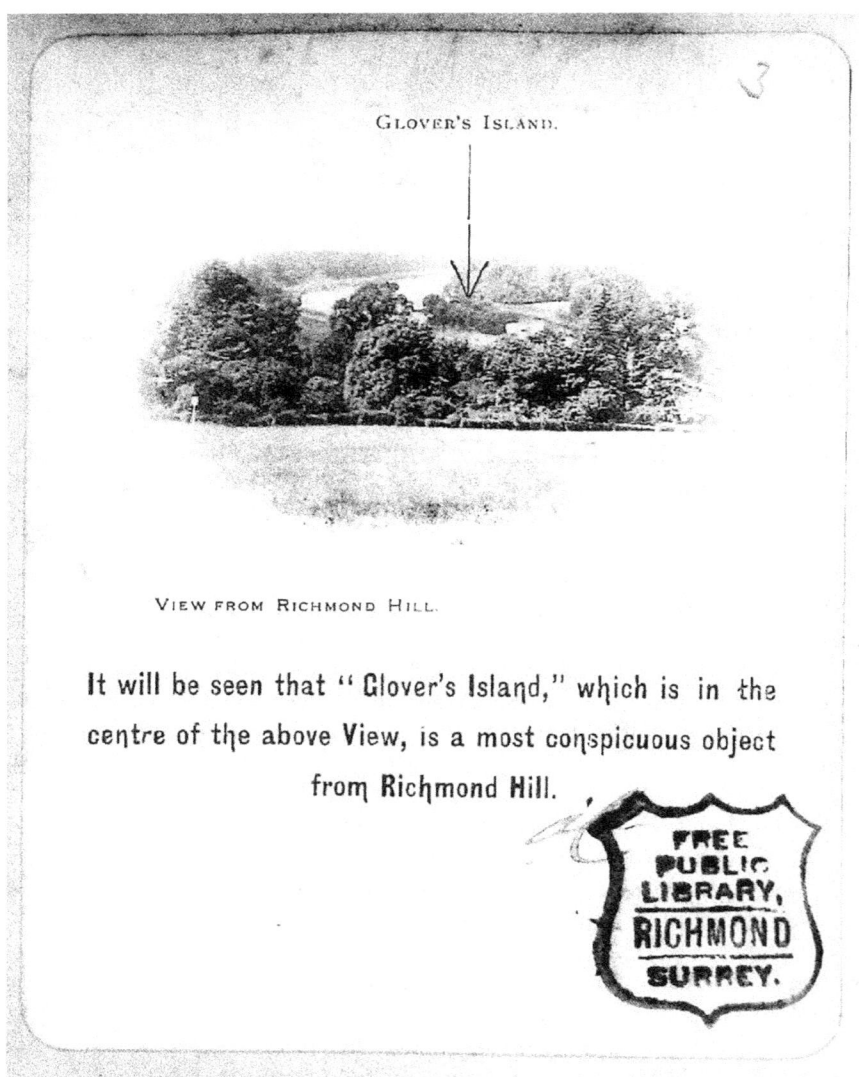

Figure 1.18 Sale card c. 1890s demonstrating the conspicuous nature of the island, and therefore its suitability for development with billboards.
Source: Image courtesy of the Library of Richmond-upon-Thames.

understandably, Glover's actions appalled local campaigners, as one local newspaper described:

> The Island lies right in the foreground of the famous view from Richmond Hill, and for that reason it has caused something like a spasm of alarm

when the owner has threatened [. . .] to sell it as the site for advertising hoardings [. . .] or for something else equally disagreeable.[218]

Another article speculated on the financial motives behind Glover's actions:

> Mr Glover may have hoped that the members of the Town Council, with their nerves shaken by dreadful apparitions of big chimneys, unsightly sheds, ugly hoardings, or fearsome sky signs [. . .] would be prepared to pay anything to prevent their waking hours being made wretched by the materialisation of this phantasmagoria.[219]

However, the high price demanded by Glover was simply too much for the Richmond Corporation to swallow. Angry, and fearing the real possibility that another purchaser would disfigure the island, Burt is reputed to have said,

> If the island were used as an advertisement station a big gallows would rise on Petersham Meadows opposite, with an effigy of the owner suspended [. . .] Anyone who attempted to use the island for a disfiguring purpose would be hounded out of Richmond.[220]

Deterred, perhaps, by such statements, the highest bid received at auction was considerably below Glover's expectations, so he promptly withdrew the island from sale.[221]

Some years later, in 1900, Petersham Ait was eventually purchased by philanthropist Max Waechter, a resident of Richmond Hill. The following year, Waechter donated the island to the town, along with his nearby house and garden, in an effort to preserve the view for the public good.[222] It is fitting that a celebration to mark the event was held at the Star and Garter Hotel on Richmond Hill and attended by notable figures of the art world, including Sir Edward Poynter (president of the Royal Academy). At this event, the town's mayor chancellor presented Waechter with a plaque which read,

> [T]his Council [. . .] desire to place on record their high appreciation of so generous an act whereby the far-famed view from Richmond Hill will forever be preserved. They would further add their conviction that with this preservation of Richmond's famous landscape Mr. Max Waechter's name will for all time be associated.[223]

In hindsight, the spirit of celebration that spring evening on Richmond Hill was perhaps a little premature – as just months later, the future of the Marble Hill estate was called into question.

Marble Hill had been recently purchased by William Cunard of the shipping family. Together with the adjacent Orleans House and Lebanon House estates, the Cunards had acquired a large part of the lands visible from Richmond Hill, as illustrated by a contemporary article and map in the *Westminster Budget*.[224] Cunard's decision to develop the Lebanon House estate[225] with suburban villas was interpreted as the forerunner of a much larger redevelopment of the Twickenham riverbank.[226] Given the wealth, power and commercial savviness of the Cunards, campaigners looked increasingly to drum up nationwide pressure for governmental assistance in securing the future of the view. The *Daily Mail* wrote, "Richmond turns to all England for help in preserving what all England has so thoroughly enjoyed", adding, "The view from Richmond Hill is the World's view, not Richmond's only. Let the work of preservation be started by the City of London or the Country at large".[227] A correspondent for the *Daily News* saw the view as the shared possession of all, and for all time, passed from one generation to another:

> Hundreds and thousands of people have acquired by long lapse of time a vested interest in the natural beauty of a certain spot. They have gazed on it often and often, it has put thoughts in their minds that chased out the little grimy pre-occupations of a mean existence, as mountain water would cleanse a vessel. Their parents may have taken them to see it; they may show it to their children, who may have little enough of nature or of beauty in their small brick-bound experience. Then, suddenly, the hand of a man unknown to them is lifted, and the trees fall [. . .] for building purposes; a man can do as he likes with his own. *But what man owns the glory that Turner painted?*[228]

These fears had been sparked by road-building activity on the Marble Hill estate,[229] which the *Architectural Review* stated was "The centre and critical point of the view", adding, "it is evident that the deep wedge of woodland formed by Marble Hill is [the view's] most necessary and indispensable part; that spoiled, the view tumbles to pieces, with an eyesore for its focus".[230]

Along with the aesthetic argument for saving the Marble Hill estate, the *Architectural Review* re-emphasised the historical and literary associations of the villa, stating, "Marble Hill is a monument to our poetry, where we may taste the orderly dream of eighteenth century classics", declaring it "an architect's rendering of the feelings of Pope in the forms of Palladio".[231] While the architectural community viewed Marble Hill House as a monument worthy of protection, the popular press also presented Richmond's view as a monument of world heritage value, worthy of the same protection:

> Why are we to lavish our picturesque sensibility, our feeling for history, romance and beauty on lands and scenes not our own, to protect against the restoration of St. Mark's at Venice or against the submersion of the Temple at Philae, and yet care nothing for such a truly national possession as the prospect from Richmond Hill? [. . .] Shall it be said of this wealthy and prosperous generation that it could spare no money

and give no thought to the preservation [. . .] of what still remains of beauty and sylvan charm to the most characteristic English landscape to be found within the four seas?[232]

Encouraged by the press campaign, a 'Richmond Hill View Executive Committee' was formed in July 1901 by a number of influential founding members, including artists Sir Edward Poynter, PRA, and Sir William Blake Richmond, Royal Academician. The work of this committee was to prepare a bill for Parliament seeking the preservation of both Marble Hill and the Dysart Estate, as well as to drum up the support of the media and other figureheads. Early proposals for the bill appear in the *Twickenham Herald*'s 'The Dysart Proposals: To Stand or Fall Together',[233] *The Times*'s 'Richmond Hill (Preservation of the View)'[234] and *Richmond and Twickenham Times*'s 'The Bill to Save and the Bill to Build'.[235] In many respects, the 'Dysart Estates Bill', or the 'Richmond Hill View Preservation Bill' as it was popularly dubbed, was a repeat of the bill thrown out by Parliament in 1896, stipulating many of the same terms previously rejected, such as the abolition of Lammas rights. However, as an article in the *Twickenham Herald* pointed out, changes to the bill ensured that all parties were likely to benefit from its enactment;[236] Richmond would receive new public lands, Ham residents would be compensated for the loss of Lammas rights and the proposal for a riverside road was to be thrown out.[237] Despite these concessions, the bill was met with some opposition. Max Waechter, in a letter to the *Daily Chronicle*, criticised the bill's terms as "sops to the different local bodies in order to buy off their opposition".[238] However, the bill was eventually passed in 1902 as the *Richmond, Petersham and Ham Open Spaces Act*. Following the success of the bill, the Marble Hill estate was secured for the nation[239] and opened as a public park under the authority of the London County Council on 30 May 1903.[240] The *Twickenham Herald*, in an account of the opening, stated that

> [The committee] felt that a national view was at stake; that a historic view was at stake, nay, that a view that was necessary to the whole world was at stake; and they never relaxed their efforts till victory was won [. . .] It was not only the glory of London, but the glory of the British Empire.[241]

The protection of the view, via the 1902 *Richmond, Petersham and Ham Open Spaces Act*, marks a significant victory for preservation advocacy groups at a time when most, including the National Trust (formed 1894) and the Society for the Protection of Ancient Buildings (formed 1877), were still in their infancy. In fact, the Act which saved Richmond Hill predates the 1913 *Ancient Monuments Consolidation and Amendment Act*, highlighting the extent to which the vista was perceived to be of national historical importance.

68 *The origins of the protected view*

It should be noted that along with the emergence of preservation bodies, the protection of Richmond Hill's view also coincides with the establishment of a British town planning profession. This is demonstrated by the discipline's first statutory recognition in the Housing and Town Planning Act of 1909,[242] and by the establishment of the first formal university programme at the Department of Civic Design, Liverpool University. By 1913, the Town Planning Association had founded the International Garden Cities Federation,[243] ensuring the place of the picturesque tradition as one of the touchstones of British town planning. One could make a comparison between the movement which sought to control the view of Richmond and the emergence of a profession concerned with the design and aesthetics of townscapes.

This was a time of renewed historical interest in the development of British towns and cities and of artistic interest in their resultant visual character, an interest which grew in reaction to the redevelopment of historic city centres in the wake of the Second World War. The *Greater London Plan* (1944) was a bold attempt to plan for post-war London in which significantly, and contrary to movements in town planning outside London,[244] author Sir Patrick Abercrombie advocated the protection of green belts and characterful urban centres. Abercrombie stated,

> The sprawling outward expansion of London has engulfed many towns and villages. Within the Suburban and Inner Urban rings they are now embedded in a vast sea of inchoate development. [. . .] Only a few have managed to resist the flow of disorderly building, and they have retained individuality. [. . .] Unyielding barriers such as permanent open spaces and rivers have defended their integrity.[245]

Of the few remaining old centres, Abercrombie references only one as an example of an intact and characterful centre, stating, "Richmond, which lies between the Thames and Richmond Great Park in one direction and between Kew Gardens and Petersham Common in the other, is an example of a well-defined community in the Suburban Ring which has stood firm".[246] No doubt Abercrombie was well aware that it was policies such as the *Richmond, Petersham and Ham Open Spaces Act* which had preserved the common lands and served to protect Richmond's well-defined rural character and views.

Further evidence of growing post-war interest in Richmond's historic visual character can be found in the publishing of a number of historic guides, including Janet Dunbar's significantly entitled *A Prospect of Richmond* (1966). Intriguingly, Dunbar connects contemporary negative attitudes towards Richmond's development with a historical lineage of anti-change sentiment. She writes,

> From the sixteenth century onward, inhabitants of the town cried Woe and behold! When familiar buildings came down to make way for a

newer look: from the eighteenth century onward, householders held Indignation Meetings when there was a danger of the Rates Going Up. Patterns of thought and behaviours repeat themselves in fascinating variation. Disapproving Richmond fingers pointed at the dissolute nobles of the 1500s, the outlandish Carolean fashions of the 1600s, the uninhibited raffishness of the 1700s, the Sabbath-breakers of the 1800s – just as they point to the gaudy goings-on of our own day.[247]

Dunbar's reference to a "pattern of thought" legitimises the message of anti-development campaigners as the unbroken historical tradition of "disapproving Richmond fingers"; loyal townsfolk campaigning to protect their town from the "outlandish" actions of external investors and developers. Dunbar's thoughts on contemporary architecture are implied via a passage on Richmond's eighteenth-century homes: "Here is a great sweep of beautiful houses, Queen Anne and Georgian. There is much variety and complete unity: each house stands happily by its neighbour, whatever the difference in style".[248] In this passage, Dunbar reveals her appreciation of the picturesque qualities of Richmond's eighteenth-century townscape. Dunbar's use of the words "variety and complete unity" incorporates much the same message as Gordon Cullen's roughly contemporary seminal examination of urban picturesque in *Townscape* (1961). Cullen uses the words "variety" and "harmony", which may be traced to William Gilpin's use of the same in *Three Essays on Picturesque Beauty* (1794).

Cullen's work, and particularly his emphasis on the qualities of a serial visual experience of townscapes, shares much with the picturesque movement in landscape architecture. His work no doubt played an influential role in the *Thames Landscape Strategy* (1994),[249] created as a management and development plan for the stretch of the Thames between Hampton and Kew, which re-envisaged the river, the old settlements and suburban developments as a single coherent picturesque landscape. The importance placed upon the history of art, architecture and landscape particularly is demonstrated by the involvement of English Heritage, the Royal Fine Art Commission and the Garden History Society in drawing up the document, and by a remarkable image in which the authors map the contributions of architects, artists and designers to the region.[250] Much of the strategy is indebted to the work of landscape architect Kim Wilkie, whose 1991 exhibition *Thames Connections*[251] proposed a river landscape "connected by an elaborate network of avenues and vistas".[252]

As such, the *Thames Landscape Strategy* imagined all the landscaped gardens of the Thames, regardless of their respective ages and stylistic and conceptual differences, as a single landscape experienced through a series of picturesque vistas. One could argue that the strategy succeeds in creating a landscape unity approaching that described by romantic eighteenth-century poets and artists, despite the fact that the reality of innumerable small, private estates and restricted access has always been very much more complicated. Thus, the *Thames Landscape Strategy* sought to fulfil

70 *The origins of the protected view*

in planning policy the poetic image of the Thames landscape, repeatedly promoted through the centuries as "a symbol of idealised English scenery, still inspiring artists, musicians and writers",[253] rather than to 'restore' it to any particular historical condition.

Among many examples of this, the strategy suggests that a view be 'restored' between a seventeenth-century avenue in Bushy Park and Garrick's eighteenth-century Shakespeare Temple at Hampton, although the two were never conceived as a single composition.[254] Along with opening new and historic vistas between landmarks, the strategy sought to increase accessibility and physical connections and to create a series of walks connecting landmarks, vistas and viewpoints in picturesque sequence, not unlike the aims of Pope at Twickenham, or Walpole at Strawberry Hill. Therefore, one could argue that the *Thames Landscape Strategy* builds upon a long history – to quote Dunbar, a "pattern of thought" – in an attempt to fulfil the picturesque values since ascribed to that history – a set of values which have, since the eighteenth century, recycled and reinforced a particular way of viewing the Richmond landscape: through a web of poetic writings and artistic images in order to fix their depictions as a design guide for the future development of the Thames.

Depictions of the Thames at Richmond, although imagined and romanticised, together produce a new reality, which has come to be perceived, somehow, as more 'authentic' than real reality. That romantic, authentic idea seems to demand its own preservation as a historical and cultural object, as well as its repeated reproduction in images, poetry and even architecture and landscape. In fact, the protection of the Richmond Hill view by an Act of Parliament in 1902 preceded the 1913 *Ancient Monuments Consolidation and Amendment Act*, understood to have been critical to the creation of the heritage industry and national bodies such as English Heritage. As such, one may view Richmond not only as an inevitable origin of the idea of the protected view but also as a key progenitor of the very idea of conservation.

Concluding remarks

This chapter has presented an intellectual and cultural history of the view from Richmond Hill in detail, placing it within the wider context of national architectural and artistic discourse. This examination has revealed the important role that the Richmond landscape played in the development of an 'English' landscape movement, and the definition of 'Englishness' more generally. Richmond not only was therefore a locally admired landscape but also came to symbolise Britain, its people and politics more generally. From the eighteenth through to the twentieth century Richmond was conflated with a classical Arcadia and viewed as a near perfect blend of urban and rural life and became a model for prototype suburban communities. This chapter has presented the evidence that it was here, in Richmond, that the English picturesque movement in art, architecture and landscape architecture developed. The important influence that the view from Richmond Hill had over the early development of this movement was recognised by the 1902 Act of Parliament which designated this particular view as Britain's first statutorily protected vista.

The aim of tracing this intellectual and cultural history of the landscape was to recover the values inherent in London's original protected vista, which itself informs subsequent protected view policy worldwide. The values inherent in the Richmond Hill vista traced in this chapter include a sense of nostalgia for some imagined past, from Caesar's army to Saxon kings and Tudor courts; the visual conventions of the picturesque, the development of which was facilitated by a concentration of wealthy London patrons who established country estates here and by the nature of those estates which were primarily for pleasure and retreat rather than agricultural profit; a developed theoretical understanding of the gaze, facilitated by contemporary scientific and philosophical inquiry in the fields of vision and aesthetics; and a growing sense that an authentic way of life could be found in a return to an imagined rural past; all of which gave rise to a number of tropes that would later characterise a peculiarly 'English' landscape movement, as well as the development of a national conservation movement. The very fact that these values underlie London's original protected vista suggests that they continue to be of relevance to an understanding of London's contemporary protected vistas, themselves subsequently informing protected view policy worldwide.

The following chapter continues the intellectual and cultural history of this particular vista by following its export to the American colonies during the eighteenth century. In doing so, it will demonstrate that the narratives and values attached to the landscape vista continue to develop and shift in response to different geographical, cultural and political contexts. As we shall see, these values are at times remarkably consistent, at others divergent, highlighting that the subjectivity of the individual plays an important part in the production of varied interpretations of landscapes and townscapes. Ultimately, policies designed to protect or enhance such vistas are themselves influenced by the values attached to them, serving to reinforce particular dominant interpretations.

Notes

1 G. J. Caesar, *The Conquest of Gaul*, trans. S. A. Handford, rev. J. F. Gardner (Harmondsworth and New York: Penguin Books, 1951).
2 B. Cunliffe, *Iron Age Communities in Britain: An Account of England, Scotland and Wales from the Seventh Century BC until the Roman Conquest* (London: Routledge, 2009).

3 Others have interpreted it as a proto-English or German word meaning 'inhabited place where the estuary begins'. For a full etymology, see www.proto-english.org/l10.html [accessed 01/04/2013].
4 M. Batey, H. Buttery, D. Lambert and K. Wilkie, *Arcadian Thames* (London: Barn Elms, 1994), p. 11.
5 Recorded as the year AD 836 or 838. H. E. Malden, *A History of the County of Surrey*, 3 (1911), pp. 487–501.
6 Interpreted as 'shining', a reference to the reflective properties of the river floodplains. Ibid., pp. 533–546.
7 Ibid.
8 Batey, Buttery, Lambert and Wilkie, *Arcadian Thames*, p. 93.
9 Malden, *A History of the County of Surrey*, pp. 533–546.
10 Ibid.
11 Batey, Buttery, Lambert and Wilkie, *Arcadian Thames*, p. 93.
12 Aided by André Le Nôtre's pupils Beaumont and La Quintenye as well as John Rose, protégé of the Earl of Essex, who studied at Versailles under Le Nôtre. Malden, *A History of the County of Surrey*, pp. 533–546.
13 Batey, Buttery, Lambert and Wilkie, *Arcadian Thames*, p. 29.
14 *Oxford English Dictionary*, 2nd Edition, vol. XII (Oxford: Clarendon Press, 1989), p. 668–669.
15 F. Koks, http://memory.loc.gov/ammem/gmdhtml/gnrlort.html [accessed 12/04/2013].
16 G. Braun, *Civitates Orbis Terrarum* (Cologne, 1572).
17 S. Edgerton, *The Mirror, the Window and the Telescope: How Renaissance Linear Perspective Changed Our Vision of the Universe* (Ithaca and London: Cornell University Press, 2009), p. 64.
18 The Renaissance man was expected to take an active interest in all the arts and sciences in order to become moral, just and closer to God. D. Kipp, "Alberti's 'Hidden' Theory of Visual Art", *British Journal of Aesthetics*, 24(3) (1984), pp. 231–240.
19 A. Young, *Tudor and Jacobean Tournaments* (New York: Sheridan House, 1987).
20 T. Longstaffe-Gowan, The London Town Garden, 1700–1840 (New Haven and London: Yale University Press, 2001), p. 124.
21 Extracted from Hampton Court Palace Records.
22 R. Strong, *The Renaissance Garden in England* (London: Thames & Hudson, 1984).
23 J. Bonehill and S. Daniels, "'Real Views from Nature in This Country': Paul Sandby, Estate Portraiture and British Landscape Art", *British Art Journal*, 22 March (2009).
24 Brothers Paul and Thomas Sandby both worked as military draughtsmen and both produced panoramas for military and non-military purposes. Mark Dorrian has suggested that even Thomas Sandby's non-military panorama of Edinburgh from Salisbury Crags, c. 1745, has a military context, having been produced in the same year as the suppression of the Jacobite Rebellion; it renders the city an object of military strategy. Dorrian, "The Aerial View: Notes for a Cultural History", *STRATES*, 13 (2007).
25 E. Barnard, *Capturing Time: Panoramas of Old Australia* (Canberra, ACT: National Library of Australia, 2012), p. 42.
26 M. Ellis, "'Spectacles within Doors': Panoramas of London in the 1790s", *Romanticism*, 14(2) (2008), pp. 133–148.
27 Longstaffe-Gowan, *The London Town Garden*, p. 63.
28 Dorrian, "The Aerial View: Notes for a Cultural History".
29 Ibid.
30 Longstaffe-Gowan, *The London Town Garden*, p. 64.

31 M. Andrews, The Search for the Picturesque: Landscape Aesthetics and Tourism in Britain, 1760–1800 (Aldershot: Scolar, 1989), pp. 61–62.
32 Mark Girouard explains that rooms directly connecting with the landscape at the ground floor begin to become fashionable only late in the eighteenth century as a result of changing attitudes in landscape design, where active exploration of a cinematic picturesque landscape was encouraged. M. Girouard, *Life in the English Country House: A Social and Architectural History* (New Haven, CT: Yale University Press, 1978).
33 A translation and adaptation of Dézallier d'Argenville's *La Théorie et la Practique du Jardinage* (Paris, 1709).
34 Longstaffe-Gowan, *The London Town Garden*, p. 120.
35 Strong, *The Renaissance Garden in England*.
36 Ibid.
37 J. Cloake, *Richmond Past a Visual History of Richmond, Kew, Petersham and Ham* (London: Historical Publications, 1991), p. 22.
38 Ibid., p. 22.
39 Ibid., p. 25.
40 J. Dunbar, *A Prospect of Richmond* (London and New York: White Lion Publishers, 1966), p. 77.
41 Ibid., p. 205.
42 D'Urfey's lyrics are published in Henry Purcell's sixth book of *The Banquet of Musick* (1692).
43 Strong, *The Renaissance Garden in England*, p. 11.
44 C. Metz, *The Imaginary Signifier: Psychoanalysis and the Cinema* (Bloomington: Indiana University Press, 1982), p. 61.
45 Strong, *The Renaissance Garden in England*, p. 70.
46 Ibid.
47 F. Bacon, "Of Gardens", in Spedding, Ellis and Heath, eds., *The Works of Francis Bacon* (London, 1890), pp. 488–489.
48 Strong, *The Renaissance Garden in England*, p. 11.
49 M. Jay, "Scopic Regimes of Modernity", in H. Foster, ed., *Vision and Visuality* (New York: New Press, 1988), p. 13.
50 Also known as the 'Renaissance Man' or 'Universal Man'.
51 Lucretius had observed the apparent convergence of parallels as seen through a straight colonnade. R. Evans, *The Projective Cast* (Cambridge, MA: The MIT Press, 1995), p. 136.
52 Edgerton, *The Mirror, the Window and the Telescope*.
53 Ibid.
54 Alberto Perez Gomez has traced a parallel change in architecture from the Renaissance to the nineteenth century, during which the use of mathematical geometry on mystical and symbolic grounds changed to its functional and technical use. A. Perez-Gomez, *Architecture and the Crisis of Modern Science* (Cambridge, MA: The MIT Press, 1983).
55 J. Berger, *Ways of Seeing* (London: BBC & Penguin Books, 1972), p. 16.
56 Jay, "Scopic Regimes of Modernity", *Vision and Visuality*, p. 7.
57 Ibid.
58 Ibid., p. 25.
59 Ibid., p. 9.
60 L. B. Alberti, *Ten Books on Architecture* (London: Tiranti, 1955).
61 H. B. Higgins, *The Grid Book* (Cambridge, MA: The MIT Press, 2009).
62 Following detailed X-ray analysis, Gabriele Morolli, professor of history of architecture at Florence University, has recently stated (2012) his belief that Francesca's *Ideal City* was in fact painted over an original architectural drawing by Leon Battista Alberti.

63 B. Berenson, *Italian Painters of the Renaissance* (Oxford: Clarendon Press, 1930), p. 135.
64 E. Panofsky, "Die Perspektive als 'symbolischen Form'", *Vortrage der Bibliothek Warburg* (1924–5), pp. 258–331.
65 H. Foster, ed., *Vision and Visuality* (Seattle, WA: DIA Art Foundation, 1988), p. xiv.
66 Jay, "Scopic Regimes of Modernity", *Vision and Visuality*, p. 9.
67 Ibid., p. 24.
68 Ibid.
69 Strong, *The Renaissance Garden in England*, p. 74.
70 Ibid., p. 118.
71 Virilio, *The Vision Machine* (Paris: Galilée, 1992), p. 73.
72 G. McPhee, *The Architecture of the Visible* (London and New York: Continuum, 2002), p. 22.
73 Reproduced in D. Mees, *Ham House Historical Garden Report* (1993).
74 Strong, *The Renaissance Garden in England*, p. 117.
75 J. B. Jackson, *The Necessity for Ruins: And Other Topics* (Amherst: University of Massachusetts Press, 1980), p. 49.
76 A 'patte d'oie', literally 'a goose's foot', is so named for its three legs meeting at a point. Andre Mollet's work at Hampton Court and his designs in *Le Jardin de plaisir* (1651) look forward to the baroque avenues of Le Notre. Le Notre designed few works in Britain but was certainly responsible for (now much-altered) designs at Greenwich and St James commissioned by Charles II.
77 Jackson, *The Necessity for Ruins*, p. 55.
78 M. Bussagli, *Piero della Francesco* (Rome, Italy: Giunti Editore, 2007).
79 P. Abercrombie, "Wren's Plan for London after the Great Fire", *The Town Planning Review* X(2), (May 1923).
80 J. Dixon Hunt and P. Willis, eds., *The Genius of the Place: The English Landscape Garden 1620–1820* (Cambridge, MA and London: The MIT Press, 1988), pp. 149–150.
81 Evans, *The Projective Cast*, p. 141 Evans's remarks reflect a prevalence in twentieth-century philosophy for the denigration of the scientific overlay of perspective in art. Jacques Lacan and Merleau-Ponty had both "maintained that all classical geometry was implicated in an attempt to capture and colonise the way we see". Evans, *The Projective Cast*, p. 125.
82 For example, the power of the landed gentry was increasingly visible in rural communities following the Enclosure Acts (c. 1750–1860), during which hundreds of thousands of acres of open common land were enclosed and the rights of commoners removed.
83 Cloake, *Richmond Past*, p. 35.
84 Ibid.
85 Ibid., p. 66.
86 According to Geoffrey Grigson, the composite word 'flower-garden' does not appear until the late seventeenth century because plants were initially tended for their medicinal or practical usage. Jackson, *The Necessity for Ruins*, p. 39.
87 Ibid., p. 47.
88 J. Dixon Hunt, *The Picturesque Garden in Europe* (London: Thames & Hudson, 2002) p. 9.
89 Jackson, *The Necessity for Ruins*, p. 37.
90 "The Adieu to the Spring Gardens at Vauxhall", *London Magazine* (Nov. 1735) in H. A. Rogers, ed., *Views of Some of the Most Celebrated By-Gone Pleasure Gardens of London* (London: Dodo Press, 1896), p. 2.
91 Cloake, *Richmond Past*, p. 34.
92 Dunbar, *A Prospect of Richmond*, pp. 87–88.
93 Cloake, *Richmond Past*, p. 34.

94 Rev. C. Jenner, *Town Eclogues* (1772) in Rogers, ed., *Views of Some of the Most Celebrated By-Gone Pleasure Gardens of London*, p. 89.
95 Cloake, *Richmond Past*, p. 34.
96 Ibid., p. 64.
97 D. Defoe, I, Letter II p. 121 in J. Bryant, *Finest Prospects: Three Historic Houses: A Study in London Topography* (London: English Heritage, 1986), p. 61.
98 Cloake, *Richmond Past*, p. 63.
99 Dunbar, *A Prospect of Richmond*, p. 88.
100 From the Renaissance onwards many artists utilised the camera obscura as a tool for capturing images of perspective scenes. Thus, the camera obscura facilitated the reproduction and resulting distribution of images of specific vistas. By the eighteenth century the compact size of the 'camera ottica' enabled artists such as Joshua Reynolds to capture accurate perspective sketches of landscape vistas in the field, which could later be reworked in the studio.
101 Cloake, *Richmond Past*, p. 63.
102 Bryant, *Finest Prospects*, p. 89.
103 Ibid., p. 85.
104 English Heritage Register of Parks and Gardens of Special Historic Interest, www.parksandgardens.ac.uk/component/option,com_parksandgardens/task, site/id,6503/tab,history/Itemid,293/ [accessed 26/01/2011].
105 Cloake, *Richmond Past*, p. 63.
106 Ibid., p. 123.
107 English Heritage Register of Parks and Gardens of Special Historic Interest, www.parksandgardens.ac.uk/component/option,com_parksandgardens/task, site/id,6503/tab,history/Itemid,293/ [accessed 26/01/2011].
108 Ibid.
109 Ibid.
110 A form of tuberculosis which affects bone.
111 Batey, Buttery, Lambert and Wilkie, *Arcadian Thames*, p. 65.
112 Virgil, G. Lee trans., *The Eclogues* (Penguin Classics, 1984).
113 Batey, Buttery, Lambert and Wilkie, *Arcadian Thames*, p. 6.
114 A. Dyce, ed., "Spring, or Damon", in *The Poetical Works of Alexander Pope* (W. Pickering, 1831), pp. 21–26.
115 A. Dyce, ed., "Summer, or Alexis", in *The Poetical Works of Alexander Pope* (W. Pickering, 1831), pp. 26–29.
116 Batey, Buttery, Lambert and Wilkie, *Arcadian Thames*, p. 67.
117 Pope refers to the "Egerian Grot" frequently in reference to his own grotto. The grotto of the nymph Egeria, near Rome, was a popular stop on the grand tour and a subject of artists and writers in the eighteenth century.
118 Batey, Buttery, Lambert and Wilkie, *Arcadian Thames*, p. 67.
119 www.poemhunter.com/poem/on-his-grotto-at-twickenham/ [accessed 28/01/2011].
120 As seen in Kent's sketch views of Pope's garden.
121 Batey, Buttery, Lambert and Wilkie, *Arcadian Thames*, p. 67.
122 A. Pope, *An Essay on Criticism* (W. Lewis, 1711), p. 7.
123 Batey, Buttery, Lambert and Wilkie, *Arcadian Thames*, p. 68.
124 M. Batey, *Alexander Pope: The Poet and the Landscape* (London: Barn Elms, 1999), p. 13.
125 Dixon Hunt, *The Picturesque Garden in Europe*, p. 15.
126 Batey, Buttery, Lambert and Wilkie, *Arcadian Thames*, p. 69.
127 Dixon Hunt, *The Picturesque Garden in Europe*, p. 26.
128 Ibid., p. 18.
129 Henry Hoare created at Stourhead, Wiltshire, between 1741 and 1780, a landscape garden directly inspired by landscape painting. Hoare wrote, "[W]hen you stand at the pantheon . . . the view of the bridge, village and church

76 *The origins of the protected view*

altogether will be a charming Gaspar picture at the end of the water". Dixon Hunt, *The Picturesque Garden in Europe*, p. 52.
130 G. Crandell, *Nature Pictorialized: "The View" in Landscape History* (Baltimore and London: John Hopkins University Press, 1993), p. 127.
131 A. Pope, *Epistles*, ed. F. W. Bateson (London: Methuen, 1951).
132 Batey, Buttery, Lambert and Wilkie, *Arcadian Thames*, p. 68.
133 Bryant, *Finest Prospects*, p. 61.
134 J. Summerson, *Architecture in Britain 1530–1830* (Harmondsworth: Penguin, 1979), p. 360.
135 Later home to architect Sir William Chambers (1781–1796).
136 Demolished c. 1847.
137 R. Desmond, *Kew: The History of the Royal Botanic Gardens* (Kew: The Harvill Press with the Royal Botanic Gardens, 1995), p. 18.
138 Bryant, *Finest Prospects*, p. 68.
139 W. Wordsworth, "Lines Written Near Richmond, upon the Thames at Evening 1790", in *Lyrical Ballads* (Washington, DC: Woodstock Books, 1997).
140 J. Langhorne, *The Poetical Works of William Collins* (New York: Trow & Co., 1848), pp. 88–90.
141 W. Collins, "Ode Occasion'd by the Death of Mr. Thomson 1749", in J. Langhorne, ed., *The Poetical Works of William Collins* (New York: Trow & Co., 1848), pp. 88–90.
142 See the introduction to this dissertation.
143 Batey, Buttery, Lambert and Wilkie, *Arcadian Thames*, p. 105.
144 T. Turner, *English Garden Design: History and Styles since 1650* (Woodbridge, Suffolk: Antique Collectors' Club, 1986).
145 D. Watkin, *The Architect King: George III and the Culture of the Enlightenment* (London: Royal Collection Publications, 2004), p. 169.
146 Ibid., pp. 170–171.
147 George III's sister.
148 Letter of 28 October 1767, quoted in M. Kohler, "German Connection", p. 29.
149 Watkin, *The Architect King*, p. 191.
150 Ibid., pp. 170–171.
151 Batey, Buttery, Lambert and Wilkie, *Arcadian Thames*, p. 31.
152 Ibid., p. 34.
153 Lancelot 'Capability' Brown was quite literally a neighbour of Garrick, moving to Hampton Court in 1764, to take up his role as royal gardener.
154 D. Garrick, "The Clandestine Marriage", in *The Dramatic Works of David Garrick, Esq: To Which Is Prefixed a Life of the Author* (London: A. Millar, 1798), vol. 3.
155 Batey, Buttery, Lambert and Wilkie, *Arcadian Thames*, p. 32.
156 Ibid., p. 59.
157 H. Walpole, *Essay on Modern Gardening* (Canton, PA: Kirgate Press, 1904), p. 75.
158 Batey, Buttery, Lambert and Wilkie, *Arcadian Thames*, p. 59.
159 W. Mason, *The English Garden: A Poem* (London, 1778), p. 4.
160 Batey, Buttery, Lambert and Wilkie, *Arcadian Thames*, p. 60.
161 Ibid., p. 60.
162 J. Macarthur, *The Picturesque: Architecture, Disgust and Other Irregularities* (London and New York: Routledge, 2007), p. 126.
163 Watkin, *The Architect King*, p. 41.
164 Ibid., p. 160.
165 Cloake, *Richmond Past*, p. 42.
166 Watkin, *The Architect King*, pp. 160–161.
167 Ibid.

168 For example, "Mesdames de Biron and Cambis have taken houses on Richmond Green" *Reports Walpole* (14 May 1790), "as well as les Boufflers and Madame de Roncherolles". Other French arrivals included Princesse d'Henin, Princesse de Bouillon, Duchesse de Biron, Comte de Lally-Tollendal, Marquise de la Tour du Pin and Comtesse de Balbi.
169 Watkin, *The Architect King*, p. 160.
170 Ibid.
171 H. Repton, *Sketches and Hints on Landscape Gardening* (1795), cited in Loudon, *Landscape Gardening and Landscape Architecture*, p. 106.
172 Watkin, *The Architect King*, p. 172.
173 Ibid., p. 175.
174 Cloake, *Richmond Past*, p. 65.
175 Watkin, *The Architect King*, p. 44.
176 Ibid., p. 44.
177 A. A. Watts, *Lyrics of the Heart* (London: Longman, 1850).
178 Woolf, *Transit of Venus*.
179 Ibid., p. 44.
180 J. Early, *Romanticism and American Architecture* (New York: A.S. Barnes & Co., 1965), p. 17.
181 T. Sprat, *The History of The Royal Society of London, for the Improving of Natural Knowledge* (London: The Royal Society, 1667; 1958), p. 113.
182 Cloake, Richmond Past, p. 69.
183 Dunbar, *A Prospect of Richmond*, p. 152.
184 Cloake, *Richmond Past*, p. 56.
185 Dunbar, *A Prospect of Richmond*, p. 148.
186 For example, Paine designed bridges at Wallington Hall, Northumberland (1755); Chatsworth House, Derbyshire, and Chillington Hall, Staffordshire (1770), among others.
187 *The London Magazine* (September 1779), in B. Cookson, *Crossing the River* (Edinburgh: Mainstream, 2006), p. 31.
188 T. Maurice, *Richmond Hill: A Descriptive and Historical Poem* (London: W. Bulmer, 1807).
189 *The Builder*, 12 July 1890.
190 However, Julius Bryant has pointed this out as a misconception, for the avenue of elms in Scott's novel was set in Richmond Park. Bryant, *Finest Prospects*, p. 66.
191 W. Scott, *The Heart of Mid-Lothian* (Edinburgh and London: Waverley Novels, 1843), p. 563.
192 Cloake, *Richmond Past*, p. 70.
193 Including *View from Richmond Park, a Wooded Landscape with a Reach of the River, Boats at Richmond, A View from Richmond Hill with the Wick* (1837), *Cholmondeley Walk* (1844) and *Kew Gardens from Richmond Hill*.
194 Bryant, *Finest Prospects*, p. 88.
195 Batey, Buttery, Lambert and Wilkie, *Arcadian Thames*, p. 98.
196 Ibid.
197 www.turnershouse.co.uk/turner2.htm [accessed 11/02/2011].
198 *Middlesex* (Ordnance Survey, 1879).
199 *Middlesex* (Ordnance Survey, 1913).
200 K. Adler, *Pissarro in London* (London: National Gallery Company, 2003).
201 N. Reed, *Pissarro in West London: Kew, Chiswick and Richmond* (Folkestone: Lilburne Press, 1997), p. 19.
202 Lucien's younger brother Ludovic Rodo Pissarro was also a formidable artist and a resident of Richmond, producing *Bedford Park, Chiswick, Pagoda Avenue, Richmond* and *Richmond Park with Caleche*, among others.

78 The origins of the protected view

203 R.A.M. Stern and J. M. Massengale, eds., *The Anglo-American Suburb* (London: Architectural Design, 1981), p. 27.
204 M. Girouard, *Sweetness and Light* (Oxford: Oxford University Press, 1977), p. 166.
205 Ibid., p. 28.
206 Stern and Massengale, *The Anglo-American Suburb*, p. 27.
207 A. G. Bell, *Richmond Park* (London: Underground Poster, 1913).
208 www.edinphoto.org.uk/0_pc_0/0_post_card_history.htm [accessed 18/02/2011].
209 *Richmond and Twickenham Times*, cutting dated 1901, Twickenham Reference Library.
210 Berryman, "The Fight for the View from Richmond Hill", p. 8.
211 'Lammas rights', of medieval origin, allowed residents of Ham to graze cattle on dedicated 'Lammas Lands'. The Dysart Estate at Ham House consisted of around 176 acres of these semi-common Lammas Lands.
212 Berryman, "The Fight for the View from Richmond Hill", p. 14.
213 Ibid., p. 17.
214 Ibid.
215 "Glover's Island: The Town Council Refuse to Purchase It", *Richmond and Twickenham Times* (14 September 1898).
216 Letter from the Mayor Albert Chancellor to Alderman Burt (24 August 1898). Also, Letter from Mayor Albert Chancellor to Alderman Burt (29 August 1898).
217 "The View from Richmond Hill", in *Local History Notes* (London: Borough of Richmond upon Thames: Richmond Libraries' Local Studies Collection, 2009), p. 4.
218 "Across the Walnuts and the Wine", *Richmond and Twickenham Times* (24 August 1898).
219 "Glover's Island", *Richmond and Twickenham Times* (17 September 1898).
220 "More Correspondence about Glover's Island", *Richmond and Twickenham Times* (20 July 1898).
221 "Glover's Island: Today at the Mart", *Richmond and Twickenham Times* (21 September 1898). Also, "Glover's Island Unsold: An Unsuccessful Auction at Tokenhouse Yard", *Daily Mail* (22 September 1898).
222 "The View from Richmond Hill", in *Local History Notes*, p. 5.
223 "The View from Richmond Hill: Mr. Max Waechter's Gift", *Richmond and Twickenham Times* (16 April 1901).
224 "The Richmond Hill View", *Westminster Budget* (26 July 1901).
225 A plan of the controversial Lebanon House development appears in the *Richmond and Twickenham Times* (6 July 1901).
226 "Richmond Hill View", *The Times* (19 June 1901). See also "The View from Richmond Hill", *Twickenham Herald* (5 June 1901), untitled article in *Richmond and Twickenham Times* (6 July 1901) and "The Spoiling of Richmond", *Daily Chronicle* (9 November 1901).
227 "Richmond's Peril: World-Famed View Threatened by Builders", *Daily Mail* (7 June 1901).
228 Untitled article in the *Daily News* (13 July 1901).
229 Untitled article in the *Richmond and Twickenham Times* (13 July 1901).
230 D. S. MacColl, "Richmond Hill and Marble Hill", *Architectural Review* X (1901), p. 25. See also untitled article in *The Times* (15 July 1901).
231 MacColl, "Richmond Hill and Marble Hill", p. 28.
232 Untitled article in *The Times* (15 July 1901).
233 "The Dysart Proposals and Marble Hill: To Stand or Fall Together", *Twickenham Herald* (13 November 1901).
234 "Richmond Hill (Preservation of the View)", *The Times* (15 November 1901). See also "The Dysart Bill", *Richmond and Twickenham Times* (23 November 1901), and "The View from Richmond Hill", *The Times* (25 November 1901).

235 "The View: The Bill to Save and the Bill to Build", *Richmond and Twickenham Times* (30 November 1901). See also "The Dysart Estates Bill", *Twickenham Herald* (11 January 1902), untitled article in the *Surrey Comet* (11 January 1902).
236 Though there was, of course, opposition. See "Ham Lammas Lands", *Daily Chronicle* (13 February 1902), and "Ham Lammas Lands", *Daily Chronicle* (14 February 1902).
237 "The Dysart Estates Bill", *Twickenham Herald* (11 January 1902).
238 "Richmond View", *Daily Chronicle* (14 February 1902). See also "Ham Lammas Lands: The Proposals of the Dysart Trustees: Shall the Thames Be Spoilt", *Daily Chronicle* (6 February 1902).
239 "The View from the Hill: The Purchase of Marble Hill Estate", *Twickenham Herald* (29 March 1903), "The Richmond Hill View: Purchase of Marble Hill", *Richmond and Twickenham Times* (26 October 1901), and "The Richmond Hill View", *The Times* (29 March 1903).
240 There were those that opposed the use of Marble Hill for public purposes due to the ample provision of public spaces at Kew and Richmond Parks. See "The View: Letter from Mr. Littler", *Richmond and Twickenham Times* (4 December 1901).
241 *Twickenham Herald* (6 June 1903).
242 D. L. Foley, "Idea and Influence: The Town and Country Planning Association", in A. K. Hoagland and K. A. Breisch, eds., *Constructing Image, Identity, and Place: Perspectives in Vernacular Architecture IX* (Knoxville: The University of Tennessee Press, 2003), p. 11.
243 Ibid., p. 11.
244 For example, in Newcastle-upon-Tyne, Coventry and others, where a modernist approach was promoted.
245 *The Greater London Plan* (London: H.M.S.O., 1945), pp. 182–183.
246 Ibid.
247 Dunbar, *A Prospect of Richmond*, p. xiii.
248 Ibid., p. 73.
249 K. Wilkie, M. Battaggia, M. Batey, D. Lambert, H. Buttery, J. Pearce, D. Goode, and D. Bentley, *The Thames Landscape Strategy* (London: Thames Landscape Steering Group, June 1994).
250 Ibid., p. 17.
251 Ibid., p. 5.
252 Ibid., p. 6.
253 Ibid., p. 5.
254 Ibid., p. 72.

Part 2
Translating images of Richmond

2 Introduction

The repeated depiction of the view from Richmond Hill in early travel guides, mass-distributed prints and later in posters and photographic postcards has made it a well-known and much-admired image both in Britain and internationally, frequently connected to themes of national and cultural identity. An eighteenth-century viewer of an image of Richmond Hill might have associated it nostalgically with the palaces of royalty, the home of celebrated poets and the subject of artists, architects and landscape designers; they might also have seen it as a landscape symbolic of the British Empire's power, epicentre of the king's very own measurement of time, and home to his state-of-the-art scientific royal observatory. Evidence of widespread popular exposure to the view from Richmond Hill, whether via pictorial or literary sources, is suggested by an examination of worldwide settlements, all of which came to be named after the 'original' town of Richmond-upon-Thames. This chapter will argue not only that the view became ubiquitous and pervasive in the eighteenth and early nineteenth centuries but also that the values encoded within the picturesque image were capable of translation from one landscape to another, from the 'original' to the 'simulacra'.[1]

In fact, the town of Richmond-upon-Thames is no 'original', having taken its name from the palace of Henry VII, which in turn was a reference to Henry's Earldom of Richmond, North Yorkshire, the dramatic skyline of Henry's palace, bristling with turrets and chivalric devices as observed in the drawings of Anton van den Wyngaerde, a romantic re-visioning of the Norman castle of Richmond, North Yorkshire.

If the naming of Richmond-upon-Thames was itself a romantic reference to another place and time, what of Richmond, North Yorkshire? Is it 'original'? In fact, as one traces the origins of the name 'Richmond', it appears ever more elusive – local historians have suggested that Richmond, North Yorkshire, takes its name from the Norman 'Comtes [translated as "Earls"] de Richemont', a town located in Normandy, France, and an honour held by the Dukes of Brittany from the twelfth to fourteenth centuries.[2]

In the same way that the authentic 'Richmond' slips away as it is traced backwards, it also becomes more complex as it is traced forwards, as travellers and colonial settlers all over the world transferred romanticised images of Richmond-upon-Thames to new locations and new landscapes. Perhaps the earliest example is not a settlement as such but a palace built for George III's sister, Princess Augusta, which she named 'Richmond Palace' near Brunswick, Germany, in 1768,[3] its landscaped gardens "laid out in the English Tast [sic]",[4] to evoke King George III's gardens at Richmond-upon-Thames, recently re-landscaped by 'Capability' Brown. As Princess Caroline's sketch illustrates, the combination of Fleischer's Palladian villa and Brown's serpentine landscape recreated a portion of the Thames landscape at Richmond, Brunswick. Its hill, rising above a broad bend in the river, flanked by meadows, grazing cattle and backed by distant views, all conform to the imagery of the Thames at Richmond. Watkin comments that "The grounds of Richmond [Brunswick] were [. . .] the first English garden of their kind in Germany",[5] and it seems that the image of Richmond-upon-Thames was central to the spread of the English picturesque throughout Europe in the late eighteenth century.

That the imagery of Richmond, particularly the compositional qualities of the view from Richmond Hill, had become a revered and instantly recognisable landscape model is demonstrated by the frequency of its reference in the journals of travellers. Settlers arriving in the 'New Worlds' of the American colonies, Southern Africa and Australasia perceived these landscapes through the prism of the old.

The prominent position that Richmond-upon-Thames held in the minds of early settlers is indicated by a 2008 newspaper article entitled 'All Roads Lead to Richmond', in which it was reported that *The Times Universal Atlas of the World* ranked 'Richmond' first in a table of the world's most prolific place names.[6] According to the atlas, Richmond has given its name to 55 towns and cities across three continents, pushing the cities of London and Manchester into second and fourth places respectively. This remains a vivid illustration of how powerful the image of the view from Richmond Hill must have been at the time of European colonisation.

A topographical analysis of 30 North American Richmonds (Figure 2.1) reveals a number of surprising similarities, often sited on the summit of a hill overlooking the bend of a river or major body of water. The geographical distribution of sites is also illuminating, almost exclusively situated in fertile, lowland regions of rolling hills. Despite the proliferation of gold-rush towns which sprang up in the high Rocky Mountains and deserts of the Midwest, there is just a single Midwestern Richmond and this too is situated in the fertile rolling hills of northern Utah's Cache River Valley. While it is no surprise that settlements have flourished in these rich agricultural areas, it seems clear that early settlers drew comparisons between the topography of these American landscapes and popular contemporary depictions of Richmond-upon-Thames, reflected in the toponymy adopted.

If topographical similarities played a part in the naming of new landscapes after those familiar from the old world, nostalgia, or a sense of longing

Figure 2.1 The Richmonds (solid outline) and Richmond Hills (dashed outline) of North America.

for the motherland, was certainly also a factor. As David Lowenthal has explained,

> Nostalgic evocations long antedate our time. Virgil immortalised the heroic and the pastoral past; Petrarch sought refuge in antiquity from his own 'wretched' and 'worthless' age; bitter-sweet regret for an Arcadian past suffused sixteenth and seventeenth century poetry and the canvases of Claude and Poussin.[7]

As we have seen, the landscape of Richmond-upon-Thames was itself permeated with nostalgic sentiment; the villas of Pope and Burlington were evocations of the classical model while their gardens called to mind Claude Lorrain's paintings and Virgil's texts.

While American author Henry James argued in *Hawthorne* (1879) that "History, as yet, has left in the United States so thin and impalpable a deposit that we very soon touch the hard substratum of nature",[8] in reality, the American continent already possessed a long and illustrious native history. Nevertheless, as James's comments suggest, settlers of the 'New World' seemed reluctant to engage with native histories and cultures, supplanting them with romantic and nostalgic narratives of their own. The importation of place names, and their associated histories, some – like Richmond – already deeply nostalgic in their own right, legitimised colonisation as seemingly inevitable, peaceful and just. Such imported histories became important in the construction of hierarchies of power within the American colonies, where any settler could "trace back their ancestry, institutions, culture [and] ideals to validate claims to power, prestige, and property".[9]

Notes

1 To use Jean Baudrillard's terminology. See J. Baudrillard, *Simulacra and Simulation* (Ann Arbor: University of Michigan Press, 1994).
2 www.britannica.com/EBchecked/topic/502797/Richmond [accessed 10/12/2012].
3 D. Watkin, *The Architect King: George III and the Culture of the Enlightenment* (London: Royal Collection Publications, 2004), p. 190.
4 Ibid.
5 Ibid.
6 "All Roads Lead to Richmond", *Daily Mail* (29 December 2008).
7 D. Lowenthal, *The Past Is a Foreign Country* (Cambridge: Cambridge University Press, 1985), p. 8.
8 H. James, *Hawthorne* (1879; reprint Ithaca: Cornell University Press, 1956), pp. 12–13.
9 Lowenthal, *The Past Is a Foreign Country*, p. 53.

3 Two American Richmonds
'Richmond Hill', New York, and Richmond, Virginia

Not only was Richmond-upon-Thames, and specifically the view from Richmond Hill, repeatedly reproduced in paintings, poetry, postcards and literature, but also it was physically reproduced by nostalgic settlers all over the 'New World'. This chapter takes another parallel path through the intellectual landscape of Richmond between seventeenth-century ideas of reproducing classical Arcadia and the twenty-first-century protected view. This path branches chronologically from the one followed in the previous chapter in the opening years of the eighteenth century. It tracks the export of Richmond's values to America. This trail charts another process of the nostalgic reproduction of picturesque images, another set of claims to authenticity, which are different to – but have striking parallels with – the process shaped by, and shaping, Richmond-upon-Thames. It leads towards ideas of the protected view whose intellectual origins are identical but whose flavour is subtly, importantly and interestingly different from the policies implemented in London.

While the precise circumstances surrounding the origins of most American Richmonds remain obscure,[1] this chapter explores two well-documented places which can be directly attributed to the influence of the landscape view. The first, a handsome country house known as 'Richmond Hill' overlooking the Hudson River on Manhattan Island, New York, would serve not only as a base for George Washington but also later as the first British ambassadorial residence and subsequently as the seat of vice presidents of the Union John Adams and Aaron Burr. As such, the connotations of the house's setting and toponymy circle around some defining moments in American history, before the house and estate slide into oblivion in the early nineteenth century. The second, the city of Richmond, Virginia, prospered as a centre of the tobacco and cotton trades, whose extensive plantations orbited around great country houses set amid landscaped grounds leading down to the tidal rivers of Chesapeake Bay. Here, the naming of the city was directly linked to visions of a prosperous genteel villa society on the model of Richmond-upon-Thames, a vision which would endure in the politics of the American Civil War, and Richmond's role as capital of the Confederacy.

The two uses of what we might call 'visions of Richmond' are related and yet subtly different. While its usage in Manhattan is gradually, and seemingly willingly, eclipsed by nineteenth-century redevelopment in the pursuit of economic development and commercial profit, simultaneously in Virginia it is actively reinforced in the promotion of the 'Southern Cavalier' identity and the politics of both 'Old' and 'New' Souths. Such divergent usages of 'visions of Richmond' demonstrate the way in which urban and landscape views may be hijacked for political means.

'Richmond Hill', Manhattan Island, New York

In the eighteenth century the area between New York City's Lower Manhattan and Greenwich Village was vastly different to its current form. Far from the regular grid of streets and apartment buildings apparent today this was principally a rural landscape, as indicated by Bernard Ratzer's *Plan of the City of New York* (1766; 1767). Principal thoroughfares followed the east bank of the Hudson River to the west, and the approximate route of Broadway to the east, avoiding a series of low hills between. One of these, southeast of the present intersection of Varick and Charlton Streets, had been known as 'Richmond Hill' since at least 1767, when Abraham Mortier, paymaster general in the British army, had built a mansion there (Figure 3.1).

Figure 3.1 'A View of the Present Seat of his Excel. the Vice President of the United States' by Cornelius Tiebout (Richmond Hill, 1789–1790).

Set in 26 acres of land[2] and crowning the hill from where there were wide-ranging views across the Hudson River and its water-meadows, the name 'Richmond Hill' may have originated in recognition of the characteristics of the local topography. For example, in his *Travel Journal* of 1732, William Hugh Grove refers to aspects of Richmond-upon-Thames in many parts of America, perceiving Yorktown, Virginia, as "like Black heath or Richmond Hill and Like that Overlooks a fine river Broader than the Thames".[3] Grove also described the Mattaponi River, Virginia, as "thick seated with gentry on its Banks [. . .] Most of These have pleasant Gardens and the Prospect of the River render them [. . .] equall [sic] to the Thames from London to Richmond".[4]

Regardless of whether the elite associations suggested by the use of the name 'Richmond Hill' resonated with Mortier, the estate was clearly considered among the most (if not the most) desirable and significant in New York, since it passed from Mortier first to Sir Jeffrey Amherst (later, Lord Amherst, at the close of the French and Indian War) and later served as the headquarters of George Washington (until the retreat of the Continental army from New York in 1776). In this remarkable turn of events Richmond Hill's function had therefore passed from aristocratic and colonial service to servicing the political and military forces of the revolutionary colonies. Of course the mansion's role in these events was strategic, limited and fleeting, but it is tempting to speculate around the change of world order represented by these shifts – could one argue that Richmond Hill's landscape view, once nostalgically reminiscent of Britain's civilised and genteel society, was now judged every bit as equal to the motherland in civilisation and gentility. Certainly, the reoccupation of Richmond Hill was a strategic objective of the British army, due to its commanding presence over Lower Manhattan. Following the stationing of troops here between 1776 and the end of the American War of Independence in 1783, the house went on to serve British interests as the home of Britain's first ambassador to the US, Sir John Temple.

The political symbolism in regaining Richmond Hill seems to set it apart from other great American houses, which like their British counterparts, tend to be associated with continuous dynastic inheritance and the perpetuation of social class. In this regard, Richmond Hill was more akin to Washington's White House or the mansions of colonial governors, rotating between agents of political power, for, having served as the residual seat of British power under Temple, it once again passed into American hands, serving as the official residence of first vice president (and second president) of the US, John Adams, and his wife, Abigail.[5]

It is from Abigail Adams that we first have a description of Richmond Hill's position and outlook. She writes,

> In natural beauty it might vie with the most delicious spot I ever saw. [. . .] The house stands upon an eminence: at an agreeable distance flows the noble Hudson [. . .]. Upon my right hand are fields beautifully

variegated with grass and grain, to a great extent like the valley of the Honiton in Devonshire.

Upon my left the city opens to view, [. . .] the Jersey shores present the exuberance of a rich, well cultivated soil. [. . .] Venerable oaks and broken ground covered with wild shrubs surround me, giving a natural beauty to the spot which is truly enchanting.[6]

To the Adams it is clear that the landscape of Richmond Hill was every bit the equal of Britain's, as Abigail makes direct comparison with "the valley of the Honiton in Devonshire". Though, of course, one cannot be certain why Abigail uses the Honiton, and not the Thames at Richmond, as her reference, it could be argued that it is more illustrative of the scale of the landscape she describes; it is humbler and more rural in quality than the full maturity of the Thames at Richmond – perhaps reflecting the Adams' perception of the youthful nation, and its latent potential for a bounteous and prosperous future.

The important thing to note is that the topographical position and outlook of the Richmond Hill estate endowed it with a position of power, sought by figures of authority on either side of the Atlantic. As a seat of first colonial imperial and then independent national power the expansive view from Manhattan's Richmond Hill served both as symbol of the authoritarian gaze and as the backdrop to important moments in the fledgling nation's history. For the purposes of this book, what is most interesting is that while the connotations of Richmond-upon-Thames's pastoral classical idyll would find resonance in the values promoted in the American South – and as explored in the following study of Richmond, Virginia – they were also evident here, in the heart of pre-industrial New York.

But times were changing. Shortly after third vice president of the US, Aaron Burr, bought the property in 1794 (Burr was familiar with the estate from the early years of the Revolutionary War), Burr filed plans for the subdivision of the estate with three new streets comprising 240 building plots. Although Burr did not carry the project through to fruition, the estate's subsequent purchaser, real estate magnate John Jacob Astor, did.[7] In 1820, Astor had the mansion relocated, apparently by rolling on timber logs, to the south-eastern corner of Varick and Charlton Streets, where it served the next three decades variously as a public tea room, opera theatre, equestrian show venue and saloon, before its demolition in 1849.[8] The fate of Manhattan's 'Richmond Hill' parallels broader transformations in the fabric of New York – the city was lurching from an agricultural to industrial economy, the population was booming, land prices were rising and there were great profits to be made from speculative development. The severance of 'Richmond Hill' mansion from its attendant landscape setting and its meteoric fall in social standing from presidential home to common ramshackle saloon in many ways reflect the degree to which northern American urban society turned away from the idealised picturesque and pastoral imagery of the colonial past towards an urbanised, industrial future – in the North at least, the 'old money' of the landed gentry was out, and 'new money' from manufacturing and trade was in. In the following study of Richmond, Virginia, it will be seen that the diverging trajectories of the North and South, which set the states upon a path towards civil war, are too reflected in the different fates of these two Richmond Hills.

Richmond, Virginia

Founded on the James River in 1733, the city of Richmond, Virginia, prospered as a centre of the tobacco and cotton trades, servicing extensive plantations on the tidal inlets of Chesapeake Bay.[9] Each plantation was like a colony in miniature, governed from the great houses at their centre, whose stately lawns leading down to tidal waterways doubled as makeshift ports for the exportation of tobacco, rice and indigo and the importation of fine English furniture.

The founding father of Richmond, Virginia, William Byrd, had spent much of his youth in England, picking up a circle of influential friends, including Sir Robert Southwell, president of the Royal Society. After inheriting his father's 26,000-acre Virginian estate in 1704, Byrd returned twice to England for long periods (first in 1714–19, second in 1721–26), conducting business as president of the Colonial Council and visiting acquaintances in estates up and down the country. Brown argues that it was during these visits that Byrd must have become familiar with the Thames landscape around Richmond.[10] Although no explicit reference of Byrd visiting Richmond survives, he certainly visited the Earl of Orkney, then governor of Virginia, at his Thames-side home of Cliveden, Buckinghamshire.[11] Byrd was also a correspondent of Archibald Campbell, third Duke of Argyll, Henrietta Howard's agent during the construction of Marble Hill House and a patron of two classical villas himself, the first at Sudbrook House, Petersham (1726–28), the second at Whitton Park, Twickenham (c. 1730). It is plausible to suggest that it was in Twickenham that Byrd reputedly met with Mrs Howard and Alexander Pope in 1719.[12] Indeed, it was at this time that Richmond and Twickenham were emerging as fashionable retreats from the bustle of the city and its affairs. It could be suggested that Byrd, well aware of the potency of this fashionable association, hoped it might encourage the marketability and prosperity of Richmond's Virginian namesake.

Byrd himself makes no mention of the connection between the two Richmonds. While commerce was clearly an important consideration for locating the city at the uppermost safe landing of the James River, there is evidence that Byrd also favoured the topography of the site and its views of the riverine landscape. A 1737 plan of Richmond, commissioned by Byrd, shows a series of large plots positioned on hills overlooking the river, clearly intended for suburban villa estates, as suggested by the English names given to them, such as Hampstead, Kingston and Guildford (Figures 3.2 and 3.3). These estates were probably intended to follow the model of Byrd's son, William Byrd III's classical villa on Gamble Hill, to which he gave the

Figure 3.2 Map of key landscape features, Richmond, VA, showing the location of Libby Hill Park.

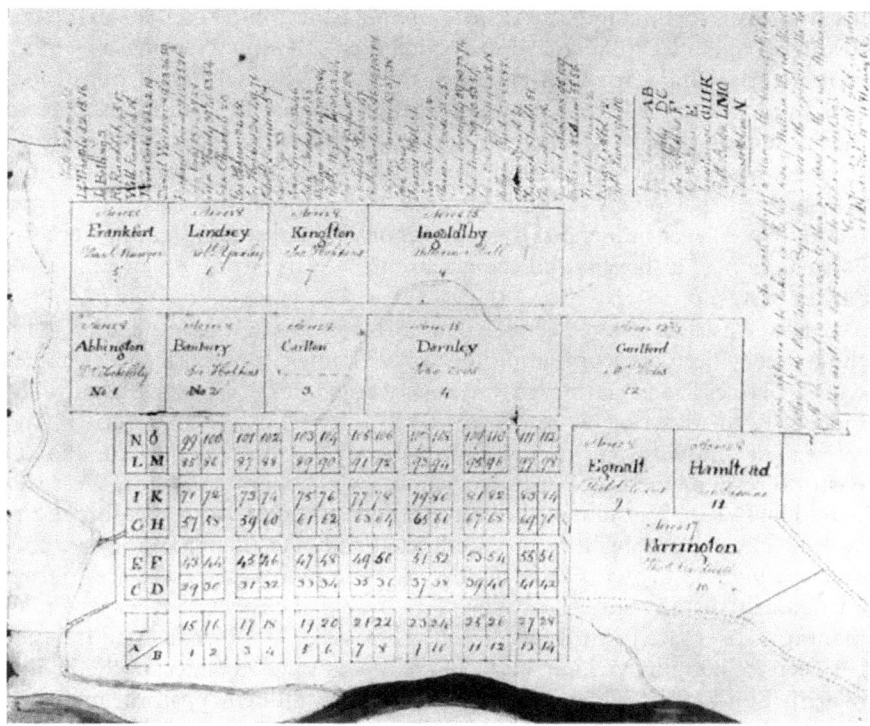

Figure 3.3 William Mayo's 1737 plan of Richmond, Virginia, commissioned by William Byrd II. The large suburban plots north of the town are given distinctly English names, such as 'Hampstead', 'Kingston' and 'Guilford'.

Source: M. Tyler-McGraw, *At the Falls: Richmond, Virginia and Its People* (UNC Press Books, 1994), p. 46.

Italianate name *Belvidere* – literally *Beautiful View*.[13] Reverend Andrew Burnaby wrote of a visit in 1759,

> Byrd has a small place called Belvedere, upon a hill at the lower end of the falls, as romantic and elegant as anything I have ever seen. It is situated very high, and commands a fine prospect of the river, which is half a mile broad, forming cataracts [. . .]; there are several little islands scattered careless[ly] about, very rocky, and covered with trees; and two or three villages in view at small distance. Over all these you discover a prodigious extent of wilderness, and the river winding majestically along through the midst of it.[14]

Regardless of whether Byrd was recalling classical associations or the Thames landscape consciously, he was certainly knowledgeable enough to discuss the classics as well as the latest fashions in art and architecture. During his first visit to England, Byrd accompanied Sir John Percival on a tour through England and Scotland in the manner of Gilpin, visiting a number of influential landscape gardens along the way.[15] Brown has demonstrated that Byrd transferred these first-hand experiences of English landscapes to the gardens at Westover, which were admired as "the finest in that Country" for "the magnificence of the buildings, the beauty of its situation, and the pleasures of the society to be found there".[16] Among the alterations Byrd made to Westover influenced by contemporary English landscapes were the construction of a 'ha-ha' and the curation of 'seats' from which to admire garden vistas.[17]

Byrd's Westover estate seems to demonstrate his self-identification with the genteel villa society of Richmond-upon-Thames, supplanting the Thames with the James River "as though the James were some far Western tributary".[18] Indeed, Byrd wrote of his return to the "solid pleasures of innocence, and retirement" at Westover in 1726, an echo of Pope's advocacy for Plinian pastoral retirement.[19] As Pope's garden at Twickenham had been, Westover would be Byrd's 'Tusculum', the scene of his retirement from London affairs and an elegant setting for the intellectual pursuits of gardening, reading and writing. As Brown has pointed out, "Virginia was, in essence, only a particularly distant English province",[20] and Byrd clearly saw his Virginian plantation as a satellite of London when he asked, "[W]here's the difference between its lying in Virginia or in Berkshire as long as I receive the Profits of it in London?"[21] Thus, Byrd transferred the affluent pastoral image of Twickenham's 'classic village' to Virginia.

In fact, Byrd's transferral of the name 'Richmond' to Virginia was an additional overlay onto a landscape which had already been mythologised from at least the early seventeenth century. The James River or 'King's River', named after James I in 1607, already tied this particular Virginian river to the king's ceremonial River Thames. Of course, even the naming of the colony 'Virginia' is indebted to Elizabeth I, the Virgin Queen. Royal associations were not limited to place names, however. From the seventeenth century, the identity of American 'southerners', and particularly the plantation gentry, was frequently compared to the 'Cavaliers' of the English Civil War. By the time of the American Civil War, this myth had gained such currency that one propagandist casually remarked that the South had been settled by "persons belonging to the blood and race of the royal family [. . .] a race distinguished in its earliest history for its warlike and fearless character, a race in all times since renowned for its gallantry, chivalry, gentleness and intellect".[22]

The translation of the Richmond Hill view onto American landscapes, or elsewhere, might be seen as a tool to obscure or obliterate native histories and to impose colonial authority and an 'English' 'Cavalier' identity. From a cynical and pragmatic point of view, the translation of an image of civility, wealth and prosperity might have been used to lure settlers on dangerous journeys to unproductive wildernesses and contested territories. The following sections will further explore the landscape of Richmond, Virginia, in order to demonstrate that the values imported with the view from Richmond Hill have at times been exaggerated and reinforced, while at others they have been suppressed and denied. They show that the view may be transformed into a political tool, the values encoded within it shaped according to contemporary cultural values and culture itself shaped by the values inherent in the view.

The view as symbol of American nationalism: Church Hill, Richmond, Virginia

This section will examine the history of the oldest district of Richmond, Virginia, Church Hill, established overlooking the James River by William Byrd in 1733, by a reading of the personal journals of British architect Benjamin Henry Latrobe, who emigrated to the Virginian colony in 1796. Latrobe's journals not only give a contemporary account of life in 1790s Richmond but also provide information regarding the early development of American forms of architecture, urbanism and landscape at a time when the nation still regarded itself as youthful. Visual perception, it is shown, was central to the ways in which the colonies expressed and formulated their identities, from landscape architecture to modern prison design. In each, the visual experience of buildings, cities and landscapes was crucial: not only in terms of aesthetic beauty but also in the notions of social reform brought about through the gaze of surveillance. These observations lead to a detailed reading of Latrobe's Virginia villas which bore a direct relationship to views of the James River landscape. Thus, in Richmond, Virginia, at least, the beginnings of an American architectural profession can be traced to intimate connections between visual perceptions of landscape, mediated through mass-produced representations of popular views – among them the view of the Thames from Richmond Hill.

It can be argued that Richmond's association with a mythologised and idealised history is reinforced by accounts of eminent local heroes who struggled for American independence, and later by the pivotal role the city played in the Civil War as capital of the Confederacy. The Church Hill district is the symbolic heart of this mythic landscape. St John's Church was constructed on an area of high ground donated by William Byrd II in 1741. Commanding extensive views over the James River, it was in this building that America's national hero Patrick Henry gave his infamous speech at the second Virginia Convention (1775), ending with the words "Give me liberty or give me death!" Among those present for Henry's revolution-inciting speech were George Washington, Thomas Jefferson and General Lee. It is notable that discontent with the old world and its colonial masters should be stoked here, on the crest of the hill overlooking Byrd's symbolically named city and the river view, reminiscent of 'Old England', that had inspired him.

The apparent lack of acknowledgement at this time regarding the provenance of Richmond, Virginia's view may represent a deliberate quashing of memories of the 'old country' in the build-up to revolution. It was an Englishman, Latrobe, who revived acknowledgement of Byrd's naming of Richmond in reference to the landscape of Richmond-upon-Thames. Latrobe, known chiefly for his later work on the White House and Capitol Building, in Washington, DC, emigrated from England to Richmond, Virginia, some 20 years after the American Revolution in 1796. Latrobe had trained in Britain under neoclassical architects Samuel Pepys Cockerell and Sir Robert Taylor.[23] It is quite likely that Latrobe was familiar with Taylor's works throughout the Thames valley region, including Asgill House and Bridge House, two riverside villas at Richmond, and No. 3 The Terrace, a prominent classical townhouse crowning Richmond Hill.[24] Regardless of whether he was aware of Taylor's work in the area, Latrobe was certainly familiar with the topography and character of the Thames. This familiarity is demonstrated by a description of the view from Church Hill in his *Virginia Journals* (1795–1798), which should be read in conjunction with two surviving watercolours Latrobe painted from the same spot (Figures 3.4 and 3.5):

> There are, I believe, few towns [. . .] in old England that have not a namesake in North America. In few cases has similarity of situation had the smallest influence upon the sameness of name. Richmond however is an exception to this remark. The general landscapes from the two Richmond-hills are so similar in their great features, that at first sight the likeness is most striking. [. . .] the windings of the James river have so much the same *cast* with those of the Thames, the amphitheatre of hills covered partly with wood partly with buildings, [. . .] are so like the range of hills on the south bank of the Thames, and the situation of Twickenham on the north [. . .], that if a man could be imperceptibly and in a instant conveyed from the one side of the Atlantic to the other he might hesitate for some minutes before he could discover the difference.[25]

That Latrobe had first-hand knowledge of this reach of the Thames is further suggested by his ability to spot the following 'differences':

> The want of finish and neatness in the American landscape would first strike his eye, while his ear would be arrested by the roar of the falls of James river below him. He would miss the elegance of Richmond bridge, and find in its place the impatient torrent tumbling over huge masses of granite [. . .]. Instead of the velvet lawns of Mr. Cambridge's Park and the precise arrangement of Twickenham, the wild trees growing among the irregular islands and the rambling edifices [. . .] would bewilder his attention. [. . .]. When however the whole country was in wood, I am convinced that it was the *general* similarity of the characters of the two situations that impressed upon this spot the name of Richmond.[26]

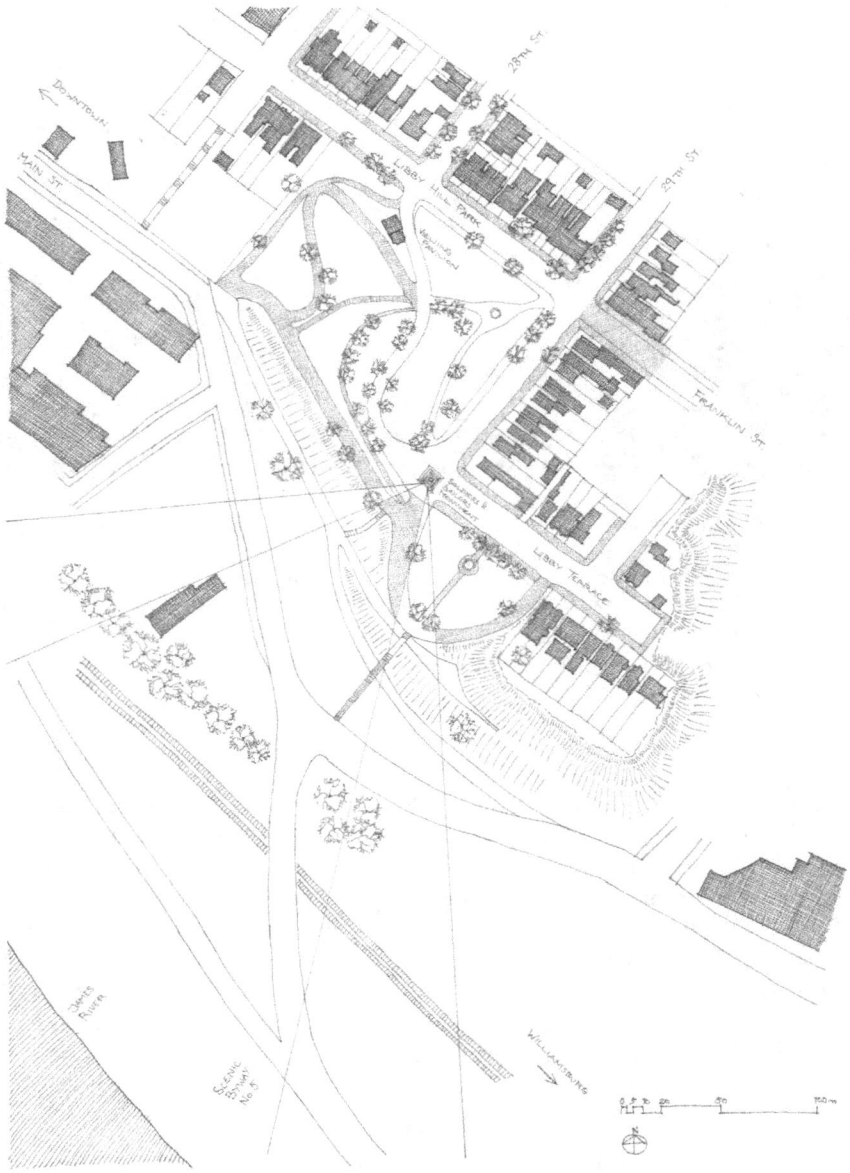

Figure 3.4 Plan of Church Hill and the view from Libby Hill Park.

Figure 3.5 Watercolour sketch of the view from Church Hill, Richmond, Virginia, by British architect Benjamin Henry Latrobe, c. 1795. Compare this view with the landscape paintings of Richmond-upon-Thames by Tillemans, Marlow, Wilson and others which date prior to 1795, with which Latrobe may have been familiar through mass-produced prints.

Source: Image courtesy of the Library of Congress, Washington, DC.

Critical of the 'inelegance' of the wilder Virginian view, Latrobe indicates his opinion of the superiority of the Thames. As an Englishman, it could be argued that Latrobe's comments once more take possession of Richmond, Virginia, for the defeated colonial power. Certainly, he speaks of the landscape as if it were European, writing of his purchase of Bushrod Washington's island in the middle of the James River, "It is a beautiful, fertile and romantic spot [. . .] its scenery would not disgrace the magic rivers of Italy".[27] Thus, the newly independent nation was promoted as a new Arcadia, invoking both a classical ideal and the genteel villa society of Richmond-upon-Thames.

The view, and its manipulation, in the work of Benjamin Henry Latrobe

As Richmond's most famous architect, Latrobe's designs, and their imitations, did much to construct the idea of that city and its landscape. It is worth spending time, here, with Latrobe's works – a prison and several villas – to show in detail how they translated the values of one Richmond to the other. In doing so, they helped to shape the landscape of the new Republic of America as well as its intellectual landscape and its design practices.

The city of Richmond's growing wealth and new-found importance as capital of the Commonwealth of Virginia (1780),[28] combined with a desperate need for reconstruction following its burning by British forces (1781)[29] and the jubilation following the colonies' new independence,[30] placed Latrobe in a lucrative position as one of America's first professional architects. Latrobe's first large commission of 1797, a penitentiary, reveals contemporary reforms founded on new principles of surveillance. British proponents of this reform, chiefly Jeremy Bentham and John Howard, argued for "the reduction of capital punishment to a minimal number of crimes, the substitution of imprisonment for the death penalty, and the transformation of jails [. . .] from sordid places of confinement to healthy, secure institutions of moral reform".[31] In the Commonwealth of Virginia, Thomas Jefferson had been promoting reform based on Philadelphia's legislative act of 1789. However, despite Jefferson's efforts, penal reform did not make an appearance in Virginia until the legislative act of 1796, which provided for the erection in Richmond of a "goal [sic] and penitentiary house".[32]

The Virginia Executive Council purchased a plot of land on a hill overlooking the James River in Richmond in 1797. Latrobe's competition-winning scheme for the site placed prisoner cells in a semicircle, watched over by a pair of bow-fronted guard residences, in a similar configuration to Bentham's fully developed circular 'Panopticon' designs of 1785.[33] Latrobe's familiarity with Bentham's designs can be attributed to his experience as surveyor to the London Police,[34] and by his apparent friendship in the 1790s with Bentham's brother Samuel,[35] also a proponent of penal reform.[36]

The revolution in visual principles which Bentham had brought about has been discussed by French philosopher Michel Foucault in *Discipline and Punish*, who shows that the Panopticon derives its power from the visual sense.[37] In effect, "visibility is a trap";[38] the prisoner "is seen, but he does not see; he is the subject of information, never a subject in communication".[39] The genius of the Panopticon is in its automatic function, whereby constant surveillance is effected irrespective of the guard's physical presence; the sight of the observation tower itself is enough to induce in the inmate a sense of being watched. Jacques Lacan might have called this powerful sense the 'gaze'. The bow windows of Latrobe's guard houses are an architectural manifestation of this 'gaze', allowing the attendant guard to command greater visibility of the semi-circular cell block beyond. This is clearly illustrated by the plan where the watch tower of Bentham's prison is substituted with what looks like a conventional domestic villa. Similarly, Latrobe commonly deployed this architectural device on residential schemes, directing the bow towards the most picturesque prospects, as Taylor had done at Asgill House, Richmond-upon-Thames (1757–58).

In many ways, the bow window arrangement functions like a fragment of Bentham's Panopticon, an architectural configuration which enhances the power of the gaze via the spatial construction of a power relationship between the viewer and the view. As Foucault explains, "power has its principle [. . .] in a certain distribution of bodies, surfaces, lights, gazes in an arrangement whose internal mechanisms produce the relation in which individuals are caught up"; the Panopticon is an additional mechanism, configured in order to "assure dissymmetry, disequilibrium, difference"[40] and so deliver subjectivity unto the inmate. Penal reformers anticipated that this system of surveillance would improve the behaviour of the prisoner; Bentham went even further, promoting its use in school and factory design as a measure to increase productivity. In the case of Latrobe's classical Virginian villas the bow window surveyed manicured landscapes tended by enslaved workers, another form of imprisonment, and another example of the manipulative power of the gaze. This observation also highlights the contradictions at work in depictions of Richmond's landscape, which was repeatedly presented as a bucolic Arcadia appealing to the picturesque sensibilities of the gentry, despite the realities of its industrial productivity and a slave-based economy.

Foucault has seen the introduction of such structures at this time as symptomatic of a cultural shift from a society governed through physical threats and punishment to a society of surveillance and discipline. Following Foucault's argument, one could argue that the introduction of the Panopticon demonstrates the new-found potency and power of the gaze in eighteenth-century thought, and is an illustration of the deliberate and calculated manipulation of both viewer and view, manifest in contemporary architectural and landscape design.

Latrobe and the picturesque

Latrobe was not a pioneer in the manipulation of the viewer's gaze, nor would the principle have been alien to him before his work on Richmond's Penitentiary. Latrobe was certainly familiar with contemporary fashions for picturesque landscape design. His extensive correspondence reveals him to have been an acquaintance of John 'Jack' Repton, Humphrey Repton's son. Writing much later, Latrobe even claimed "intimate acquaintance" with Humphrey Repton himself in 1794.[41]

Whatever the truth may be concerning Latrobe's acquaintance with Repton, it is clear that he was a "devotee of the picturesque".[42] Evidence remains in the form of 14 volumes of sketchbooks and correspondence. Of particular note is an apparently unfinished and unpublished work, *An Essay on Landscape* (1798–99), written as an instruction in landscape painting to a friend, Ms Susanna Spotswood. This work, one of the earliest drawing books to be written in America,[43] shares many similarities with Gilpin's famous travel guides.[44] Indeed, at this time the boundaries between travel writing on landscape, landscape perception and garden design were increasingly blurred; Latrobe, for example, also edited and provided illustrations for William Bruce's *Travels to Discover the Source of the Nile* (1790).[45] The works of both authors instructed the reader not only in the historical and political narratives of landscapes but also in how to create pictorial compositions worthy of the great Italian painters, such as Claude Lorrain.

Though Latrobe's *An Essay on Landscape* was never published, his work did influence indirectly the course of American landscape painting and perception. Carter has pointed out that Latrobe's pupil William Strickland produced the title vignette for Fielding Lucas's *The Art of Colouring and Painting Landscapes in Water Colours* (1815). In addition, Benjamin's son John Latrobe authored *The Progressive Drawing Book* (1827–28), profusely illustrated with English as well as American views, signifying the transatlantic absorption of the picturesque taste. Carter notes, "John H. B. Latrobe based at least eight of his fifteen plates of American scenery on drawings by his father, an English-born amateur who had carved the Picturesque point of view into the American landscape".[46]

Latrobe's Virginia villas

Latrobe's advocation of picturesque conventions in landscape art and architecture may also be apparent in his built architectural works. In particular, Latrobe's design for an irregular villa intended for a hilltop site in Richmond, Virginia (1797) – conceived in direct relation to the landscape – could be interpreted as an exceptionally early example of picturesque architectural planning.[47] Published in Latrobe's folio of work entitled *Designs of Buildings Erected or Proposed to Be Built in Virginia 1795–1799*, the villa is one of a number of schemes proposed for Richmond's Church Hill district. The title page depicts many of these projects clustered around the hill as an Arcadian scene of classical villas set within an undulating landscape.[48]

It has been suggested that the irregular villa may have been intended for the architect's own home, supported by the setting of a perspective drawing which seems to indicate the site Latrobe himself owned on Church Hill. Certainly, Latrobe was planning to build himself a home, writing that it was his intention to "have a little house upon my beautiful little hill here by the end of summer [1798]".[49] The idea that the house was for Latrobe himself is also supported by the unusual nature of the plan, a curious choice for a client at a time when symmetrical planning was still mainstream. In fact, Snadon and Fazio have described the villa as "without doubt one of the most imaginative domestic solutions proposed in America in the eighteenth century", adding that "it antedates most published English experiments with such an asymmetrical type".[50] Each room's orientation is carefully considered, so that each possesses its individuality of form and, accessed one after another, reveals a sequence of distinctive landscape vistas (Figure 3.6).

Figure 3.6 Benjamin Henry Latrobe's 'Irregular Villa', designed for a site on Church Hill, Richmond, Virginia, in 1797.

If landscape vistas from the villa were an important consideration of its internal planning, one could also argue that the irregularity of exterior form created by Latrobe's blind openings, stepping volumes and projecting bows was intended to enhance the stereometry of kinetic and oblique views of the villa from within its landscape setting, suggested by Latrobe's own perspective views. Robert Adam might have called this concept of kinetic architectural form 'movement'. As Adam explains in *Works in Architecture* (1773),

> *Movement* is meant to express, the rise and fall, the advance and recess, [. . .] of form [. . .] so as to add greatly to the picturesque of the composition. For the rising and falling, advancing and receding, [. . .] have the same effect in architecture, that hill and dale, fore-ground and distance, swelling and sinking have in landscape: That is, they serve to produce an agreeable and diversified contour, that groups and contrasts like a picture, and creates a variety of light and shade, which gives great spirit, beauty and effect to the composition.[51]

That Latrobe considered the 'movement' of his villa's composition from a kinetic viewpoint[52] is suggested by the presence of perspective construction lines faintly visible on the ground floor plan.

Of the projects collected in Latrobe's *Designs of Buildings Erected or Proposed to Be Built in Virginia* folio, only one, 'Clifton', was completed to his satisfaction. Both the landscape plan and perspective watercolours of Clifton demonstrate the importance of the naturalistic landscape, enhanced

Figure 3.7 Perspective drawing by B. H. Latrobe, for 'Clifton', Church Hill, Richmond, Virginia, c. 1798–99.

by the provision of undulating serpentine pathways from which the house was to be observed within its setting (Figure 3.7).[53] However, the reality of Clifton's site was far from Latrobe's idealised vision; research has shown the site to have been bordered by a three-storey tobacco factory, along with the noise and pollution of a wash house and smokehouse.[54] Latrobe's design clearly sought to screen and disguise these intrusions into the Arcadian landscape he imagined, directing views from the peripheral pathways towards the house itself and the James River beyond, to create, as had Walpole at Strawberry Hill, a picturesque oasis within what was actually becoming a busy industrial suburb.[55]

Thomas Jefferson in Richmond

The importance Latrobe placed upon the visual sense in both his Penitentiary design and his Virginian villas is also evident in the work of Thomas Jefferson. In 1785 Jefferson had been asked to procure designs for a government building to be erected on a hilltop overlooking the James River at Richmond.[56] Following a European Grand Tour of classical ruins and picturesque landscapes, Jefferson submitted plans based on the Maison Carrée at Nîmes,[57] which he stated "is allowed without contradiction to be the most perfect and precious remain of antiquity in existence".[58]

Just as Jefferson had first seen the Maison Carrée on his travels in Europe, so too his importation of the Roman temple was explicitly designed to appeal to the tastes of the picturesque tourist. An example of this is Jefferson's statement that "it is noble beyond expression and would have done honor to our country as presenting to travellers a morsel of taste in our infancy, promising much for our maturer age".[59]

With Latrobe's classical villas and Jefferson's gleaming white Roman temple perched high above the river, the James River landscape was becoming established almost as an English landscape garden informed by Italian landscape painting. Jefferson surely recognised this, as he had toured English picturesque gardens on his travels, stating that "The gardening in that country is the article in which it excels all the earth".[60] Extracting ideas from these gardens, Jefferson imagined a garden pavilion for his 'Plinian' villa-estate at Monticello, Virginia, where "the roof may be Chinese, Grecian, or in the taste of the Lantern of Demosthenes at Athens".[61] He also considered building "a small Gothic temple of antique appearance" and noted in his journal the pyramid he had seen at Stowe.[62] Though the square surrounding Jefferson's Capitol building in Richmond received no formal landscape plan, the view of the river was certainly integrated into Jefferson's design. In its original configuration the raised podium of the portico was reached by a pair of imperial stairs on the broad sides of the building. This arrangement shares similarities with Lord Burlington's Chiswick House, where the stairs lead the visitor to the first-floor porticos, from which to take in vistas of the landscape beyond. Similarly, the Capitol's portico served as a viewing terrace from which to view the expansive river landscape. Writing later, in 1846, Scotsman George Mackay noted that the river was "so directly beneath you that it almost seems that you could leap into it".[63] This viewing function of Jefferson's Capitol is today regrettably lost, the result of a dense crowding of later and much taller buildings, and the addition of steps to the portico.

As well as serving as a place from which to view the landscape, Richmond's Capitol embellished it in a manner typical of the picturesque. This, I suggest, was not lost on Latrobe, whose watercolour sketch of the Capitol from the proposed site of his island villa has all the compositional hallmarks of picturesque landscape painting: a foreground tree carefully positioned to frame the view, a middle ground of water and clumps of trees enlivened by the distant classical temple (Figure 3.8). As Latrobe wrote in *An Essay on Landscape*,

> Having satiated your eye with this prospect, retire within the Grove, so that the foreground shall consist of trees, and shadowy earth. The landscape is immediately lightened up with a thousand new beauties, arising from the novelty of the contrast. This particular effect, of seeing a distant view glittering among near objects is familiar to every observer. The Landscape is now become a perfect composition.[64]

Just as the disparate villas and gardens of the Thames were imagined to be united in one great picturesque landscape from the viewpoint on Richmond

Figure 3.8 Benjamin Henry Latrobe was particularly drawn to purchase Bushrod Washington's island for its picturesque views. In this watercolour by B. H. Latrobe, Jefferson's Capitol forms the centrepiece of an Arcadian landscape, which may be compared easily to English landscape gardens, such as those at Stowe.

Hill, so too Latrobe unites the city, the river, the villas and their gardens in one great Arcadian landscape composition.

One contemporary writer would describe Richmond as "a beautiful little city, built up of rich and tasteful villas, and embellished with all the varieties of town and country, scattered with a fine and exquisite skill".[65] This view of a prosperous Arcadian landscape is similar to the impression Alexis de Tocqueville had on his arrival to New York by way of the East River in 1831. De Tocqueville was delighted by "a number of little palaces of white marble, several of which were of classic architecture". However, his enthusiasm was dampened when he learned, upon closer inspection, that the "marble temples" had walls of whitewashed brick and columns of painted wood. As Early states,

> In the deception De Tocqueville found evidence of the "hypocrisy of luxury", a vice he believed inherent in democracies where "appearance is more attended to than reality". [. . .] Showiness was almost inevitable in a period that characteristically valued the aura of nostalgic associations surrounding particular architectural forms more than the forms themselves.[66]

De Tocqueville found that the Arcadian image was just that, a romantic image projected onto the landscape. The point, perhaps, was that these buildings were designed as elements of a much larger whole, as objects placed within the landscape according to rules of visual composition. The actual fabric of these structures mattered less than the fictive reality of which they formed a part, a new classical landscape claimed from the ancients, via the Thames, for a great American city. For all that this classical authority was imagined as a romantic conceit, it was no less authentic to its authors than the original.

What is important to note here is that the very foundations of an American architectural profession, and a mode of vision for the viewing of American landscapes and townscapes, grew from culturally engrained examples of Anglo-Palladian architecture and the 'English landscape' movement. Specifically, the Virginian capital of Richmond was shaped via the mediated images of Richmond-upon-Thames. Despite a direct translation of many of the values encoded in the picturesque view onto the landscape of Richmond, Virginia, it will be seen that these values were not static but in constant flux. In the following sections, the dynamic nature of the vista's shifting cultural and political values in the build-up to and aftermath of the American Civil War will be examined via a study of picturesque images of the Virginian landscape and, more specifically, the view of the James River from Church Hill.

Libby Hill's Greek Revival villas: Richmond as classic city

Richmond, Virginia, has long been admired for its scenic position, and Church Hill in particular, the location of historic St John's Church, became one of the city's most fashionable spots for admiring the view, home to the suburban villas of a new elite. This chapter will follow the next steps in the intellectual history of the view's development and the shift in its imaginative construction from a rural landscape to a city suburb. It will account for the designation of Libby Hill Park, the construction of a viewing terrace and serpentine carriageways. The chapter will argue that through this process, Church Hill's expansive prospect was concentrated into a narrowly defined and controlled vista, while at the same time its associated values were reinforced through the construction of scenic parks, monuments and a proliferation of inexpensive, mass-produced images.

Within the district of Church Hill may be found one of Richmond's smallest but perhaps most important public park, an area of gardens laid out at the edge of steeply sloping Libby Hill. Overlooking the bend of the James, which so resembled the river's serpentine course at Richmond-upon-Thames, the viewing terrace at Libby Hill Park demonstrates, more than anywhere else, why the city received its name (Figure 3.9). Established in 1851, Libby Hill Park was one of the first to be designated in a system of municipal public

Figure 3.9 The panoramic view of the James River from Libby Hill Park, Church Hill, Richmond, Virginia.

parks.[67] Its goal was to preserve for public use an area of open ground from which to observe the view of the James River, as much had passed into the private ownership of property developers and others, including Latrobe, who had packed the hillside with the villas of an early industrial elite.

Many of Church Hill's villas were built from the wealth of Richmond's flourishing nineteenth-century industries, including its famous ironworks and tobacco factories. Contemporary artists made a point of depicting the city's smoking chimneys, warehouses and railway viaducts as advertisements of its industrial prosperity. Indeed, Libby Hill afforded the finest panorama of Richmond's prosperous semi-rural villas set against the background of this industrious activity, marking it out as *the* viewpoint of choice for touring draughtsmen.

Church Hill's plethora of classical villas is a testament to Richmond's "Flush Time", a period of unprecedented growth following the War with Britain (1812–1814). Though only the Wickham-Valentine and Brockenbrough houses remain, these white stuccoed mansions, often with two-storey porticos facing the river, played a significant role in defining the character of Richmond's river views. The contemporary proliferation of classical villas is demonstrated by the remark of a character in James Fenimore Cooper's *Home as Found* (1838), who states, "An extraordinary taste is afflicting this country in the way of architecture, nothing but a Grecian temple being now deemed a suitable residence for a man in these classical times".[68] Though the Greek Revival style was prevalent throughout much of the east coast of America at this time, Virginia is often credited as its birthplace, and Jefferson as its founding father. One historian of the Greek Revival has written that

> [Many] dispute the origin of the neo-classic style in America, but here in Richmond there can hardly be a doubt that residences of this type were inspired by the model Jefferson gave in the Capitol. The columns of a Roman façade, set on a bold Richmond hill, fired the imagination of not a few ambitious gentlemen.[69]

In Richmond too, one can trace Jefferson's influence upon architect Robert Mills, the author of several early Greek Revival villas and, as architect of the Washington Monument and US Treasury, America's most influential Greek Revival architect. Of Richmond's two remaining villas, the Brockenbrough House is attributed to Mills, Latrobe's protégé and rival in his late career. A grand but plain house with a two-storey colonnade facing over the formerly open hillside towards the river, the Brockenbrough House is chiefly known for its infamous role as 'White House of the Confederacy' during the American Civil War. The villa's setting is much changed; the river views from the rear portico have been blocked in recent years by tall buildings and the steep hillside regraded. Though of a different building, Mordecai's account of a similarly sited house on Ross Street, Richmond, gives an impression of its former setting:[70]

> The house [. . .] had no claim to antiquity, but it excited admiration by the beauty of its elevated position and its Italian aspect. A centre building with wings, and a portico in the rear [. . .], commanding an extensive view of the city beneath, of the country around, of the river, its islands and its falls and its smooth water; [. . .] these combined to form an exquisite landscape.[71]

Richmond's villas, such as the one Mordecai describes here, not only enjoyed spectacular views but also were themselves studied for their picturesque qualities. The mass production and widespread distribution of prints of Mills's buildings during the first decades of the nineteenth century[72] contributed to the popular notion, promoted at this time, that Richmond was a city of elegant classical buildings set within a picturesque Arcadian river landscape.[73]

The literary portrayal of Libby Hill and the visual construction of the 'South'

As Richmond's population boomed and a prosperous middle class developed, the value of land on fashionable Church Hill escalated, encouraging shrewd developers to infill large villa plots with denser compact housing. The upper classes, tired of their increasingly old-fashioned mansions, and aware of the value of their plots for middle-class housing, soon began to move away towards the West.[74] This moment is captured in local author Ellen Glasgow's *Romance of a Plain Man* (1909). Set during the late 1800s on Church Hill, it is a love story centred on an affair between an upper-class woman and a 'plain' man. It captures a moment, after the Civil War, in which the hierarchical society of the American South, considered old-fashioned by the northern victors, was in flux. In *Away Down South*, James Cobb has written that in both North and South, authors such as Glasgow and Thomas Nelson Page "churned out treacly romantic portraits of the Old South".[75] Francis Pendleton Gaines also notes this tendency towards romanticism, writing that "estates swelled in size and mansions grew proportionately great. Gentlemen were perfected in lovely grace, gay girls in loveliness, slaves in immeasurable devotion".[76] Fenimore Cooper was also guilty of this hyperbole when he wrote that the South had "more men who *belong to the class of what is termed the class of gentlemen*" than "any other country of the world".[77] The collective works of these writers have been dubbed the 'Southern Renaissance', when, "in the absence of a critical historical tradition, southern writers began to ask how such an appealing and glorious past could have degenerated into such a dismal and defective present".[78]

Such romanticised visions of the Old South were berated as such by northern reviewers at the time, who tended to view the South as "a primitive and exotic land distinctly apart from the rest of America".[79] In discussing Glasgow's novels, a 1909 *New York Times* reviewer lamented that

> it is a pity that a novelist of Miss Glasgow's gifts should select a theme, no matter how true it may be locally, so at variance with our National spirit and so impossible in any other locality. For the spirit of caste dominates the whole story.[80]

This damning review reveals how, some 40 years after the end of the Civil War, southern society was still perceived in the North as alien to the "National spirit". This alien South was still later represented in Wilbur Joseph Cash's *The Mind of the South* (1941) and Howard Zinn's *The Southern Mystique* (1964) as "a savagely racist, intellectually stunted, emotionally deranged society unwilling to admit it was sick, much less heal itself".[81] Cash ridiculed the Old South fantasy as a "sort of stage piece out of the eighteenth century" where "every farmhouse became a Big House, every farm a baronial estate, every master of scant red acres [. . .] a feudal lord".[82]

Despite negative press from northern reviewers, Glasgow's novels contain much of interest to historians of Richmond in particular and the South in general. Chiefly, Glasgow's nostalgic view of the caste system illustrates the middle-class white southern perception that a supposedly noble, agrarian,

Jeffersonian and 'American'[83] society was being eroded by the Wordsworthian 'dark and satanic' modernising forces of the 'Yankee' North. Glasgow writes,

> Our prosperity, with our traditions, had crumbled around us, yet there were still left the ancient church, with its shady graveyard, and an imposing mansion or two inherited from the forgotten splendour of former days. [. . .] The other [modern] Richmond – that "up-town" I heard sometimes mentioned – I had never seen, for my early horizon was bounded by the green hill, [and] by the crawling salmon-coloured James River at its foot.[84]

Glasgow imagines Church Hill as a 'ghost town' haunted by memories of a splendid past. In many ways, Glasgow's juxtaposition of the modern industrial "up-town" with the crumbling mansions of old Richmond is representative of the divide between the modernising forces of the industrial North, the unseen enemy beyond the visible landscape, and the pastoral nostalgia for an imagined 'Old South'. Thus, Glasgow's novels contributed to a wave of anti-modern sentiment, common at this time among Southern Renaissance writers, who tended to promote features of pre-industrial pasts.

Photography and the city

Richmond's earliest photograph, a daguerreotype taken from a spot on Church Hill, demonstrates the rapid development of the neighbourhood with speculative row housing by c. 1855. This pre-crash property boom in cities of the 'New South' was a favoured subject of 'Southern Renaissance' authors, in particular Phillip Alexander Bruce's *The Rise of the New South* (1905), Mildred Rutherford's *The Old South: What Made It, What Destroyed It, What Has Replaced It* (1916) and the novels of Thomas Wolfe.

It is important to note here that the widespread assumption that the 'Old South' declined as a result of the North's modernising policies is misleading. The glorious past described in the writings of Southern Renaissance authors is as much a figment of their imaginations as the exclusive association of industrialisation with the North. For example, the common picturesque description of Richmond's landscape in later novels is often at odds with eyewitness accounts of the city, which was, even at the height of its supposed glory in the 1850s, a rather ramshackle affair. Former president John Tyler described the "surface on which the city stood [as] untamed and broken", adding that

> Almost inaccessible heights and deep ravines everywhere prevailed. The capitol square was [. . .] but rudely, if at all, enclosed. The ascent to the building was painfully laborious. The two now beautiful valleys were then unsightly gullies, which threatened, unless soon arrested, to extend themselves across the street.[85]

Far from the tidy image conveyed in the writing of authors and journalists, and in lithographic illustrations circulated in the newspapers,[86] it is clear that Richmond had its share of problems. The popular picturesque description compensated for the visual shortfalls of the city.

The impact of the invention of photography, and the possibility of its infinite reproduction,[87] on the perception of the city cannot be underestimated. In *Kodak and the Lens of Nostalgia* (2000), Nancy Martha West suggests that, through advertising, the Eastman Kodak Company taught consumers to "apprehend their experiences and memories as objects of nostalgia, for the easy availability of snapshots allowed people for the first time in history to arrange their lives in such a way that painful or unpleasant aspects were systematically erased".[88] Equally, the photograph captured the realities of American cities and taught its citizens to understand what was, and was not, picturesque (or photogenic). As cultural theorist Marshall McLuhan has written,

> This immense tidying-up of our inner lives, [. . .] has had its obvious parallels in our attempts to rearrange our homes and gardens and our cities. To see a photograph of the local slum makes the condition unbearable. The mere matching of the picture with reality provides a new motive for change.[89]

Where the landscape artists of previous generations could 'tidy' up unsightly portions of Richmond with a brushstroke, like the unkempt wasteland which had encircled Jefferson's Capitol, photography made such spaces new objects of civic shame. It is no coincidence that a movement of civic beautification – the 'City Beautiful' movement of the late 1890s – swept through American cities at this time.[90]

The early years of the photograph coincided with the professionalisation of American advertising; marketing experts, brand names, labels and packaging were all in their infancy.[91] Newly tidied-up cityscapes would feature heavily on millions of photographic postcards. According to the special collections department of Virginia Commonwealth University Library, photographic postcards began to be widely used in the US after the introduction of the Private Mailing Card Act in 1898. In the next few years the demand for postcards grew as a craze for collecting them spread throughout the country. This 'golden age' of postcard publishing and collection lasted from 1898 through to the mid-twentieth century. One estimate has put the number of different postcard views of Richmond, Virginia, produced during this period at around 2,000.[92] In America, as in the UK and mainland Europe, the effect of the photographic postcard was to turn city views into commodities to be consumed. As West writes,

> [B]eginning at mid-century, [. . .] objects assumed an increasingly symbolic value, emerging as signs for or symbols of a seemingly endless

variety of social meanings. Such a transformation occurred because formations such as advertising emerged during this period to represent commodities as spectacles, as objects that possessed unprecedented special meanings.[93]

The trend for increasing commodification is reflected by the Great Exhibition of 1851 and the series of American 'world's fairs' which followed. Richmond too held an exhibition in 1892, at which all manner of commercially available products could be viewed. A contemporary newspaper image depicts the city itself, its landscape and its architectural objects, as a series of commodities to be viewed, presented to the observer as if arranged for perusal in a gallery.[94] Through the mass production and distribution of photographic prints, the city view as commodity could now also be owned by anyone, anywhere. At the same time, the photographic image of a city could be nostalgic, a visual cue preserving the personal memories of a particular time and place.

Kodak's success can, at least in part, be attributed to the success of the illustrated magazine industry, which exploited new photo-reproduction technologies, such as the improvement of the halftone process (1890) and the photogravure process (1895). Boorstin has described these technical innovations as "part of a great, but little-noticed, revolution", dubbing it "the Graphic Revolution", a period in which "Man's ability to make, preserve, transmit, and disseminate precise images [. . .] grew at a fantastic pace".[95] An equally important factor in the success of these photographic magazines was their marketing as the natural accompaniment to leisure time.

The railway tourist or Sunday picnic party, exposed to Kodak's magazine advertisements, now sought to capture (and preserve the memory of) the landscapes they saw before them, particularly as periodicals such as *Outing Magazine* and *Outdoor World and Recreation* had begun to promote the camera as an essential accessory of the outdoor excursion.[96] By the time Kodak introduced the $1 Brownie camera in 1900, the amateur photographer was trained to see, and equipped to capture, scenes of picturesque, historic and/or natural interest, like those of Richmond's public parks, and Libby Hill was no exception.[97]

A study of Richmond's many postcard views demonstrates a shift in popularity from western viewpoints of the city towards the more idyllic rural view from Libby Hill in the east. With the arrival of heavy industry in the western part of the city, attracted by the canal and abundance of free water-driven power, western viewpoints became increasingly industrialised, as demonstrated by the cover image of Gamble Hill Park in *Harper's Weekly* (1887). Set against the headline "The New South", this image glories in the sublime scale of Richmond's factories, presenting them as a spectacle to be observed from the foreground park bench. Post–Civil War, the defeated South was committed to a programme of 'reconstruction' and the industrialisation of its primarily agricultural economy. In this image, mechanisation is presented as a liberating force, freeing an increasingly prosperous middle class from the drudgery of labour-intensive work.

If the 'New South' politics of reconstruction promised future prosperity, its potency was reliant upon deep-rooted nostalgic sentiment for a former golden age. As Cobb suggests, "Defeated and embittered, southern whites drew determination and hope from the New South's promises of an affluent golden age just ahead", just as they "also found pride and reassurance in [the South's] celebration of a carefully constructed golden age behind, the glorious and heroic heritage of the Old South and the Lost Cause".[98] If the Gamble Hill image stands for the 'New South', the Libby Hill view could emphasise a nostalgic, picturesque rurality, a heavily romanticised image of the 'Old South' in which the Confederate cause found expression.

Monumentalising the view: Libby Hill as memorial to the Confederate cause

In 1894, a memorial to Confederate soldiers and sailors – and implicitly to the Confederate cause – was constructed on Libby Hill. This memorial effectively sought to claim a particular politics for the landscape of Richmond and its picturesque images. Its new re-imagination of the idea of Richmond's landscape, rooted in familiar claims to nostalgia and authenticity, is worthy of note.

Though admired often for its picturesque qualities, Libby Hill also afforded a near cartographic bird's-eye view of the city, leading to its use by a series of photographers to record the destruction of the city in the wake of the American Civil War (1865) (Figure 3.10). These photographs demonstrate a fascination with ruination, depicting the shattered remains of the city's grand buildings in a deeply moving fashion. This incredible photographic record of Richmond's Civil War destruction formed the basis for the collections of the Southern Historical Society, established soon after in 1869. The society's comment that its collections would form "a complete arsenal from which the defenders of our cause may draw any desired weapon"[99] would seem to corroborate photographer Susan Sontag's much later observation that the language of photography borrows much from the military (you 'aim' and 'shoot' the camera).[100] The creation of historical societies, and the assembly of these visual 'arsenals', also represented a militaristic defence of a southern collective memory, or "a Confederate historical memory that would vindicate both the Confederate cause and those who served it".[101] One could argue that regional identities were strengthened rather than weakened by the Civil War. Cobb has written, "[I]f the defeated southern states had emerged from the Civil War as a relatively cohesive 'South', the triumphant North had simply affirmed its credentials as 'America'".[102] Thus, in the immediate aftermath of the Civil War, Richmond posited itself as anti-North, the 'real America' or even anti-American, adopting the varied imagery and associations of ancient Greece, Rome and Augustan England. Richmond's Civil War photographs

Figure 3.10 The destruction of Richmond in the wake of the American Civil War (1865) was captured by hundreds of photographs. Jefferson's damaged Capitol takes centre stage in many of these, inviting comparisons between the fall of the South and of classical Rome or Carthage.
Source: Image courtesy of the Virginia Historical Society.

lamented the destruction of a supposedly glorious 'Old South' (despite the fact that the city had been burned by retreating Confederate forces), romanticising the ruins of the Southern Union in the fashion of a fallen empire. As if to underline this, Jefferson's war-ravaged Capitol, captured by Unionist cannon, and then by their cameras and photographic film, plays a symbolic lead role in many of the images.

In an explicit reference to imperial Rome, city engineer Wilfred Cutshaw, charged with the development of the municipal parks, designed the Monument to Confederate Soldiers and Sailors, erected on Libby Hill in 1894.[103] This took as its model Alexandria's 'Pompey's Pillar', erected for Emperor Diocletian in AD 293, standing 73 feet high and topped with a bronze figure. As if to highlight this classical reference, contemporary postcards depicting the monument claim that "it occupies one of the seven hills from which Richmond (like ancient Rome) is built", adding that "from its summit may be obtained a magnificent panoramic view of the city and surrounding country, while at its foot, sweeping [. . .] in a wide and graceful 'bend', flows the historic James river".

Central to Cutshaw's argument for a monument on Libby Hill was the site's visibility within the landscape, and thus its visual power. A correspondent to the *Richmond Dispatch* (1886) remarked,

> There alone will it be the common property of our people, for there it can be seen by more of them and from more parts of the city than any other. [. . .] From the deck of the river steamers its towering form will greet the eye as soon as the bend [. . .] is passed.[104]

One can also detect a sense that Cutshaw and the other advocates of the Libby Hill location intended the monument to act as a viewpoint itself – that the monument was a celebration of Richmond's landscape setting. The aforementioned newspaper correspondent continues:

> It is a lovely spot, and from it the view of the river, landscape and city is unsurpassed. A lady once standing there when the evening sky was all aglow and flushing all nature with its radiance remarked to me: 'I have seen most of the celebrated views in this country and in Europe, but not one of them is more beautiful than this'.[105]

The role of the monument as viewpoint is made explicit by a history of the project, published in 1894, which documents the creation of the viewing terrace and carriageways that encircle the base of the monument, in order that "the monument [and landscape] may thus be viewed by a carriage on every side".[106]

Windsor Farms: suburban projections of 'Old England'

The development of the terrace and carriageways around the Confederate Soldiers and Sailors Monument aligns with a broader movement in 'parkway' design. The appearance of carriageways and the motorcar in postcard views of Richmond's parks demonstrates how designers increasingly considered the 'windshield' view of the city. As Boorstin has noted, the immense physical endurance and "athletic exercise" of travel had evolved into a "spectator sport".[107] The ease of access to nature enabled by the motorcar is reflected by the growth of outdoor recreation movements throughout the early 1900s and the spread of the suburbs, whose developers promoted them as ideal sites for indulging in gardening, walking and naturalistic photography. An advertisement in a contemporary newspaper promised readers that suburbs such as 'Westbrook Lawn' offered "the opportunity of a lifetime for those who desire to live outside the city limits *with all city conveniences*",[108] while a third used the tag line "Back to Nature and the Farm" to sell lots at "The Village of Bensley: 'The Suburb Beautiful' ".[109]

In Richmond, Virginia, the Garden City movement is best demonstrated by landscape architect John Nolen's design for a suburban estate commissioned by tobacconist T. C. Williams. Given a suitably agrarian name, along with the connotations of an idealised aristocratic 'Old England', a 1926 plan of Nolen's 'Windsor Farms' survives in the collections of Virginia Commonwealth University. The plan demonstrates how, as in British examples such as Parker and Unwin's Hampstead Garden Suburb, streets radiate in a curvilinear pattern about a central square and club house. The combination of naturalistic landscaping and historical architecture lend the suburb the appearance of a number of small 'country house' estates with the feel of an 'Old English village'.[110] Describing the trend for romantic historicism in suburban architecture, Lowenthal has written,

> Architects on both sides of the Atlantic made tangible this nostalgic myth by reviving an Old English vernacular. Mock-Tudor became the predominant domestic style of the 1920s and 1930s, "quaint" and "old-fashioned" became terms of praise; "to be up-to-date" now meant to look as old as possible.[111]

Remarkably, Windsor Farms' reference to Old England was more than simply in the name and its visual cues; two of the constituent country house estates were reconstructed from architectural fragments shipped across the Atlantic.

Before we examine these two reconstructions, something should be said about the context of 1920s American visual culture. The design of the Windsor Farms estate, with its curving roads lined with blossoming apple trees and quaint homes, conforms to a visual recipe popularised by contemporary postcard and photographic views. Of particular influence was the work of Harvard-educated Congregational minister Wallace Nutting, who amassed a fortune from the mass production of his photographs, photographic calendars and guidebooks. These typically took the form of rural landscape views, the sinuous curve of a country lane a particular favourite subject. The colonial homestead, with all its refined elegance amid picturesque naturalistic gardens, was also a popular choice; Nutting's *States Beautiful* guidebook series, including *Virginia Beautiful* (1930), reads as an itinerary of colonial plantation estates intermingled with rural landscapes and picturesque lithographs.

Nutting was not alone in his popularisation of nostalgic and picturesque scenes. In fact, as early as 1922 the Eastman Kodak Company had sent a team of marketing representatives

> to drive along the country's most travelled roads and scout out particularly scenic areas. Acting on their recommendations, Kodak's advertising department erected 6000 signs to tip off motorists that a scenic view

lay ahead. Composed simply of black lettering against a plain white background, the signs read 'Picture ahead! *Kodak as you go*'.[112]

Kodak's pairing of photography with motoring promoted American landscapes as pictures, visual commodities subject to aesthetic and artistic scrutiny, as well as nostalgic mementos of past holidays or events. In this way, Kodak played a direct role in the construction of what Urry calls the "tourist gaze".[113] As a 1917 Kodak advert caption stated, "Wherever the purr of your motor lures you, wherever the call of the road leads you, there you will find pictures, untaken pictures that invite your Kodak".[114]

Unlike Kodak, Nutting also produced internal views, staged at a series of historic properties in New England and further afield, typically depicting nostalgic reconstructions of bygone daily life, such as Nutting's *Trimming the Pie Crust* (1915). In this view, the historic setting is complemented by reproduction furniture to Nutting's own design, available along with his photos through the company's successful catalogue.[115] Enthusiasts of the Nutting 'look' could even spend the day motoring through the New England countryside to one of his five showroom houses, genuine historic buildings furnished with Nutting products and prints available for purchase. The very act of approach, speeding through the picturesque scenery of New England, acted as the prelude to Nutting's consumer experience. One could argue that contemporary suburban developments, with their serpentine roads lined with blossoming cherry trees, sweeping lawns, and names deliberately rich with historic and aesthetic allusion, were designed to reproduce the visual effects of leisure motoring, as popularised by figures such as Nutting.

Certainly, the aforementioned reconstruction of two historic English buildings on the Windsor Farms estate demonstrates contemporary enthusiasms for the nostalgic, historic and picturesque. The first such structure, Agecroft Hall, a fifteenth-century manor house formerly from Pendlebury near Manchester, was purchased at auction by developer T. C. Williams in 1925 (Figure 3.11). Its demolition and sale sparked protests in Britain and a debate in the House of Commons, but nevertheless it was agreed that the Hall's perilous derelict state was not to be preferred. The Williamses and their architect, Henry G. Morse, salvaged only the most picturesque and interesting fragments of the house, re-erecting them to a new plan, designed to suit the twentieth-century requirements of the suburban family. Immediately next door, Alexander Weddell and his wife, Virginia, were also reconstructing the salvaged architectural fragments of a building they had acquired at auction in 1925, all that remained of Warwick Priory, an Elizabethan mansion incorporating medieval fabric.[116]

Naming it Virginia House, the building reflects the confluence of two separate agendas, a home for the couple and, in a philanthropic gesture, a headquarters for the Virginia Historical Society. For the latter, the Weddells proposed a reconstruction of George Washington's English ancestral home,

Figure 3.11 Sixteenth-century Agecroft Hall, as reconstructed at Windsor Farms, Richmond, Virginia.

Source: Image courtesy of Library of Congress, Washington, DC.

Sulgrave Manor, which was incorporated into the building's western façade. This curious replication of a medieval manor house merged with the real fragments of an Elizabethan mansion creates a curious tension in scale between the building's two facades. Jacqueline Taylor has suggested this tension reveals the different symbolic functions of the house: the Sulgrave Manor portion firmly associates Virginia with a heroic past, while Warwick Priory demonstrates Alexander Weddell's aspiration to be associated with aristocratic circles and a constructed ancestry.[117] Both together form a picturesque ensemble to be viewed for its symbolic associations (Figure 3.12).

Leaving no heirs, the Weddells' plan to host the Virginia Historical Society somehow pre-inscribed an air of historical integrity and legitimacy to the structure. This is heightened by a historical description of the house written by Alexander himself, to act as a guide on public open days at Virginia House, when visitors were admitted to view treasures of the Weddell's private collection. To accompany the exhibition, Alexander Weddell authored a catalogue entitled *Richmond Virginia in Old Prints* (1932), which gives

Figure 3.12 The motorist's view, c. 1920s, of Virginia House, Windsor Farms, Richmond, Virginia, showing reconstructed elements of Warwick Priory.
Source: Postcard image courtesy of Virginia Commonwealth University.

an insight into the Weddells' visual perception of the city, its history and landscape.

Strikingly, Weddell's catalogue begins with a passage which equates Richmond, at the close of the Civil War, to the eulogies of great fallen cities of classical legend. This nostalgic romanticism for a former golden age is immediately connected to the picturesque image:

> It will be noted at first glance that Richmond has been depicted more often and, on the whole, with somewhat more artistic spirit than most American cities [. . .]. Aside from the historical appeal of many events in the annals of the city, the first reason for this would seem to be the setting of the little town [. . .] which [. . .] affords a situation beautiful and picturesque. Hills made for hard climbing but for fine prospects. The crescent bow of the rocky river bed was the despair of navigators but the dream of architects.[118]

This vision contrasts with Weddell's description of the city's destruction, perhaps as a plea to support the preservationist efforts of the Virginia Historical Society and also of the National Society of the Colonial Dames of America. If the Weddells were advocates of historical preservation, their home demonstrates their admiration of Garden City planning: "[W]hen the motor car liberated the wealthy Richmonder from his thraldom to distance, he rediscovered the knolls that overlook the James and crowned them with the fine houses that castellated the skyline from Maymont to Westham bridge".[119] In Weddell's mind, Richmond's new suburban developments had 'rediscovered' picturesque architectural and urban planning. The construction of 'fine houses' such as his own Virginia House might be imagined as restoring the image of the city, repairing the scars left by the Civil War and more broadly by an age of industrialisation.

William Lawrence Bottomley: re-imagining 'colonial' Richmond

Just as the 'reconstructions' at Windsor Farms claimed an idea of the past and became assumed into that imagined past, so too were new suburban homes. An aerial photograph of the fledgling estate, dated c. 1928, reveals a third house under construction on a plot neighbouring Virginia House. This house, the work of William Lawrence Bottomley, is one of four Bottomley designed for the riverside bluffs of Windsor Farms. Bottomley, born in New York in 1883, had trained at Columbia University and the American Academy in Rome. In 1908, he enrolled at the Ecole des Beaux Arts and completed extensive travels throughout the European continent. No doubt it was during this time that Bottomley familiarised himself with the works of European architects, and particularly with the works of English architects of the eighteenth century. Though Bottomley produced several designs for high-rise buildings in New York during the 1930s, he is chiefly remembered for his 'James River Georgian' villas, works which have played a major part in the aesthetic imagination of Richmond.

Bottomley's early works in Richmond were mainly clustered along the imposing Monument Avenue, site of the memorial to General Lee described previously, a grand project of civic beautification conceived in the 1890s. Along with the monuments to the great and good of the Confederate South, one could view Bottomley's scattering of neo-Georgian townhouses, four on the south side and five on the north, as a nostalgic allusion to a glorious and orderly past. The authors of *The Work of William Lawrence Bottomley in Richmond* (1985), however, suggest that Bottomley's architecture recalls not so much a romantic vision of a prosperous antebellum South as the more distant 'golden age' of colonial Virginia, stating that his homes are "more English than American Georgian [. . .] [with details] which might have come from a plate in William Salmon or Batty Langley".[120]

In later years, Bottomley's principal commissions were for increasingly large suburban villas, including Milburne, Windsor Farms and perhaps his best known and most influential house, Nordley, whose roof may just be discerned to the right of the 1928 aerial photo. Built in 1923, Nordley's commissioner had wanted an Elizabethan house in the manner of neighbouring Virginia House and Agecroft Hall. However, Bottomley soon talked them round, stating that "the revised house would be very picturesque in mass [and] [. . .] it would add to the charm of the place to have a Virginia Palladian house".[121] When it came to Nordley's landscape design too, Bottomley envisaged an informal and picturesque garden in the English manner, suggesting,

> I would have this garden mysterious, secluded, romantic, in strong contrast to the formal balanced lines of the house. Imagine sitting there in the Spring on a moonlight night, the view veiled by a silvery haze. White statues and vases embowered in foliage glowing faintly against the dark foliage and the James with its great expanse of silver water flowing slowly by.[122]

Bottomley's romantic vision for Nordley was not lost on Richmond's 'Southern Renaissance' novelist Ellen Glasgow, who described the house, giving it the pseudonym "Dare's Gift", in a short story published by *Harper's Magazine* in 1925. Glasgow writes,

> Following the steep road, which ran in curves through a stretch of pines and across an abandoned pasture or two, I came at last to an iron gate and a grassy walk leading [. . .] to the open lawn planted with elms. With that first glimpse the Old World charm of the scene held me captive. From the warm red of its brick walls to the pure Colonial lines of its doorway, and its curving wings mantled in roses and ivy, the house stood there, splendid and solitary [. . .] the heavy cedars crowding thick up the short avenue did not stir as the wind blew from the river; and above [. . .], a lonely bat was wheeling high against the red disk of the sun.[123]

Though the house was just two years old, Glasgow's description presents the scene as replete with "Old World charm", clearly alluding to the fiction of great age. The curving road crossing abandoned pastures which begins the piece is, in the mind's eye of the reader, the serpentine drive of a once great, now fading, plantation estate, not the freshly laid suburban streets and vacant lots of newly developed Windsor Farms. Thus, Glasgow's description historicises Nordley and its neighbouring suburban villas through the use of nostalgic and picturesque imagery.

Within a few years, Bottomley's architectural works were deemed so enchanting, so picturesque, that his houses had become decisive to the image Richmond held of itself – as an elegant eighteenth-century villa society – eclipsing the few 'authentic' architectural remnants of that era. O'Neal and Weeks write that Bottomley "helped create some of the best new parts of a proud old city, and his urban/suburban villas have a cumulative effect which set the mark for an entire city".[124] Or, to quote Cobb, Richmond "entered the twentieth-century bedecked in the grandiose architectural splendour meant to invoke the Old South Golden Age".[125] This historicising of Bottomley's work might be viewed as simple misidentification, as his Windsor Farms homes share a region of the city with a pair of 'reconstructed' examples of colonial domestic architecture: Wilton and Ampthill Plantations. While Virginia House and Agecroft Hall romanticise Virginia's European roots, the Wilton and Ampthill reconstructions declare the importance of Virginia's own, though linked, early history. And yet, set in accordance to a romantic vision of their 'authentic' eighteenth-century appearance, one could argue that they too allude to visions of colonial 'Englishness'.

The enduring re-inscription of Richmond's romantic image

Ampthill, constructed by Henry Cary sometime before 1732, was formerly located on a riverside plantation some 6 miles downstream of Richmond. In 1928, the property was purchased for the development of the du Pont Rayon Factory and the house was threatened with demolition. Saved by a descendent of the Carys, Ampthill was carefully dismantled and reconstructed on a site at Windsor Farms, Richmond, close to the reconstructions of Agecroft Hall and Warwick Priory. Employed to oversee the project was architect Thomas Tileston Waterman, described as possessing "a passion for the preservation of endangered architecture".[126]

It was probably under the guidance of Perry, Shaw & Hepburn at Virginia's Colonial Williamsburg that Waterman honed his particular methods of reconstruction. Ampthill shares similarities with Williamsburg projects, where the building was returned to a romantic vision of its 'original' or 'authentic' form. For example, Waterman reinstated features it was presumed to have once had, yet retained the flanking wings – which Waterman himself noted as later additions. F. C. Kaynor suggests that Waterman justified such historical discrepancies by placing "himself mentally in the eighteenth century", which allowed him to address current "architectural problems as he thought they would have been addressed by eighteenth-century people".[127] Waterman's publication of the Ampthill 'restoration' in his *Domestic Colonial Architecture of Tidewater Virginia* (1932), presented as a work of academic building archaeology, lends a certain legitimacy to the act of romanticising colonial Virginia, while also publicising his 'restoration' works to prospective clients.

No doubt the inclusion of neighbouring Wilton plantation, built by William Randolph III in 1753, in Waterman's book did not go unnoticed by the plantation's 1932 purchasers, a local branch of the Colonial Dames of America. Having rescued the house from demolition (apparently, Bottomley had advised a previous owner to tear the house down in order to reuse the brick), the Dames promptly entrusted Waterman with its careful dismantling and reconstruction 6 miles upstream in Richmond.

The founding of the National Society of the Colonial Dames of America in 1891[128] reflects the contemporary popularity of movements in historic preservation. Strikingly, these societies conceived of themselves as historic gene pools, composed of the descendents of America's most notable colonial families. The NSCDA's motto "Daughters Conserve the Virtues of Their Elders" eloquently sums up the society's familial attitude towards conservation. It had been the NSCDA that had funded the restoration of Washington's Sulgrave Manor, Northamptonshire, in 1923, incidentally the very project which had inspired Weddell's reconstruction of Sulgrave in his own Virginia house.

Wilton opened to the public in 1952 as a living museum complete with costumed actors and furnished with reproduction antiques. Gardens, little based on real historical evidence but rather on English models, were constructed to surround the house. This provided a suitably picturesque foil to the scene, where the visitor could slip into a rose-tinted vision of Virginia's past – an imagined time when ties with Old England were still strong and Virginia planters lived supposedly comfortable, elegant and prosperous lives. Richard Guy Wilson has interpreted the use of colonial imagery by the NSCDA as "the expression of an Anglo-white-gentrified and elite class who, traumatised by their displacement from power, employed colonial imagery to maintain status".[129]

The particular brand of romanticised 'preservation' enacted by societies such as the NSCDA could be viewed as a reaction to the rapid destruction of historic buildings following the stock market crash of 1929, when many owners viewed demolition as the only viable option. Parallels may be drawn between the outpouring of regret following Richmond's destruction at the close of the American Civil War and the perception of 1930s preservation groups that a new phase of destruction had returned.

Meanwhile, recognising rates of high unemployment among architects, draughtsmen and surveyors, the US government initiated a relief programme under the auspices of the Civil Works Administration,[130] proposing a national survey of America's built heritage. Coincidentally, the new affordability of the motorcar, along with the dramatic infrastructural improvements which had encouraged motor tourism in the manner of Nutting's pictorial and historical guides, now also aided the architectural researcher in reaching remote and ruinous plantations.

Many of the drawings Waterman had made for *Domestic Colonial Architecture of Tidewater Virginia* were absorbed by the Historic American Buildings Survey (HABS) following his appointment as assistant director. Thus, Waterman's romanticised aesthetic, its sensibility imbued with the imagined values of historic Richmond, merged with the goals of the HABS program in seeking to survey not only a series of the most vulnerable American buildings, threatened by demolition or neglect, but also conspicuous symbols of American identity and patriotism. Among these was St John's Church of Church Hill, Richmond, surveyed on 29 March 1934, the location, as we saw previously, of Patrick Henry's revolution-inciting speech. In total, the HABS program documented 67 historic structures in Richmond, more than any other American city (compare with Williamsburg's 24 entries). Many of those surveyed were domestic villas of the eighteenth and nineteenth centuries, implicitly reinforcing a romantic vision of genteel, colonial Richmond.[131] The early work of the HABS surveyors, published in Waterman's *English Antecedents of Virginia Architecture* (1939), *The Mansions of Virginia* (1945) and *Dwellings of Colonial America* (1950),[132] presented an architectural portrait of Virginia as a land of elegant plantation homes set amid picturesque landscapes. As historian Fiske Kimball has written, "[A] whole province of great mansions, most of them never drawn or published before, is re-discovered. The background of a vanished civilisation is exactly set forth".[133] Kimball therefore acknowledges Waterman's work as an investigation of a once glorious past, lending legitimacy to his romantic aesthetic.

As I have argued, a fledgling American conservation movement coincided with developments in infrastructure and the new availability of the motorcar. The ability, and desire, to tour the landscape in search of scenic and historic landmarks was actively promoted by camera and automobile manufacturers, while at a governmental level both road-building projects and historical surveys were implemented as forms of work relief. Richmond's historic buildings and scenic landscape setting were recognised early in this process, reflecting nostalgic calls that symbols of a former golden age were threatened by industrialisation. In the following chapter, this renewed nostalgia for the past will be explored, particularly in relation to the American invention of the scenic parkway, which paired modern automotive technology with a nostalgic and picturesque mode of vision. In this way the picturesque vista was reborn as a model with which to shape whole itineraries through the American landscape.

Cinematic itineraries in the nostalgic picturesque: Colonial Parkway

In the 1920s, the National Park Service, and other bodies, realised the potential of Tidewater Virginia's historic and natural sites as the weekend destinations of Richmonders. As such, no exploration of the impact of the 'windshield' view upon the architectural and urban form of Richmond could be complete without a study of these weekend annexes of the city, where romantic visions of 'colonial' Virginia – and a particular idea of vision – were nurtured and consolidated. This chapter will examine the influence of the kinetic view from the motor car upon a growing heritage industry, and demonstrate that nostalgic picturesque vision was a central theme of modernist projects from parkways to interstate highways.

The Historic American Buildings Survey (HABS), overseen by Waterman and Thomas Vint, ultimately realised the proposal for a national survey of built heritage first suggested by landscape architect Charles E. Peterson.[134] In 1930, Peterson served as resident landscape architect at Yorktown, Virginia, where he was "involved with the establishment of the newly created Colonial National Monument (dedicated Colonial National Historical Park in 1936)".[135] As part of the park's establishment, Peterson proposed that a scenic parkway be developed to link the two principal sites, Yorktown and Jamestown, with the colony's former capital, Williamsburg.

At the heart of the proposed parkway, architects, historians and archaeologists had been working since the 1920s on the semi-historical reconstruction of Virginia's colonial capital, Williamsburg, fuelled by a veneration of its romantic imagery and an idea of its historical authenticity. At a cost of $79 million, funded by the American philanthropist and oil magnate John Rockefeller Jr, the 'Colonial Williamsburg' project attempted to turn back the clock to the 1790 revolution, demolishing hundreds of genuine historic buildings and reconstructing supposedly more 'authentic' buildings in their place. In one such controversial reconstruction, the Capitol building was 'recreated' in its first iteration, destroyed by fire in 1747, and not its second incarnation, in which the declaration of independence was signed. The architects Perry, Shaw & Hepburn, whose office included the young Waterman, chose to reconstruct this earlier building as it is depicted in a greater proportion of historic illustrations, justified as lending greater authenticity to the reconstruction. Carl Lounsbury has suggested that the architects simply felt that the first structure was "inherently more interesting architecturally".[136] Certainly, there has been much debate over the accuracy of the building: how much is devised from archaeological evidence and how much by the architect's aesthetic taste. In many respects, it mirrors traits of romantic 'restoration' exhibited throughout late eighteenth and nineteenth-century Britain, which sought to alter the physical remnants of the past, idealising them in accordance with an imagined original intent and to suit an idea of the social aspirations of the present.

While the Colonial Williamsburg project restored, copied and reconstructed elements of the town, the Colonial Parkway project went a step farther, creating a whole fictional landscape so that the unfolding scenery of colonial Virginia's 'golden age' could be experienced from the modern vantage point of the motor car.[137] Established in 1930 and completed only in 1957, Colonial Parkway links three corners of America's 'historic triangle', the site of the first colonial settlement at Jamestown, the colonial capital of Williamsburg and the site of General Cornwallis's surrender at Yorktown. As such, the parkway represents a historical timeline of colonial America – the drive itself a metaphorical journey through time. More practically, the aim of the parkway was to allow the motorist access between the three sites while carefully directing and shielding his or her view, immersing the motorist in a romantic simulation of 'authentic' eighteenth-century landscapes.[138] This immersive aim of the Colonial Parkway project is highlighted by Louis Cramton's comments that he

> would like the visitor to be able to drive on to Williamsburg [. . .] without the impression of the early days being driven from his mind by a succession of hot-dog stands and tire signs, [. . .] [protected by]

trees shutting out all conflicting modern development, [and] not to be a glaring modern pavement but [. . .] giving the impression of an old-time road.[139]

This was despite the fact that the parkway follows no historic route, traversing marshes and creeks for scenic value, problematic areas typically avoided by colonial road-builders. In the course of 'returning' the landscape to its imagined colonial appearance, contemporary rural businesses, such as vegetable gardens and working farms, were forced to close in order "to produce lifeless pastoral illusions composed of placid meadows, winding streams, and artfully located plantings".[140]

The moving image: parkways and cinema

Roughly contemporary with the construction of the parkways, the emerging film industry soon realised that audiences accustomed to the appreciation of scenic and historic vistas from the comfort of the motor car could be better reached via drive-in movie theatres. Coincidentally, Richmond figured prominently in American cinematic history. Virginia's mix of historic architecture, Civil War battlefields and attractive mountains and seascapes, along with its proximity to Washington, rendered the state a popular film location among early production companies. In the late 1890s, the rivals Edison Company and the American Mutoscope and Biograph Company both shot short films at locations near Richmond.[141] Despite a general migration of film companies either west to Los Angeles or north to New York, a surprising number of early twentieth-century films were located in Virginia. Some of the more notable twentieth-century productions include D. W. Griffith's *America* (1924), *Brother Rat* (1938) and *Giant* (1956).

Like the parkway projects, where viewers were encouraged to believe in the 'authenticity' of the staged landscape, film producers aimed to transport the viewer to other locales and eras. As Patrick Brogan has written,

> Forgetting that camera angles are selected, tapes and films edited and distorted, we attend to them as raw glimpses of what actually happened. The feeling that the past is open to perusal as never before creates an illusion that *we*, at last, can know what it was *really* like.[142]

Even director D. W. Griffith said of his epic *Birth of A Nation* (1914), "You will see what actually has happened [. . .] there will be no opinions expressed, you will merely be present at the making of history [. . .] The film could not be anything but the truth".[143] Griffith's statement demonstrates the visual power film held over early audiences, a force recognised by the leaders of the National Park Service (NPS) who, concerned with the visual experience of the parks and methods by which historical information could be conveyed, began increasingly to look to Hollywood as a source of inspiration.

Cultural historian Jeannie Kim has pointed out that reorientation of national recreational spaces in favour of the car "quietly transformed what was described as a democratizing gesture into a form of leisure that was directed toward a specifically white, middle-class nuclear family".[144] Despite visitor records which indicated such segregation, and the occasional cry of dissent, little was done to rectify the situation.[145] The parks' rhetoric, particularly apparent in the publications of historic sites such as Colonial Parkway, acted only to reinforce this form of elitism by presenting visitors with narrow and romantic depictions of white colonial gentry. In parallel to this rhetoric, the oil paintings of Sidney E. King, commissioned by the NPS in 1954 and timed to coincide with the 1957 visit of Queen Elizabeth II, depict highly romanticised Anglophilic scenes of colonial Virginia. At the time, King's paintings were praised for their historical accuracy; archaeologists, architects and historians collaborated on their details while King himself made study visits to view examples of seventeenth-century architecture in England. However, King's is a sanitised world, free of the real squalor, segregation and slavery which had existed in the early colonies.

Scenic byways: projecting the romantic vision

Virginia's parkway projects blend technologically advanced highway engineering with a picturesque aesthetic and cinematic vision. Where the budget for infrastructural projects on this scale was not available, state governments simply dedicated existing routes as 'scenic byways'. Such dedications justified a general upgrading of rural roads while appealing to a public that had grown weary of manufactured parkway scenery. As Timothy Davis writes,

> Asserting that parkways were "deadly dull to drive on," a 1950 *Harper's Magazine* column [. . .] urged motorists to escape the homogenized and pasteurised parkway landscape in order to discover the "real America" that lay along the unconstrained byways where vernacular cultures were allowed to flourish.[146]

If parkway landscapes were now being viewed as 'pasteurised', 'homogenised' and perhaps even 'globalised', scenic byways were promoted as 'authentic' American landscape experiences. However, one could argue that the visual criteria for America's scenic byways – colonial farmsteads, historic battlefields, agricultural fields, orchards and picturesque vistas – demonstrate the byways as equally complicit in a staged representation of supposedly authentic American landscapes – like the parkways, just the latest manifestation of Nutting's photogenic rural lanes.

In Richmond, Virginia, 'Scenic Byway 5' begins at the foot of Libby Hill Park and stretches as far as Williamsburg, hugging the James River and a string of colonial plantations, including Shirley, Berkeley and Byrd's Westover (Figure 3.13).[147] If Colonial Parkway is understood as a romantic

Figure 3.13 Map of the Tidewater region of Virginia, showing the route of Scenic Byway 5, connecting Libby Hill Park, Richmond, to the James River plantations, Colonial Parkway and the colonial state capital of Williamsburg.

recreation of a colonial route, Scenic Byway 5 is popularly recognised as the 'authentic original', despite the fact that much of the route was laid only in the 1920s. In fact, the colonial route from Richmond to Williamsburg took a more direct and straighter route further inland. The route of the modern byway, then, may be viewed as a reflection of early motor tourism, affording the Richmond day tripper a curated colonial plantation experience and picturesque river vistas en route to Williamsburg via a leisurely, sinuous road. In a study of its scenic byways, Richmond Regional Planning Authority stated, "With Richmond serving as a hub of transportation [. . .] the region can, and should, promote places of historical and cultural significance, and what better way to get there than by a scenic byway?"[148] As such, the motor-tourist departing Richmond by Scenic Byway 5 immediately entered a romantic vision of eighteenth-century Virginia with the vista of the James River from Libby Hill forming the symbolic opening act – an introductory summary of Virginia's historic colonial landscape.

Unlike the parkways, the designation of scenic byways did not directly allow for the restoration of buildings or landscaping works. However, the government label 'scenic' has contributed to gentrification. For example, the erection of historical markers and viewpoints along byways drew attention to historic structures, increasing their desirability and encouraging restoration. The *Scenic Roads Study* concluded that "Historic places and rural communities connected by regional scenic roads are great avenues for economic development and promotion of the historic qualities of the region".[149] In the case of Scenic Byway 5, a whole district of former industrial warehouses which border the James River below Libby Hill has benefitted from the 'scenic' designation, now restored as upmarket apartment buildings while similar, yet inconspicuous, warehouses one street away remain in dereliction. If the motorist is tempted to consider Richmond's wealth of nineteenth-century industrial heritage at this point, he/she is quickly redirected by the city-limit signpost positioned precisely at this location. In the form of a fluted and loosely Tuscan-order column, surmounted by a small pediment, one could argue that the city-marker directs the minds of visitors – in none too subtle fashion – to the idea of a classical and Arcadian interpretation of the landscape, setting the tone for the unfolding vistas en route to Colonial Williamsburg (Figure 3.14).

The operators of motels, restaurants and inns along scenic byways were quick to cash in on the desire to provide for the motor-tourist an immersive visual experience, seizing the opportunity to extend it to their lodgings, mealtimes and rest stops. Thus, the 'colonial' motel was born. In fact, the colonial plantation model was easily adapted to the needs of the modern motel; at the centre, a great house (containing the public facilities), surrounded by outbuildings (tourist chalets), fronted by an expanse of lawn (replaced with tarmac) bordered by the river (substituted

Figure 3.14 Richmond as generalised 'historic' landscape: the Richmond city-limit post on Scenic Byway 5 demonstrates – in none too subtle fashion – the recurring theme of Richmond as classical city, and the Virginian plantations as Arcadian landscape.

for a pool) (Figure 3.15). Boorstin has investigated the rapid spread of the motor court, stating that "In 1935, [. . .], there were about ten thousand motels or tourist courts; after twenty years there were some thirty thousand".[150] The popularity of these motels as destinations in their own right is evident from the number of postcard views produced from 1950 through the 1970s, many of which illustrate their 'picturesque' nostalgic qualities. For example, a postcard for Dutch Gap Tourist Court depicts the type of detached 'colonial' style motel chalets popular at this time; where every family could experience the lifestyle of the colonial squire albeit with the added luxuries of bathrooms, hair dryers and clock radios. Further demonstration of the tourist's desire to re-live a romanticised colonial lifestyle is suggested by another postcard view of Colony Inn, Richmond, featuring eighteenth-century figures in a suitably nostalgic pen and ink sketch.

The implication is that, through the cultivation of idyllic visual experiences, parkways and scenic highways have promoted a nostalgic scenic architecture,

Figure 3.15 Postcard of Richmond Auto Court, c. 1960s, showing a typical 'colonial plantation' motel arrangement, with the great house/reception at centre, the dependencies/chalets arranged symmetrically about it, the riverfront substituted for a swimming pool, and the sweeping lawns substituted for a great sweep of tarmac.

from the brick veneer applied to the bridges of Colonial Parkway to the 'colonial' motel. In turn, these simulated landscapes have themselves become legitimised as significant cultural landscapes in their own right. For example, Colonial Parkway is now recognised as a statutorily protected historic monument. As Davis has written, "In classic postmodern fashion, the simulacrum is now celebrated as much as its ostensible antecedent".[151]

It is no coincidence that the sequential visual experience of the parkway coincided with a period of booming cinema audiences. If the parkways can be likened to a cinematic sequence, an analogy could be made between the architecture of their attendant buildings and the theatricality of cinematic film sets. Soon, roadside traders were erecting their own stage-set fantasies designed to attract the motorists' gaze, as Robert Venturi has explored in his seminal work *Learning from Las Vegas* (1977).[152] Many examples of this may be found in the developments which sprang up along Richmond's highways, including a colonial revival funeral parlour and freight handler's office, both dating from the late 1940s.

Interstate image corridors: the persistence of parkway vision

The locations of parkways and byways might lead one to assume that this form of visual manipulation affected rural areas only. However, parkways were conceived and engineered by urban planners whose target audience was the suburban motorist. As such, parkways were urban products whose visual aesthetic imposed an influential force upon the idea of the city as well as ideas of landscape.

In Richmond, contemporary planning policies ensure visual control is maintained over unfolding vistas of the city, as observed from the interstate highways which pass through it. Known as 'interstate image corridors', these policies could be seen as a reaction to what Boorstin has called the interstates' "thorough dilution of travel experience".[153] Established under the Federal Aid Highway Act of 1944, the interstate highway network has been described as a utilitarian exercise in modern highway engineering.[154] As such, Boorstin has argued that the experience of travel was reduced from an ever-changing visual experience to a mere period of time, passing road signs the only visual records of landscapes traversed. In response, contemporary city plans designate where views should be enhanced, screened or protected, in order to present to traffic, hurtling past at 80 miles per hour, a promotional snapshot of the city as colonial capital and stronghold of a romanticised South.[155] As Richmond's 2010 Master Plan stated,

> Careful attention to these major entryways into Richmond has broad implications for the City's ability to maintain a high quality visual environment and attract and retain new residents and businesses. Image corridors are key transportation corridors that should display a high-quality appearance to enhance the image of Richmond.[156]

One could argue that the resurrection of visual criteria – as demonstrated by vocabulary such as "visual environment", "image corridors" and "appearance" imposed by contemporary planning policy upon the utilitarian highways of the 1940s – owes a debt to the picturesque visual planning of the early American parkways, reintroduced and popularised by architectural theorists on both sides of the Atlantic from the 1950s.

British architectural criticism in the 1950s was marked by a renewed cynicism towards the urban sprawl of modern cities, led in substantial part by the staff of the *Architectural Review* (*AR*), including Nikolaus Pevsner, Hubert de Cronin Hastings and Gordon Cullen. Arguably the most influential of the *AR*'s features, certainly in terms of its transatlantic influence, was the polemical 1955 *Outrage* edition, in which authors Ian Nairn and Cullen attacked the featureless "low density mess"[157] of suburban sprawl. Following the success of *Outrage* on both sides of the Atlantic, Nairn and Cullen were approached by *Fortune* magazine to tour and comment on the visual planning of selected American cities from Chicago to San Francisco. The projected book for this ambitious project, given the working title *Townscape USA*, though eventually published as *The American Landscape: A Critical View* (1965), would have fitted neatly into a developing American discourse at this time. Other contributions to this discourse, which sought to reinvigorate American architectural criticism with regards to urban form, include Jane Jacobs's *Death and Life of Great American Cities* (1961), Peter

Blake's *God's Own Junkyard* (1964) and Lynch, Appleyard and Myers's *The View from the Road* (1964).[158]

Nairn used the project's fee to undertake a monumental road trip from Philadelphia to Los Angeles, an experience which would cement his hatred of urban sprawl. In a similar project undertaken by the *AR* some years earlier in 1939, artist John Piper set out to photograph every visual structure en route from London to Bath, as part of the journal's grandiose agenda of "visual re-education" to "re-establish the supremacy of the eye".[159] In a parallel of Nairn's commission, a critical component of this project had been to stimulate architectural discourse on the visual state of the nation's great arterial routes. Piper's 'before and after' shots, plus his accompanying dialogue, demonstrate how a painterly aesthetic was actively promoted by the *AR* and its editors, an aesthetic interchangeably known as 'Visual Planning', 'Exterior Furnishing' and 'Picturesque Planning', though best remembered as the title to Cullen's influential *Townscape* (1961).[160] It is in these projects and the resulting proliferation of motoring guidebooks that one might trace the influence of the American parkways. Though the British government did not go in for the building of scenic highways as such, architectural critics on both sides of the Atlantic argued for a visual re-evaluation of roadscapes based upon a picturesque aesthetic the *AR* editors themselves traced directly back to the lineage, now familiar here, of Repton, Payne Knight and Price.[161]

Viewed in this light, Richmond's 'interstate image corridors' might be interpreted as a continuation of townscape principles which sought to create an edited – almost cinematic – visual experience of the city. One could argue that a similar, edited, cinematic experience can be achieved by walking the streets of Richmond's suburban communities. One such example is the aptly named West Broad 'Village', a romantic attempt at the reproduction of a whole town, with a main street "not unlike the bustling main streets of colonial America".[162] Though the pretence of West Broad is towards a traditional vision of American towns, the two-dimensionality of this romantic imagery is revealed by its construction; much of Main Street comprises a series of steel and concrete-framed structures dressed with a thin façade of 'historical' townscape motifs. As John Fortier has written,

> To an American, the landscape [. . .] seems saturated with "creeping heritage" – mansarded and half-timbered shopping plazas, exposed brick and butcher-block décor in historic precincts [. . .]. Long uprooted and newly unsure of the future, Americans *en masse* find comfort in looking back; historic villages and districts become "surrogate home towns that contain a familiar and reassuring landscape".[163]

If West Broad Village could be interpreted as a kind of cinematic set, it is the middle ground between Williamsburg's 'historically accurate' reconstruction and the pure fantasy of Disneyland. One could argue that were West Broad Village to have a cinematic equivalent, it might be found in the double exposure image: fragments of romanticised eighteenth-century Williamsburg superimposed upon the sinuous curves and picturesque landscaping of the American parkway. As Boym has written, "A cinematic image of nostalgia is a double exposure, or a superimposition of two images – of home and abroad, past and present, dream and everyday life".[164] In the case of West Broad Village, one finds familiar nostalgic imagery thinly applied over the steel and concrete skeletons of its modern buildings.

Concluding remarks

Following an exploration of Richmond Hill's history, this chapter has traced the transposition of that view onto the American landscape, and followed how this particular view's meaning has been mediated and translated from one landscape to another. This translation of a common set of values is apparent in landscape and architectural works, in fine art, literature and diverse forms of popular media from the newspaper to the postcard. Continuing from this, it has traced the development of the picturesque view from a static to a kinetic mode of vision, via photography, the car and the cinema screen. These new technologies have not so much produced a scientific future as reinvented the past, re-inscribing familiar tropes as well as established conventions for the viewing of landscapes and townscapes. Just as the static idea of the picturesque view has always exerted power – intellectually, culturally and over architectural and landscape forms – this chapter has shown that the moving picturesque viewpoint has exerted similar power, in service of similar values, in ways which are both different and strikingly consistent. The visual conventions deployed in the creation of supposedly 'modern' landscapes, such as the suburb and American highway, can, as this chapter has shown, be linked to the picturesque conventions observed in the Richmond landscape. Thus, the values inherent within London's first protected vista remain at work within contemporary cityscapes on either side of the Atlantic.

Notes

1 Many are reputedly named after Charles Lennox, Duke of Richmond and governor general of British North America (e.g., Richmond, MA; Richmond, NH; Richmond, ON, and Richmond, QC). Others trace the name to Richmond, Virginia, one-time capital of the Confederate states (e.g., Richmond, KY; Richmond, MO; Richmond, OH, and Richmond, OR).
2 Obtained on a 99-year lease from Trinity Church.
3 G. A. Stiverson and P.H. Butler III, eds., "Virginia in 1732: The Travel Journal of William Hugh Grove", *Virginia Magazine of History and Biography*, 85 (January 1977), p. 18.
4 Ibid.
5 From June 1789 to until August 1790, before the capital moved from New York to Philadelphia.

6 J. Owen Grundy, "The Glory that Was Once Richmond Hill's Is Long Since Faded and Forgotten, Part 1", *The Villager* (New York City), 13 September 1945.
7 M. Hale Smith, *Sunshine and Shadow in New York* (New York: J. B. Burr, 1869), p. 121.
8 M. C. Henderson, *The City and the Theatre: The History of New York Playhouses* (New York: Back Stage Books, 1973, 2004), p. 65.
9 This region, commonly referred to as 'Tidewater' Virginia, extends through much of Maryland, Virginia, the Carolinas and Georgia.
10 C. Allan Brown, "Eighteenth-Century Virginia Plantation Gardens: Translating an Ancient Idyll" in T. O'Malley, M. Treib eds., *Regional Garden Design in the United States* (Washington: Dumbarton Oaks) p. 129.
11 Ibid.
12 Ibid., pp. 133–134.
13 Showing the relationship of the classical house and landscaped grounds to the extensive view over the bend of the James River (to the left of the image).
14 A. W. Weddell, *Richmond Virginia in Old Prints* (Richmond: Johnson Publishing Company, 1932), p. 117.
15 Including those at Cliveden, Buckinghamshire and Blenheim Palace, Oxfordshire. M. R. Wenger, ed., *The English Travels of Sir John Percival and William Byrd II: The Percival Diary of 1701* (Columbia, MO: University of Missouri Press, 1989).
16 H. C. Rice, ed., *Travels in North America in the Years 1780, 1781 and 1782* (Chapel Hill, NC: University of North Carolina Press, 1963), p. 430.
17 L. B. Wright and M. Tinling, eds., *The Secret Diary of William Byrd of Westover, 1709–1712* (Richmond, VI, 1941), p. 540. Similarly, the house has details derived from English precedents, particularly from *Palladio Londinensis: Or the London Art of Building* (1734). T. T. Waterman, The Mansions of Virginia, 1706–1776 (Chapel Hill, NC: The University of North Carolina Press, 1945), pp. 150–153.
18 Brown, "Eighteenth-Century Virginia Plantation Gardens: Translating an Ancient Idyll", p. 134.
19 Ibid.
20 Ibid., p. 134.
21 William Byrd II to Sabina, 28 March 1718, Woodfin and Tinling, *Another Secret Diary*, p. 337.
22 J. Quitman Moore, "Southern Civilisation: Or the Norman in America", *DeBow's Review*, 32 (Jan–Feb 1862), p. 14.
23 Sir Robert Taylor was many years senior to Cockerell. Latrobe joined Cockerell's practice after the death of Taylor, which facilitated his meteoric rise from draughtsman to partner. M. W. Fazio and P. A. Snadon, *The Domestic Architecture of Benjamin Henry Latrobe* (Baltimore, MD: JHU Press, 2006).
24 F.H.W. Sheppard, ed., *Survey of London: St James Westminster* (London: English Heritage, 1960), p. 309.
25 E. C. Carter II, J. C. Van Horne and C. E. Brownell, eds., *Latrobe's View of America, 1795–1820: Selections from the Watercolours and Sketches* (New Haven, CT: Yale University Press, 1985), pp. 120–121.
26 Ibid., pp. 120–121.
27 E. C. Carter II, *The Virginia Journals of Benjamin Henry Latrobe 1795–1798* (London and New Haven: Yale University Press, 1977), p. vii.
28 Moved inland from the former capital of Williamsburg, to protect the city from British attack.
29 Led by 'traitor' Benedict Arnold.
30 Virginia declared its independence from the British Empire on 15 May 1776, though the Constitution and Bill of Rights were not ratified until 25 June 1788.
31 J. A. Cohen and C. E. Brownell, *The Architectural Drawings of Benjamin Henry Latrobe* (New Haven, London: Yale University Press, 1994) p. 98.

32 Ibid., p. 98.
33 Another similarity noted by Cohen and Brownell which may suggest Latrobe's familiarity with Bentham is the treatment of the external elevation and of windows set within blind arches, and the contrast between the external and internal elevations.
34 Revealed in a letter to Robert Mills, 12 July 1806.
35 Cohen and Brownell, *The Architectural Drawings of Benjamin Henry Latrobe*, p. 100.
36 In fact, Samuel Bentham constructed his own Panopticon structures, including a St Petersburg school in 1806.
37 M. Foucault, *Discipline and Punish: The Birth of the Prison* (London: Penguin Group, 1977).
38 M. Foucault, "Panopticism", in N. Leach, ed., *Rethinking Architecture: A Reader in Cultural Theory* (London: Routledge, 1997), p. 361.
39 Ibid., p. 362.
40 Foucault, *Discipline and Punish*, p. 11.
41 M. W. Fazio and P. A. Snadon, *The Domestic Architecture of Benjamin Henry Latrobe* (Baltimore, MD: JHU Press, 2006), p. 86.
42 Cohen and Brownell, *The Architectural Drawings of Benjamin Henry Latrobe*, p. 16.
43 There were over 100 by 1800. Carter, *The Virginia Journals of Benjamin Henry Latrobe*, p. 465.
44 For example, W. Gilpin, *Observations on the River Wye, and Several Parts of South Wales, etc., Relative Chiefly to Picturesque Beauty: Made in the Summer of 1770* (London: A. Strahan, 1800).
45 W. Bruce, *Travels to Discover the Source of the Nile* (Edinburgh and London, 1790).
46 Carter, *The Virginia Journals of Benjamin Henry Latrobe*, p. 466. Though Latrobe is often credited with introducing the picturesque to America, it had already arrived, as is evident in the picturesque language adopted by Thomas Jefferson, particularly in *Notes on the State of Virginia*, ed. William Peden (Chapel Hill, NC: University of North Carolina Press, 1955), pp. 19, 24–25.
47 For a related argument on the picturesque planning of Latrobe's Hammerwood Park, East Sussex, see Fazio and Snadon, *The Domestic Architecture of Benjamin Henry Latrobe*, p. 122.
48 To the right, the winged figure of Philadelphia raises up victoriously an image of Latrobe's Bank of Pennsylvania, his first great commission and, one suspects, a symbol of Philadelphia's gain as Richmond's loss.
49 Cohen and Brownell, *The Architectural Drawings of Benjamin Henry Latrobe*, p. 81.
50 Fazio and Snadon, *The Domestic Architecture of Benjamin Henry Latrobe*, p. 237.
51 R. and J. Adam, *Works in Architecture* (London, 1773), vol. 1, no. 1.
52 Latrobe's design for another palatial house in Richmond, his 'Mill Hill' project, shares attributes with Adam's description of 'movement', with projecting polygonal and rectangular bays heightening the dynamic stereometry of the building.
53 In the manner of Horace Walpole's Strawberry Hill, Twickenham.
54 Cohen and Brownell, *The Architectural Drawings of Benjamin Henry Latrobe*, p. 295.
55 In 1772 Walpole's Strawberry Hill suffered from the consequences of an accident at a nearby gunpowder factory. A. Chalcraft and J. Viscardi, *Strawberry Hill: Horace Walpole's Gothic Castle* (London: Frances Lincoln Ltd., 2007), p. 38.
56 Completed in 1788.
57 These had been drawn under his direction by Charles-Louis Clerisseau, who had studied and measured the Roman temple for his book *Les Monuments de Nîmes*

(1778). C. Clerisseau, *Les Antiquités de la France, Monuments de Nîmes* (Paris: Philippe-Denys Pierres, 1778). J. Early, *Romanticism and American Architecture* (New York: A.S. Barnes & Co., 1965), p. 13.
58 *The Papers of Thomas Jefferson* (Princeton: Princeton University Press, 1954), IX, p. 221.
59 M. Tyler-McGraw, *At the Falls: Richmond, Virginia and Its People* (Chapel Hill, North Carolina: UNC Press Books, 1994), p. 72.
60 E. Dumbauld, "Jefferson and Adams' English Garden Tour", in W. H. Adams, ed., *Jefferson and the Arts: An Extended View* (Washington, DC: National Gallery of Art, 1976), p. 139. See also Early, *Romanticism and American Architecture*, p. 39.
61 Ibid.
62 Ibid.
63 T. T. Potterfield, *Nonesuch Place* (Charleston, South Carolina: History Press, 2009), p. 21.
64 Carter, *The Virginia Journals of Benjamin Henry Latrobe*, p. 473.
65 Brown, "Eighteenth-Century Virginia Plantation Gardens: Translating an Ancient Idyll", p. 125.
66 Early, *Romanticism and American Architecture*, p. 27.
67 "St John's Church Historic District", *Discover Our Shared Heritage Travel Itinerary* (National Park Service), www.nps.gov/nr/travel/richmond/St.Johns.htm [accessed 17/03/2011].
68 Early, *Romanticism and American Architecture*, p. 45.
69 Weddell, *Richmond Virginia in Old Prints*, p. xxix.
70 Samuel Mordecai, quoted in A. Weddell, *Richmond Virginia in Old Prints*, p. 30.
71 Ibid., p. 30.
72 Mills exhibited a drawing of the church at the Society of Artists, Philadelphia, in 1812 and set about publishing it as an engraving, describing it as "a handsome picture, capable of ornamenting any room". J. M. Bryan, *Robert Mills: America's First Architect* (New Jersey: Princeton Architectural Press, 2001), p. 107.
73 Ibid.
74 Demonstrated by contemporary newspaper advertisements for 'modern' properties in the west of the city – for example, a 1910 Blanton & Company advert for property in "Monument Annex". "Rapidly Richmond Moves Westward", *Richmond Times-Dispatch* (7 August 1910).
75 J. C. Cobb, *Away Down South* (Oxford: Oxford University Press, 2007), p. 77.
76 F. Pendleton Gaines, *The Southern Plantation: A Study in the Development and the Accuracy of a Tradition* (New York: Columbia University Press, 1925), pp. 63–64.
77 J. F. Cooper, *Notions of the Americans: Picked up by a Travelling Bachelor* (London: Colburn, 1828), in Cobb, *Away Down South*, p. 24.
78 Cobb, *Away Down South*, p. 130.
79 Ibid., p. 1.
80 "Class and Caste in Old Virginia", *New York Times* (26 June 1909).
81 Cobb, *Away Down South*, p. 1.
82 W. J. Cash, "The Mind of the South", *American Mercury* (October 1929), p. 185.
83 In the sense of the Jeffersonian ideal of the American yeoman farmer, living comfortably from the land.
84 E. Glasgow, *Romance of a Plain Man* (New York: Forgotten Books, 2017), p. 3.
85 Weddell, *Richmond Virginia in Old Prints*, p. 31.
86 Prior to photography and the development of the photographic magazine, newspapers were an important medium in the circulation of lithographic images. The invention of the rotary press, which could print simultaneously on both sides of a continuous sheet, dramatically increased the speed with which images could be reproduced and distributed. For example, the New York *Tribune*'s high-speed press, installed in the 1870s, could turn out 18,000 papers per hour.

138 Translating images of Richmond

The first reproduction of a photograph in a newspaper did not occur until 1880. D. J. Boorstin, *The Image, or What Happened to the American Dream* (New York: Atheneum, 1962), p. 13.
87 First enabled by the wet collodion process, introduced in 1851.
88 N. M. West, *Kodak and the Lens of Nostalgia* (Charlottesville and London: University Press of Virginia, 2000), p. 1.
89 M. McLuhan, *Understanding Media: The Extensions of Man* (Cambridge, MA: MIT Press, 1994), p. 197.
90 McLuhan is of the opinion that the invention of photography directly influenced the City Beautiful movement in landscape and architecture. McLuhan, *Understanding Media*, p. 197.
91 West, *Kodak and the Lens of Nostalgia*, p. 29.
92 Virginia Commonwealth University Library exhibition entitled *Rarely Seen Richmond: Early Twentieth Century Richmond, Virginia as Seen through Vintage Postcards*. See also K. Henderson, "The Art of the View: Picture Postcards of Virginia, 1900–1925", *Virginia Cavalcade*, 40(2) (Autumn 1990), pp. 66–73.
93 West, *Kodak and the Lens of Nostalgia*, p. 4.
94 "Welcome Friends!: Richmond Throws Open Her Gates to the Exposition Visitors", *The Richmond Dispatch* (6 October 1892).
95 Boorstin, *The Image, or What Happened to the American Dream*, p. 13.
96 Ibid., p. 32.
97 By 1905 Kodak had sold over 1.2 million cameras to roughly one-third of the population of the US. Ibid., p. 41.
98 Cobb, *Away Down South*, p. 68.
99 Ibid., p. 100.
100 S. Sontag, *On Photography* (New York: Picador, 1977).
101 Cobb, *Away Down South*, p. 100.
102 Ibid., p. 215.
103 "St John's Church Historic District", *Discover Our Shared Heritage Travel Itinerary* (National Park Service), www.nps.gov/nr/travel/richmond/St.Johns.htm [accessed 17/03/2011].
104 Ibid.
105 "The Statue of Lee: What Is the Best Site in Richmond for It?" *Richmond Dispatch* (28 March 1886).
106 "How It Was All Done: A History of the Confederate Soldiers and Sailors Monument", *Richmond Times-Dispatch* (30 May 1894).
107 Boorstin, *The Image, or What Happened to the American Dream*, p. 85.
108 "Westbrook Lawn", *Richmond Times-Dispatch* (18 September 1910).
109 "Village of Bensley", *Richmond Times-Dispatch* (18 September 1910).
110 M. N. Stanard, *Windsor Farms: Hauntingly Reminiscent of Old England* (Richmond, VA: Windsor Farms, 1926).
111 D. Lowenthal, *The Past Is a Foreign Country* (Cambridge: Cambridge University Press, 1985), p. 9.
112 West, *Kodak and the Lens of Nostalgia*, p. 65.
113 J. Urry, *The Tourist Gaze* (London: Sage Publications, 2002).
114 West, *Kodak and the Lens of Nostalgia*, p. 67.
115 T. A. Denenberg, "Consumed by the Past: Wallace Nutting and the Invention of Old America", in R. G. Wilson, S. Eyring and K. Marotta, eds., *Re-creating the American Past: Essays on the Colonial Revival* (Charlottesville and London: University of Virginia Press, 2006), p. 37.
116 Formerly the Priory of the Augustinian Order of the Holy Sepulchre of Jerusalem founded in 1109, and rebuilt by Thomas Hawkins after the dissolution of the monasteries in 1536.

117 J. Taylor, "Virginia House: The Reconstruction of Social and Historical Narratives", *Re-creating the American Past: Essays on the Colonial Revival* (Charlottesville, VA: University of Virginia Press, 2006), p. 248.
118 Weddell, *Richmond Virginia in Old Prints*, p. xxviii.
119 Ibid.
120 H. Stafford Bryant Jr., "Two Twentieth Century Domestic Architects in the South: Neel Reid and William L. Bottomley", *Classical America*, 1(2) (1972), p. 31.
121 Ibid., p. 113.
122 O'Neal and Weeks, *The Work of William Lawrence Bottomley in Richmond*, p. 133.
123 E. Glasgow, "Dare's Gift", in R. K. Meeker, ed., *Collected Short Stories of Ellen Glasgow* (Baton Rouge, LA: Louisiana State University Press, 1963), p. 74.
124 O'Neal and Weeks, *The Work of William Lawrence Bottomley in Richmond*, p. i.
125 Cobb, *Away Down South*, p. 87.
126 C. C. Lavoie, "Architectural Plans and Visions: The Early HABS Program and Its Documentation of Vernacular Architecture", *Perspectives in Vernacular Architecture*, 13(2) (Anniversary Issue, 2006/2007), p. 18.
127 F. C. Kaynor, "Thomas Tileston Waterman: Student of American Colonial Architecture", *Winterthur Portfolio*, 20(2/3) (1985), p. 143.
128 Along with the Daughters of the American Revolution and the Society of Colonial Daughters.
129 R. G. Wilson, S. Eyring and K. Marotta, eds., *Re-creating the American Past: Essays on the Colonial Revival* (Charlottesville and London: University of Virginia Press, 2006), p. 6.
130 A. Robbinson, "A 'Portrait of a Nation': The Role of the Historic American Buildings Survey in the Colonial Revival", in Wilson, Eyring and Marotta, eds., *Re-creating the American Past: Essays on the Colonial Revival* (Charlottesville and London: University of Virginia Press, 2006), p. 99.
131 *Historic American Buildings Survey: Catalog of the Measured Drawings and Photographs of the Survey in the Library of Congress* (National Park Service: Historic American Buildings Survey, 1941).
132 T. T. Waterman, *English Antecedents of Virginia Architecture* (American Philosophical Society, 1939); Waterman, *The Mansions of Virginia 1706–1776*; T. T. Waterman, *Dwellings of Colonial America* (Chapel Hill: The University of North Carolina Press, 1950).
133 A. Robinson, "A 'Portrait of a Nation': The Role of the Historic American Buildings Survey in the Colonial Revival", *Re-creating the American Past*, p. 114.
134 E. Carr, *Mission 66: Modernism and the National Park Dilemma* (Amherst: University of Massachusetts Press, 2007), p. 22.
135 C. C. Lavoie, "Architectural Plans and Visions: The Early HABS Program and Its Documentation of Vernacular Architecture", *Perspectives in Vernacular Architecture*, 13(2) (Anniversary Issue, 2006/2007), p. 18.
136 C. Lounsbury, *The Reconstruction of Williamsburg's First Colonial Capitol, 1928–1934: A Critique* (1989), http://research.history.org/DigitalLibrary/View/index.cfm?doc=ResearchReports%5CRR1137.xml [accessed 15/09/2010].
137 The Colonial Parkway project can be seen as an extension of the Williamsburg reconstruction. Architects involved in both projects reputedly socialised together throughout the 1930s, sharing thoughts and philosophies.
138 The parkway's general design owes much to the work of American landscape architects Frederick Law Olmsted and Calvert Vaux. In their design for Central Park, pedestrians are separated from carriageways by unobtrusive underpasses and bridges, which become picturesque landscape features in their own right.

139 H. Eckenrode, "Origin of the Colonial National Monument", 16 October 1933, file 101 C-2, "History General-1930-November 1952", collection of the Colonial National Historical Park.
140 T. Davis, "A Pleasant Illusion of Unspoiled Countryside: The American Parkway and the Problematics of an Institutionalised Vernacular", in A. K. Hoagland and K. A. Breisch, eds., *Constructing Image, Identity, and Place: Perspectives in Vernacular Architecture IX* (Knoxville: The University of Tennessee Press, 2003), p. 235.
141 www.vatc.org/film/filmhistory.asp [accessed 01/06/2011].
141 Lowenthal, *The Past Is a Foreign Country*, p. 368.
143 P. Sorlin, *The Film in History: Restaging the Past* (London: John Wiley & Sons, 1980), pp. viii–ix.
144 B. Colomina, A. Brennan and J. Kim, eds., *Cold War Hothouses: Inventing Postwar Culture, from Cockpit to Playboy* (New York: Princeton Architectural Press, 2004).
145 Ibid.
146 Davis, "A Pleasant Illusion of Unspoiled Countryside", p. 240.
147 The byway takes on added significance from the fact that two US presidents, Henry Harrison (signer of the Declaration of Independence) and John Tyler, both lived at plantations along the route. Berkeley plantation is also credited as the site of the first Thanksgiving, a particularly patriotic association of the route. *Scenic Roads Study* (Richmond Regional Planning District Committee, June 2004), p. 4.
148 Ibid., p. 2.
149 Ibid., p. 3.
150 Boorstin, *The Image, or What Happened to the American Dream*, p. 113.
151 Davis, "A Pleasant Illusion of Unspoiled Countryside", p. 242.
152 R. Venturi, *Learning from Las Vegas: The Forgotten Symbolism of Architectural Form* (Cambridge, MA: MIT Press, 1977).
153 Boorstin, *The Image, or What Happened to the American Dream*, p. 114.
154 Ibid., p. 112.
155 Planning and Development Review, Richmond Master Plan (Richmond, Virginia: City of Richmond, 2010), p. 29.
156 Ibid.
157 I. Nairn, cited in G. Darley, "Ian Nairn and Jane Jacobs, the Lessons from Britain and America", *The Journal of Architecture*, 17(5) (2012), 734.
158 Nairn, cited in Darley, "Ian Nairn and Jane Jacobs, the Lessons from Britain and America", pp. 733–746.
159 James Richards, "The Second Half Century", *The Architectural Review* (January 1947), p. 23. See also S. Parnell, "AR's and AD's Post-War Editorial Policies: The Making of Modern Architecture in Britain", *The Journal of Architecture*, 17(5) (2012), 763–775.
160 R. Elwall, "'How to Like Everything': Townscape and Photography", *The Journal of Architecture*, 17(5) (2012), p. 672.
161 Peter Rayner Banham, writer for the *Architectural Review*, entitled his history of architectural criticism between 1945 and 1965 "The Revenge of the Picturesque". J. Macarthur, "The Revenge of the Picturesque, Redux", *The Journal of Architecture*, 17(5) (2012), 643–653.
162 www.westbroadvillage.com/main-street/index.shtml [accessed 03/09/2010].
163 J. Fortier, *Fortress of Louisbourg* (Toronto: Oxford University Press, 1979), p. 19.
164 S. Boym, *The Future of Nostalgia* (New York: Basic Books, 2001), p. xiv.

4   Richmond, NSW

A critical question that the themes of this book bring to the fore is 'Why was the image of Richmond used so often to describe other landscapes?' In this study of Richmond, New South Wales, Australia, I discuss the ways in which landscapes have been overlaid with Western meaning by explorers, cartographers and settlers. Such a translation of European vision to the Australian landscape served as both convenient shorthand for the description of topographical features in an age before photography and a means to construct colonial imperial identities, which in doing so excluded others from possession of the land.

The Hawkesbury River

About 50 miles to the south of Sydney, rainwater falling on west-facing mountain slopes forms numerous streams which eventually feed into the Nepean, the Grose and finally the Hawkesbury River. By this point, the river has changed direction, flowing first north, and then east, to meet the ocean at spectacular Broken Bay north of Sydney.

Aboriginal peoples, including the Guringai or Eora, the Wannungine and the Darkinung, had long recognised Broken Bay and the Hawkesbury River as excellent places of settlement, enjoying fresh water and abundant fishing. Numerous middens, rock shelters and rock engravings scattered along the foreshore are testament to the frequency of indigenous occupation. Further inland, along the Hawkesbury River, it is known that Aboriginal peoples cultivated indigenous root crops, such as the yam, along the river banks,[1] regularly clearing the land through traditional burning practices. In *The Hawkesbury River: A Social and Natural History* (2017), Peter Boon writes that

> The more fertile land [. . .] was probably burnt frequently with a mosaic of low-intensity fires to provide the green pick that attracted game and to keep vegetation in the park-like state that made animals easier to hunt [and colonisation easier].[2]

By contrast, the steep sandstone geology of Broken Bay, with its thin soils and dense bush cover, would have proved less suitable for cultivation and hunting, so burning was likely much less frequent. Such indigenous land management practices perhaps explain the perceptions of early European explorers, who saw nothing but uninhabited wilderness in the sandstone country, and who misinterpreted the park-like lands of the Hawkesbury as both entirely *natural* and reminiscent of (equally man-made and managed) 'naturalistic' landscapes at home in Britain.

As such, the discourse of European 'discovery', 'exploration' and 'pioneering' continues to be common among descriptions of the Hawkesbury region, regularly presented as the backdrop to heroic events in Australian national history. Historians have typically presented this landscape, the destination and then setting-off point for great explorers, the home of hardy pioneers and some of the nation's earliest colonial settlements, as the "cradle of Australia".[3] Even where the intention has apparently been to recognise the indigenous history of the landscape, such as in the protection of land, in 1894, which would later become Ku-ring-gai Chase National Park, the focus was upon preservation of the natural 'wilderness' and the few archaeological vestiges of indigenous peoples long disappeared. Even the very name is emblematic of this kind of thinking; 'Guringai' was proposed by Frederick Eccleston Du Faur for the "genuine Aboriginal ring about this word, [. . .] [which] I think no better could be found for commendation as doubtless the tributaries of the Hawkesbury would be favourite, fishing and hunting grounds for this *vanished race*".[4] Powell and Hesline (2010) argue that the bastardisation of the word 'Guringai' into 'Ku-ring-gai' was an invention of "the amateur ethnologist John Fraser in 1892 from his own spelling of the word 'Guringai', [. . .] and from 'Kuri', meaning adult initiated men".[5] The addition of the word 'Chase' was intended to indicate that it was an area of open bush and not an English 'park' with its implications of enclosed and managed landscapes. Essentially, the development of Ku-ring-gai Chase could be seen in relation/reaction to the Europeanised landscapes of Australia's early national 'parks', such as the sanitised Edwardian boathouses and lily ponds of the nation's first – Sydney's Royal National Park. But, one could argue, Ku-ring-gai Chase is no less a romantic and manufactured European vision of the Hawkesbury – the curation of a rugged wilderness devoid of people, only hauntingly reminiscent of the 'noble savages' of a "vanished race".

'Discovery'

It is to Captain James Cook that the discovery and naming of Broken Bay have traditionally been credited, despite excellent research that has shown Cook in fact referred to another location, having sailed past the Hawkesbury, unremarked, by night.[6] Whatever the case may be, the first recorded European to properly investigate the bay was Governor Phillip, who embarked on a longboat from the ship *Sirius* on 2 March 1788. Deducing that a fine river may lead into the bay, and given Sydney Cove's poor access to fresh water for arable farming, Phillip ordered several further expeditions by boat and overland between 1788 and 1789. On his second expedition of 15 April 1788, Phillip, assisted by Lieutenant Ball and John White, took an overland route north-east from Sydney, reaching about 15 miles inland over four days. On the third day, they reached an outlook with a fine, ranging view over the plains which would become known as 'Prospect Mount', beyond which a distinctive hill acted as a landmark. Historian Ernest Favenc captured the moment:

> [A] remarkable hill, destined to become a well-known early landmark, Phillip called Richmond Hill. In the brief view he had of the range, there was suddenly born in Phillip's mind the conviction that a large river must have its source therein, and that upon the banks of such a river, the soil would be found more arable than about the present settlement.[7]

Although it has been argued that Phillip named the hill, like those he named 'Carmarthen' and 'Lansdowne', after political figures of the day, it is important to note the connection between contemporary connotations of the name 'Richmond' and Phillip's imagined river landscape. In the light of the early chapters of this book, it is possible to infer that Phillip was well aware of the landscape and topography of Surrey's Richmond Hill, a renowned and much-reproduced view of the River Thames made famous from at least the beginning of the eighteenth century for its illustrious royal, noble, artistic and literary associations. Phillip's naming of the distant hill is consistent with Favenc's comment that he was convinced there was an abundant, fertile riverine landscape to be discovered to the north-west. At the same time, it already laid claim to these uncharted territories for the British Empire, though via the explorer's gaze and without having actually stepped foot there.

The picturesque and the panoramic

Of course, Phillip's reference to a well-known topographical feature in Britain should be viewed as part of a broader tendency for European explorers to view 'new' landscapes through the prism of the 'old'. In *The Cartographic Eye: How Explorers Saw Australia* (1996), author Simon Ryan describes a vision which "far from being a fresh and innocent transcription of the natural world [. . .], is constructed in terms of the *picturesque* and the *panoramic* – two European conventions of seeing, which possess ideological agendas of the own".[8] Once understood, Ryan argues that such conventions

> deconstruct [explorers'] claims to the authority of originality and immediacy, for [. . .] the vision [. . .] is culturally mediated. Moreover, they

are techniques which reveal the nexus between power and surveillance [. . .] and, once the nexus is realised, it is possible to see that 'innocent' aesthetic responses are actually expressions of imperial greed.[9]

Such modes of vision were, in fact, intrinsic to the practices of exploration; in the densely forested sandstone country of eastern New South Wales exploration generally proceeded from one high point to the next. At each point, summit trees were laboriously cleared to open a panoramic vista through the trees,[10] allowing a new high point on the horizon to be fixed as destination. The routes of successful exploratory missions thus became a chain of landmark panoramic vistas, while failed missions were often the result of the inability of European explorers to assemble the landscape into a neat and memorable series of scenes – in other words, the visual impenetrability and monotony of the bushland plains disorientated European explorers, while indigenous peoples were able to navigate freely and effectively.

If the panoramic mode of vision was intrinsically linked to the practices of exploration, the picturesque was often a means by which to appeal to the senses of a broader public, through adding detail to published exploration accounts. Although poet Barron Field insisted that the Australian landscape was un-picturesque,[11] William Gilpin had criticised the naval explorer Phillip Parker King for failing to add 'high colouring' to his descriptions,[12] which might aid the reader. Ryan has argued that explorers' accounts of Australia do often remark upon the picturesque qualities of views, constructed through the use of picturesque vocabulary expected by readers.[13] For example, in his *Journal of an Expedition into [. . .] Tropical Australia [. . .]* (1848), explorer Thomas Mitchell described a scene whose

> outlines were wild, the tints sublimely beautiful. [. . .] grass, verdure, driftwood and water – were so opposed to the dark hues of the [. . .] rocks, that a Rusdael [sic], or a Gainsborough, might there have found an inexhaustible stock of subjects for their pencil. [. . .] May the object of our journey be successful [. . .] and that more of [nature's] graces may thus be brought back within the reach of art.[14]

Mitchell's writing shows him to have been at great pains to demonstrate his knowledge of landscape art, which one could view as a means by which he could separate himself out as a gentleman of taste. It doing so, Mitchell's writing also sheds light on the motives behind colonial naming practices. For example, in one instance Mitchell describes a "beautiful headland [. . .] just such as painters place in middle distance",[15] naming it 'Mount Salvator' in a clear appeal to the learned readers' familiarity with the landscape paintings of Salvator Rosa, a favourite of contemporary connoisseurs of the picturesque.[16]

Such projections of the picturesque took possession of the Australian landscape through viewing it as "ready-made for the occupation of a European power and its agriculture".[17] For example, in his journal of 1844–47, explorer Charles Sturt described

> flat after flat of the most vivid green, ornamented by clumps of trees, sufficiently apart to give a most picturesque finish to the landscape. Trees [. . .] dropped over the river, forming long dark avenues, and the banks of the river, grassed to the water, had the appearance of having been made so by art.[18]

Although many analyses of European responses to the Australian landscape have emphasised how different and strange the land seemed,[19] the use of picturesque description projects English class privilege onto the Australian landscape; as Ryan has argued, "If the land resembled an estate, then surely the appropriation of land had received a natural confirmation".[20]

Three 'Richmond Hills'

Beyond its use as a convenient descriptive convention, picturesque language could thus convey the potential of new landscapes for colonial expansion – as Ryan writes, "[I]f the land was picturesque it was ripe for transformation into wealth".[21] Mitchell even specifically noted the potentiality of the picturesque prospect, writing that a view of "an open country has a double charm in regions for the most part covered with primeval forests, calling up pleasing reminiscences of the past, brighter prospects for the future".[22] Governor Phillip's 'Richmond Hill' seems the perfect example of this ability of picturesque language to connote the latent potential of the landscape, and to drive the processes of exploration and settlement.

Over a period of 25 years, from 1788 onwards, Phillip's 'Richmond Hill' became the desired destination and later navigational aid for successive expeditions to the Hawkesbury region. The very name conjured up imagery of a rich and fertile land, capable of solving the settlement of Sydney Cove's greatest need – productive arable land. In fact, the location of Richmond Hill moved at least twice. In another expedition of 1788 Phillip reached a hill from the summit of which could be seen the Carmarthen and Lansdowne ranges. Deducing that the party must be on Richmond Hill they "drank to those noble men after whom those mountains had now been named".[23] However, Bowd has argued that it could not have been possible to see this hill from Prospect Mount, and concludes that Phillip, as a sailor, "was apt to mistake distances and landmarks [on land]".[24]

The third location of Richmond Hill was determined during Phillip's most noteworthy expedition, along the Hawkesbury River to its confluence with the Nepean River, which embarked from Broken Bay on 28 June 1789. On the eighth day rowing upstream, the party found themselves at the foot of a hill "covered with lofty trees but free from scrub; the country all around being pleasant to look upon, rich with grass, and without any of those rocky patches which met their eyes so often in other directions".[25] Apparently swept away by "the charms of the scenery" the party proceeded some distance up the hill before they camped.[26] When they summited the hill to take in the view the next morning, Phillip recognised his Carmarthen and Lansdowne Hills, naming the hill on which they stood Richmond Hill. The party was suitably impressed by the view of the landscape, the stately river winding through meadows clear of scrub and punctuated by stands of mature trees. The soil, too, was good; a small patch was sown with a few potatoes, some Indian corn, melon and other seeds under Phillip's instruction,[27] in order to prove the fertility of the land already well established and understood by its indigenous occupants.[28]

In another expedition of April 1791, upon arriving at Prospect Mount the party was able "to discover plainly the object of our pursuit, Richmond Hill, distant about eight miles, in a contrary direction from what we had been proceeding upon".[29] Unsure of the errors in their directions the party retraced their steps, intending to follow the Nepean River to Richmond Hill, though the expedition was abandoned after six days in the bush. The following month (May 1791), a party returned to the site of abandonment, and continued to the banks of the Hawkesbury, which they followed up to Richmond Hill.

In all these expeditions, Phillip had been struck by a park-like country "as fine as any I ever saw", with stands of mature trees scattered throughout grassland.[30] The same sort of landscape had similarly appealed to Cook at Botany Bay, where he remarked upon a "country finely diversified in wood and lawn" and "some of the finest meadows in the world".[31] As George Burnett Barton writes of one occasion, Phillip "was so pleased with the undulating landscape before him [. . .] that he [. . .] gave it the name of Belle Vue – probably in recollection of some pleasant landscape in the old world".[32]

The successive relocation of Richmond Hill throughout the course of these expeditions is intriguing. I would argue that it is reflective of the meaning which Phillip endowed with its name. In the first instance, the unexplored 'Richmond Hill' – viewed from a distance – was symbolic of the intended destination; Phillip's promise of an imagined bounteous riverine landscape would be worth the considerable effort, and unknown dangers, entailed in traversing the 'empty' 'wilderness' (although, of course, the landscape was neither 'empty' nor 'unknown' to Aboriginal communities). The lack of the promised river on reaching the second 'Richmond Hill' inevitably sealed its fate, eclipsed by the discovery of the third, close to the confluence of the Nepean and Hawkesbury Rivers. Here, the landscape offered all that Phillip had both anticipated and promised, the prospect of productive agriculture allowing for the continued prosperity of the colony of New South Wales. To those familiar with images and literary depictions – both at home and abroad – of the Thames landscape at Richmond, Surrey, the prospect of a new 'Richmond Hill' somewhere 'out there' in an otherwise hostile landscape could perhaps be as potent a force for exploration and exploitation as that of the gold 'rushes' of the following century. As such, the search for 'Richmond Hill', similar to the possession of the landscape through exploration and naming practices (e.g., after British nobility and political figures), may be viewed as a particular form of colonial project, and perhaps as one of Phillip's principal aims as colonial governor for furthering the development of the colony.

Among numerous other expeditions to the Hawkesbury region, the colony's second governor, John Hunter, undertook at least two either side of an extended stay in England. No doubt informed by contemporary British aesthetic fashion as a keen amateur artist himself, Hunter remarked of his 1796 expedition that "the different views & landscapes from the banks of this river are extremely beautiful and would much amuse a good painter".[33]

In the intervening years between Governors Phillip and Hunters' expeditions much had changed along the upper reaches of the Hawkesbury. Not least, a number of permanent settlers had taken up occupation of the land, constructing huts and clearing the bush for agriculture. Of these pioneering individuals the most notable were former convicts James Ruse, who had established Experimental Farm at Parramatta, and his neighbour at Parramatta, Charles Williams. The reasons behind Ruse's and Williams's relocation to the upper Hawkesbury remain unclear, but the region was of course well known by this time due to numerous expeditionary accounts.[34] It is tempting to speculate how much Phillip's visual construction of a bounteous riverine landscape – a new 'Richmond Hill' – could have influenced these entrepreneurial settlers to move further west in pursuit of profit. As Boon points out,

> In any case, it seems that the decision to settle the area [. . .] was a private one and not part of official government policy. The paradox is that [Governor] Grose [. . .] later proudly claimed ownership of the expansion.[35]

Developing the Hawkesbury landscape: Governors Grose and Macquarie

By 1797, at least 600 settlers had taken up residence on the upper Hawkesbury, spread about a government wharf and barracks a few miles downstream of Richmond Hill.[36] Growing up 'ad hoc' around a riverside square, this village, with its views of rolling grassland, was unofficially known as 'Green Hills', and would later be formalised under Governor

Macquarie with the more stately name of 'Windsor'. In many ways the contrast between informal, ramshackle 'Green Hills' and stately 'Windsor' is reflected in the contrast between presentations of early settler society. Historians and popular culture, particularly fictional novels and television drama, have tended to perpetuate stereotypes, characterising individuals as lazy, idle and drunken former convicts, the towns as rowdy and lawless, and the landscape as equally threatening as beautiful. However, this could as much be viewed as a construction of cultural identity; a hardened stoicism, both in terms of people and landscape, emerges in history writing which has much to do with the formation of a distinctive Australian culture.

In fact, Governor Grose *did* complain that he had a problem with Hawkesbury settlers "who have evidently no other view than the purpose of raising a sufficient supply to pay their passages to England".[37] The solution was to grant settlers 30-acre plots of land with the stipulation that grantees reside on and cultivate the land. It is the surveys of these land grants that provide some of the earliest plans of the Hawkesbury settlements. Intriguingly, James Grimes's survey plan of 1796 makes first reference to 'The Terrace', a road built to follow the river from Green Hills to Richmond Hill, along which were strung many of the earliest Hawkesbury land grants. The name 'The Terrace' seems to refer to the topography of the northern riverbank upon which the road was built, following an escarpment of high ground overlooking a great bend in the river's course (Figure 4.1). Perhaps it is no coincidence that we should find this name, given that 'The Terrace' overlooking the Thames on Surrey's Richmond Hill had already achieved much fame via its artistic depiction and connection to literary works such as James Thompson's *The Seasons* (1730).

Certainly, comparisons were directly made between the landscape of the Hawkesbury and that of the Thames at Richmond (Figure 4.2). In 1789, Captain Watkin Tench had described his first impression of the Nepean River as "nearly as broad as the Thames at Putney".[38] Perhaps the most obvious connection was made by Governor Macquarie – upon the naming of his five new townships in the upper Hawkesbury (1810) he explained that

> I gave the name of Windsor to the Town intended to be erected in the District of the Green Hills [. . .] from the similarity of this situation to that of the same name in England; the Township [. . .] I have named Richmond, from its beautiful situation, and as corresponding with that of its District [in England]; [. . .].
>
> Having sufficiently celebrated this auspicious Day of christening the five Towns [. . .] I recommended to the Gentlemen present to exert their influence with the Settlers in stimulating them to lose no time in removing their Habitations, Flocks & Herds to these Places of safety and security, and thereby fulfil my intentions and plans in establishing them.[39]

Figure 4.1 View of the Hawkesbury River from The Terrace, between Richmond and Windsor.

Figure 4.2 View of the Banks of the River Hawkesbury after J.W.Lewin (1813).
Source: British Museum.

Macquarie's act of establishing the five Hawkesbury towns, two named after admired British landscapes (with obvious royal connections), and the remaining three (Castlereagh, Pitt-Town and Wilberforce) named after prominent British politicians, indicates the development of the Hawkesbury region as a colonial enterprise. It's important to note, however, that here, perhaps more than anywhere in the development of the Australian colonies, was the colonial project *par excellence* – Macquarie's vision extended to the regular grid layout and architectural detail of the new towns, including the provision for "a central square, six chains on each side, which was to be surrounded by a church, schoolhouse, gaol and guard house". Each building typology was rigorously specified – brick or weatherboard walls not less than nine feet high, with brick chimneys and shingle roofs. Architectural historian J. M. Freeland has stated that this was no less than "the earliest building regulation controlling building in Australia and applied only to the five Hawkesbury towns".[40]

As a result, the five 'Macquarie Towns' of the Hawkesbury would become home to some of Australia's finest Georgian buildings, including Francis Greenway's St Matthew's Church, Windsor and its adjacent rectory, the Macquarie Arms Hotel and a sprinkling of numerous genteel brick neoclassical villas (Figure 4.3). There can be no doubt that in their design, architects and craftsmen looked to the contemporary fashions of Britain, making use of pattern books published in England and distributed throughout the colony. Given the clear fluidity of patterns and images via publishing practices it is surely not a stretch to suggest that the landscape of the Hawkesbury was viewed, and manipulated, in the same way – in

Figure 4.3 One of Windsor's elegent Georgian villas.

relation to images of idealised British landscapes and, in particular, the view from Richmond Hill, Surrey. After all, it was the landscape of Richmond-upon-Thames that had served as the cradle and test-bed for many of the latest fashions in architecture and landscape design, as well as landscape painting and aesthetic discourse.

The Frontier Wars

The emergence of an ordered, structured colonial community along the Hawkesbury at this early date (Windsor is widely considered the third oldest British colonial settlement on the Australian continent after Sydney and Parramatta) has tended to occupy historical and architectural narratives of the region, depicted as the "cradle of Australia".[41] These ordered processes, by which Grose and Macquarie intended to control the sporadic initial development of the Hawkesbury region, would, however, bring with them chaotic consequences; although official policy urged the maintenance of good relations with Aborigines, the imposition of colonial settlements upon the landscape was devastating to indigenous communities.

Firstly, Europeans arriving by ship brought with them successive waves of disease. Describing the smallpox epidemic of 1789, Collins wrote that

> On visiting Broken Bay, we found that [smallpox] had not confined its efforts to Port Jackson, for in many places our path was covered with skeletons, and the same spectacles were to be met with in the hollows of most of the rocks of that harbour.[42]

It has been estimated that more than 80% of the Aboriginal population in the Sydney region might have died as a result of the disease, leading to the depopulation of vast areas and the abandonment of their lands.[43] The resulting loss of oral histories and traditional knowledge is indicated by the fact that there is no known word for the clan who formerly occupied the land at Richmond – James Kohen simply names it the 'North Richmond tribe', demonstrating how total was the European eclipse of aboriginal presence in the landscape.[44]

Where disease had preceded, 'war' followed. While violent incidents had occasionally taken place around Port Jackson and Parramatta, along the Hawkesbury River from at least 1794 to 1816 there was a sustained period of "armed conflict, murder and mutual retribution between Aborigines and the British", which would become known as the 'Frontier Wars'.[45] Although conflict would escalate into mindless 'tit-for-tat' reprisals, the original motives seem surprisingly clear; writing in 1795, Reverend Fyshe Palmer described that

> The natives of the Hawkesbury lived on the wild yams on the banks. Cultivation has rooted out these, and poverty compelled them to steal

Indian corn to support nature. The unfeeling settlers resented this by unparalleled severities.[46]

It is probable that many early events went unrecorded, though it seems that the tipping point came with the robbing of food from a colonist's hut in 1794 – a punitive expedition resulted in the murder of seven or eight Aborigines. The following October, an Aboriginal boy was kidnapped by a group of Hawkesbury farmers who had him stripped and bound, dragged naked through a fire, thrown – still bound – into the river, and then shot dead as he struggled in the water.[47] Launching an enquiry at Parramatta, Lieutenant John Macarthur heard evidence from just two individuals: Robert Forrester, who admitted shooting the boy, and Alexander Wilson, a Windsor settler who justified the crime as "as an act of mercy".[48] Without further testimony the matter was promptly quashed. Perhaps in retaliation, in May of the following year two farmers were killed as they attempted to stop Aborigines stealing maize. Between 1794 and 1799 it is probable that around 20 British and more than 40 Aborigines had been killed along the Hawkesbury alone, with conflict reaching its peak around 1800, in what would be known as the 'Black Wars'.[49] A series of atrocities on both sides in 1805 (typically the pillage or burning of a colonial farm, followed by murderous punitive expeditions to exact non-discriminate revenge on any and all Aborigines) caused Governor King to officially ban contact between Hawkesbury farmers and Aborigines.[50]

Officially, conflict had come to an end by the close of 1816, even despite the fact that earlier in the year Macquarie had ordered two separate expeditions to exact "exemplary and Severe Punishments on the Mountain Tribes who have lately exhibited so Sanguinary a Spirit against the Settlers".[51] However, Aboriginal elders did agree to bring an end to the raids and Macquarie reassured the government in London that "all Hostility on both Sides has long since Ceased".[52] It is around about this time that a change in policy towards the Aborigines becomes apparent in the granting of land to two Dharug men at Richmond, and the establishment of an Aboriginal reserve and township at Boongaarrunbee (later known as 'Black Town'). On the one hand these moves attempted to relieve the poverty of Aborigines on the Hawkesbury, but on the other they are in line with typical colonial practices of racial segregation and isolation. Far from prospering, the Aboriginal community of the Hawkesbury declined to around 200 people by the 1820s, and by 1900 there were just two initiated Dharug men remaining. As Hirst has written, "the Aboriginal and European ways of life were incompatible in almost every respect and the displacement of one form of life by another was abrupt and complete".[53]

Depicting the Hawkesbury

Despite the traumatic genesis of the Hawkesbury settlements, and the paradox presented by the stereotype of the drunken idle settler, the architectural and landscape images commonly presented of the region during this period are of genteel villa estates and idyllic riverside meadows. The endurance of such images is arguably the result of the architectural refinement of many of the settlements' early buildings and the real beauty of the Hawkesbury landscape. However, it is also in large part due to the way in which the landscape was described by travellers – utilising the aesthetic language of painting made popular in British travel accounts – and the attraction of the region for travelling artists from the early decades of the nineteenth century onwards.

Artist John William Lewin arrived in Sydney in 1800, courtesy of a wealthy British patron with interests in cataloguing the natural world and entomology. Although Governor Macquarie recommended Lewin as the colony's first official artist, he was formally rejected by the government in London, prompting him to found the colony's first art school, in 1812. Of Lewin's works, his best known is the earliest illustrated book on Australian birds, published principally for a British audience. Likewise, his landscapes, including *A View of the River Hawkesbury N. S. Wales* (1802), could arguably be said to have targeted British audiences in their appeal to acculturated picturesque tastes, claiming 'wild' native landscapes as artefacts of colonial study.

Another early British artist that travelled to the Hawkesbury, William Westall, had been admitted to the Royal Academy School of Art in 1799, roughly contemporary with artist John Constable. Two years later, as topographic artist aboard Captain Matthew Flinders's HMS *Investigator*, Westall was one of the first Europeans to circumnavigate the Australian continent. Again, here is the artist in the official service of a colonial project, capturing the Australian landscape for a predominantly British audience; more than a dozen of Westall's pencil sketches show Hawkesbury scenes, including *Hawkesbury River, View No. 13* (1802), which shows a typical raised view over a sinuous bend in the river.

Of course, paintings, sketches and descriptions didn't *have* to be made on site, and could just as easily be made in Britain sometime after the fact. For example, artist Joseph Lycett, sentenced to 14 years transportation for forgery, was by 1818 doing government work and producing landscape paintings for wealthier Sydney clients. Pardoned by Macquarie in 1821 (perhaps as a result of Lycett's production of three drawings that Macquarie had sent to Lord Bathurst in London as a gift), Lycett returned to Britain, where he published a 12-volume series of antipodean scenes entitled *Views in Australia* (1824). Lycett's targeting of an elite British readership is demonstrated by his dedication of the work to the same Lord Bathurst, and the high price commanded by such a publication at the time. Following the argument that Lycett depicted the Australian landscape from a mix of memory and preparatory sketches, and in the tradition of 'artistic license' manipulated it to conform to the aesthetic tastes of his patrons, it is important to note Bathurst's personal context; Bathurst had grown up on the Cirencester estate of his grandfather Allen Bathurst, who had frequently entertained Alexander Pope and Jonathan Swift. Pope had even played a part in the landscape design of the estate, which included within its bounds the principal source of the River Thames. It should be of little surprise, then, that Lycett developed numerous views of the Hawkesbury River with uncanny resemblance to the admired landscapes of the Thames, and presented in an aesthetic style Pope and Swift would both have understood and admired – for example, a *View of Windsor upon the Hawkesbury River* (1824), *View of Nepean River, at the Cow Pastures, New South Wales* (1824) and *View of Wilberforce, on the Banks of the River Hawkesbury New South Wales* (1825).

Likewise, the typical painterly language deployed by Reverend John Dunmore on approaching a section of the Hawkesbury River at Wiseman's Ferry in 1827 could easily have been spoken by that other touring clergyman and amateur artist, William Gilpin, in his well-known *Observations on the River Wye [. . .] 1770*. As if it were a painted canvas, Dunmore describes how

> The rays of the setting sun were glowingly reflected in the smooth glassy surface of the broad river, when this beautiful scene suddenly burst upon our view. Patches of wheat [. . .] appeared to the right and left along the main river, [. . .] as far as the eye could trace it along the mountains [. . .] while the yellow tints [. . .] and the deep healthy green [. . .] beautifully contrasted with the sombre shades of the forest, and the grey rocks that were ever and anon peering forth.[54]

Alongside those, like Dunmore, with an obvious affinity for landscape art, other trained artists came to the Hawkesbury region in the service of supposedly objective science. For example, Conrad Martens arrived in Sydney in 1835, after serving for two years as expeditionary artist on board the *Beagle* with Charles Darwin. For the next 30 years Martens practised as a professional artist, searching out inspiration in landscapes across the Australian colonies. As a topographical artist with a working knowledge of maritime vessels, many of Marten's most accomplished works depict maritime and riverine subjects, interpreted by some as representations of Britain's maritime prowess and the technological machinery of empire. Even where maritime activity is conspicuously absent, such as in *Wisemans Ferry* (1838), there is a sense in Martens's work that the landscape has been 'conquered', or at least partially tamed by colonial enterprise – for example, in his depiction of a road cut across the formidable hills in *Pass above Wisemans Ferry, Hawkesbury River* (1839). Further examples of this are Martens's numerous commercial commissions for paintings of colonial homesteads, which seem to express the owners' superior status in having turned a 'fearsome' and 'empty' land to profitable agriculture (i.e., their status as 'landed gentry', rather than as mere 'colonists'), and their exemplary 'taste' in cultivating the picturesque potential of its landscapes (perhaps, even, no longer inferior to the landscapes of Britain).[55]

The trend followed by these early artists in visiting the Hawkesbury for inspiration grew towards the later years of the nineteenth century; as Peter Boon writes, the river acted as "a muse to countless creative folk".[56] Austrian artist Eugene von Guérard painted *Govett's Leap and Grose River Valley, Blue Mountains, New South Wales* in 1873, a view which had already been depicted by William Romaine Govett (1836 – after which it is named) and George Penkivil Slade (1868) and which would become the regular haunt of travelling artists, including William Raworth (1874) and Thomas George Glover (1878).

It is somewhat surprising that even from an early date, the nature of these groups of travelling artists was surprisingly organised; artist and member of the Academy of Art Du Faur had established an artists' camp in the Grose Valley in 1875, with the specific aim of facilitating artists' access to Hawkesbury River and Blue Mountain scenes. Alongside numerous paintings, including William Charles Piguenit's *Hawkesbury River with Figures in a Boat: On the Nepean* (1881) and *The Upper Nepean, New South Wales* (1889), the outputs of Du Faur's camp include some of New South Wales's earliest commercial photography. The immense difficulty of photographing the Hawkesbury region at this time (it took five men to carry the heavy glass plate negatives of E. W. Searle, along with vast quantities of toxic chemicals required) indicates the practice of photography as a colonial science; photography offered greater detail, accuracy and objectivity than painting, and stable glass negatives were capable of being catalogued and stored.[57] However, this is not to say that photography went untouched by subjective perception; photographs were often 'staged' as if to show 'the moment of discovery' and carefully directed to capture pleasing image compositions. In this sense, the supposed objectivity of early landscape photography was no less informed by culturally engrained aesthetics than painting, leading T. Bonyhady to describe Joseph Bischoff's *The Valley of the Grose* (1875) as "among the most compelling colonial landscape photographs [in the World]".[58]

Other camps and excursions were led by artist Julian Rossi Ashton, who preferred to camp in the meadows close to the Hawkesbury River around Richmond, described by *The Picturesque Atlas of Australasia* (1886) as "the river of the artist and the tourist".[59] As a contributor to the *Atlas*, Ashton produced *The Hawkesbury, at Wisemans Ferry* and later produced many riverine views, including *The Afterglow, Foulweather Reach, Hawkesbury River, New South Wales* (1884), *A Waterhole on the Hawkesbury River* (1885) and *Sentry-Box Reach, Hawkesbury River, New South Wales*. Notable attendees at Ashton's camps included British artist Charles Conder, founding member, alongside artists Tom Roberts, Arthur Streeton and Frederick McCubbin, of the Heidelberg School of Australian Impressionism. Conder's depictions of the Hawkesbury at Richmond include *Springtime*

1888, Pugh's Lagoon, Richmond and *The Farm, Richmond, New South Wales* (1888), all of which exhibit peculiarly nostalgic and riparian characteristics – almost as if depicting the home counties of Britain – where, incidentally, Conder would later migrate, to live out the remainder of his life in suburban Surrey.

Another frequent visitor to the region, Conder's friend Arthur Streeton, took up residence in the Traveller's Rest below Richmond Hill on numerous occasions from the early 1890s.[60] Perhaps the most famous of his Hawkesbury River paintings is *The Purple Noon's Transparent Might* (1896), originally called *Hawkesbury Landscape* (Figure 4.4). Painted at The Terrace above Richmond, where a steep escarpment gave excellent views across the meandering river, Streeton described

> The glory of the river and plain spread before me[.] Far below were the tops of river-oaks, and water like the blue of a black opal. The

Figure 4.4 Arthur Streeton, *The Purple Noon's Transparent Might* (1896).
Source: National Gallery of Victoria.

brightness of noon, the power of deep blue, [. . .] wrought me to a pitch of excitement [. . .] it seemed like working in a fiery trance.[61]

Streeton's depictions of the Hawkesbury River[62] are today widely considered to be among Australia's most significant artworks, works which not only are beautiful but also somehow contribute to the formation of the nation's history and identity. Somehow it has become near impossible to discuss the Australian landscape without discussing Streeton's superior skill in capturing the quality of light and colour. In *New Worlds from Old: 19th Century Australian and American Landscapes* (1998) Johns et al. have claimed that "No-one before Streeton [. . .] had realised the artistic potential of the panoramic view of the valley from the escarpment of the high riverbank, known as The Terrace".[63] However, as I have attempted to show, even before white explorers had set foot in the Hawkesbury region, they had already begun to overlay the imagery of Britain's Richmond Hill upon its landscape. In fact, the artistic potential of the river was one of the very first observations to be made by British explorers, and even the very use of the name 'The Terrace' seems linked to the famous 'Terrace' on Surrey's Richmond Hill, which had been long admired for its views since at least the seventeenth century.

That views of the Hawkesbury River were widely known and appreciated in the late nineteenth century – beyond the circles of artists – is clear from the arrival in Richmond of Phillip Charley in 1891. Charley's story is often presented as a classic of the Australian 'rags-to-riches' paradigm and 'fair go' mentality, as Charley, having been sent to the outback by his doctors on the recommendation to seek a drier climate, went on to discover Australia's largest silver deposit at Broken Hill, becoming one of the colonies' richest men by the age of just 23. With his profits Charley bought property along the Hawkesbury at Richmond, including Richmond Hill itself, upon the summit of which he set about building a palatial country house, 'Belmont Park' (Figure 4.5). Below the terraced gardens, wraparound veranda and belvedere tower, Charley had the riverside grounds landscaped in the fashion of an English country park, planting stands of English oaks set within meadows. In choosing to construct the house on the summit of the hill, rather than on the site of the existing homestead, Charley was clearly tapping into the power of the raised view over the Hawkesbury River as status symbol (extending his gaze across his estates and connecting him to the heroic events of Governor Phillip's expeditions) and, like Streeton, placing the river centre stage as object of aesthetic delight.

Of course, it is important to iterate that for every successful commercial artist, such as Streeton, and later Sydney Long, who frequented the Hawkesbury region in the late 1890s,[64] there were myriad others. 'The Windsor Group' refers to nine artists of mixed notoriety who, travelling

Figure 4.5 Phillip Charley's Belmont Park mansion, built on the summit of Richmond Hill, 1890s.

by train from Sydney, often took organised painting weekends to the region between 1935 and 1945.⁶⁵ The impact of these groups lies not in a single work or artist but in the cumulative power of a body of work which repeatedly depicted the Hawkesbury region in a particular way – as viewed through the lens of European picturesque vision; these are images of idyllic summer afternoons, lazy river scenes and nostalgic views of colonial buildings, as if untouched by the twentieth century.

The persistence of the Hawkesbury picturesque

Such images of the Hawkesbury persisted, and were strengthened, throughout the latter decades of the twentieth century. In particular, the 1980s–1990s saw an influx of wealthier residents, profiting from Sydney's ongoing expansion, who bought up and renovated increasingly fashionable historic houses along the Hawkesbury. In many instances such renovations were heavy-handed and overly informed by nostalgic colonial vision – for example, in the addition of upper stories, filigree cast-iron verandas, shutters and other trimmings now often mistaken as 'original'. Even where renovations were apparently academic in intention the decision to strip away layers of accumulated history (inserted shop fronts, dormer windows, closed in verandas etc.) seems to be informed as much by visions of a colonial ideal as by historical authenticity.

It is perhaps most revealing that one Richmond craftsman who undertook many of these alterations, Dennis Mahboub, even built himself a home from the salvaged fragments of these altered buildings (Figure 4.6). Constructed over a period of 30 years (1980–2010) on a sandstone cliff upstream of the confluence of the Hawkesbury and Grose Rivers, Mahboub's remarkable home has all the hallmarks of a Hawkesbury settler's home – rough-hewn sandstone blocks, delicate sash windows, timber slab walls and a wrap-around veranda, crammed with Australiana and antiques. One could be forgiven for mistaking this rambling homestead for a genuine colonial-era structure which has evolved organically over time, but the extraordinarily scenic unfurling of the building's approach, spatial planning and sequence of contrived views across the landscape all indicate it as the work of a single mind. Here, perhaps, is the most concrete and succinct expression of late twentieth-century 'Hawkesbury picturesque' vision, reflected (much less successfully) in numerous buildings since. Take Windsor's kitsch, postmodern 'Riverview Shopping Centre' (2006), for example, whose Disneyesque colonial streetscape conceals a conventional retail warehouse behind. Such elaborations on the truth are equally evident in literary and television fiction – for example, in Kate Grenville's quasi-historical novels *The Secret River* (2005, adapted for television by ABC in 2015) and *Sarah Thornhill* (2011), which follow the transformed fortunes of a transported convict whose children become affluent landholders on the river.

160 *Translating images of Richmond*

Figure 4.6 Local craftsman Dennis Mahboub's remarkable colonial style home (constructed from 1980 onwards), overlooking the Grose River above Richmond.

What is important to understand is that the depiction of the Hawkesbury which persists today – as an effortlessly idyllic, quaint landscape – belies the truth of its creation. This had been a landscape transformed and managed by aboriginal farming practices, explored and settled despite significant hardships and carefully planned via the colonial mechanisms of surveying, land grants, township plans and building regulations. In this sense, British colonial practices (informed by a culturally engrained aesthetic) supplanted aboriginal management of the landscape. This is apparent in both depictions of the landscape and in cultural products (the arts, architecture, literature, photography, television and cinematography) which reflect, and conform to, the aesthetics of 'Hawkesbury picturesque' vision.

'No trucks through historic square!'

On a warm summer morning in 2017 traffic is streaming through Windsor's Thompson Square, apparently undeterred by banners strung across historic verandas and placards tied to picket fences (Figure 4.7). Thompson Square has become 'ground zero' for a 24-hour, six-year-long sit-in protest, conducted from the Community Action for Windsor Bridge's (CAWB)

Figure 4.7 Placards and banners rail against the construction of a new road bridge through Windsor's historic (and scenic) Thompson Square. A classical villa is the obvious billboard for these sentiments. View of the CAWB War Office in Windsor's Thompson Square.

dedicated 'War Office'.[66] The group's campaign – the longest running in Australia's history – targets the New South Wales government's proposals to erect a new bridge across the Hawkesbury, which campaigners claim would be "destructive to the unique and fragile heritage of an important part of our nation's history"[67] through altering the town's historic physical and visual relationship to the river. What is interesting for the purposes of this book is the means by which campaigners have presented their arguments; during the somewhat bizarre opening of the group's 'War Office', campaigners modelling themselves on infamous nineteenth-century bushrangers 'The Wild Colonial Boys' rode horses across Windsor Bridge and hoisted the Eureka flag in Thompson Square,[68] symbolic of a form of vigilante attack on the state government. Such a theatrical statement was clearly based upon culturally engrained – somewhat nostalgic and embellished – national stereotypes and historical themes.[69] For example, local resident Nina Butler described Thompson Square as

> the birthplace of the great Australian ideal of a 'fair go'. Thompson was just a convict but he rolled his sleeves up and [became a successful

businessman]. This place is integral to the spirit of our country and I think that's worth fighting for.[70]

Alongside these events a display of historic photographs and paintings of the Hawkesbury River took centre stage, erected prominently within the square, accompanied by descriptions which lamented the ongoing erosion of the town's historic and picturesque river views. Despite the obvious paradox that the town's existing bridge was constructed in 1874, and the current road cut through the square in the 1920s, leader of CAWB Harry Terry has stated, "You look out here and you can see what it looked like in 1814 [. . .]. The history is right here in front of you".[71] Even the group's website is headed by a historic photograph of the river and town, to which a digital 'watercolour' filter has been applied – a typical example of the tendency to view the Hawkesbury region through a painterly and nostalgic lens.[72]

While bridge proponents argue that the few available crossings act as bottlenecks, forcing traffic to queue through the historic centres of the towns, and constricting the economic growth of the region, bridge opponents view the proposed construction as a blot on the picturesque aesthetic and heritage values of Windsor's views, arguing that the construction of a crossing elsewhere would facilitate the restoration of Thompson Square to its original form. With an Upper House Enquiry proceeding into the future of the bridge proposals in 2018, it seems that there is still some way to go before the dispute is settled, though it does seem that the heritage argument put forwards by CAWB has gained traction within the state government. Either way, it is easy to draw parallels between the current movement to save Windsor's riverside and the early twentieth-century 'Indignation' campaigns which led to the protection of Richmond Hill's view over the River Thames, Surrey; both have been based upon the notion that these river landscapes have been significant to landscape art movements, and possess national and international historical significance more broadly.

Concluding remarks

The tendency to view the Hawkesbury River landscape with the same painterly and nostalgic vision by which Richmond Hill, Surrey, has been viewed should, in the light of this chapter, be understood as more than simply coincidence. In fact, before Europeans had even set foot within this landscape they had projected a vision of Richmond Hill upon it – the upper Hawkesbury would, they insisted (to invested parties both at home and in London), be a prosperous agricultural land capable of sustaining the colony of New South Wales in the long term. The careful administration of the Hawkesbury settlements' development also ensured that they evolved in line with this predetermined vision; land grants of 30 acres set the landscape on a path towards genteel villas set within generous grounds, while regulations determining layout and building construction set the parameters for Richmond's and Windsor's handsome townscapes.

Throughout the course of the region's development, comparisons between the visual characteristics of the Hawkesbury and Thames landscapes were routinely made, with the effect of writing out the aboriginal history and contribution to the landscape. This was perpetuated by the work of travelling artists who tended to depict – at first – 'empty' natural wildernesses and later quaint colonial farmsteads, both streams of which contributed to national movements in landscape art. When local residents amassed fortunes from exploiting the land (either along the Hawkesbury or elsewhere in Sydney or further afield in the gold mines and cattle stations of New South Wales) it ought not to be surprising that they looked to the fashions and established patterns of aristocratic Britain for their models – for example, Phillip Charley's construction of Belmont Park (built 1892), a sandstone mansion atop Richmond Hill and his landscaping of the surrounding riverside estate in the English picturesque manner. Polo, stud farming and river regattas (even motor excursions in, reputedly, Australia's first Rolls Royce) are all considered to have completed Charley's vision of British gentlemanly life along the river (reminiscent of Kenneth Grahame's *Wind in the Willows*, 1908) at the far-flung edges of empire.

This is the Hawkesbury vision which persisted in the late twentieth-century craze for 'restoring' heritage buildings and in the pseudo-historical forms adopted for new buildings, and which continues to persist in the cultural products of landscape art, literature, television and cinematography today; the Hawkesbury's landscape views have become inextricably linked with colonial history, heroic national figures and personal 'rags-to-riches' tales, so much so that the proposal for a new road bridge across the river at Windsor has been charged as an attack on the very fabric of Australian identity. Yet, although views of the Hawkesbury are presented as *benign* amenities with aesthetic and heritage value to *all*, obvious questions remain about to *whom* these landscape views have been and are valuable, and what are the *values* embedded within such perceptions – perceptions which ultimately displaced traditional indigenous understanding of the landscape and continue to wield a controlling power over its architectural and urban development.

Notes

1 For example, George Burnett Barton, recounting Governor Phillip's expedition along the Hawkesbury of 1789, writes, "The banks at this part of the river had the appearance of being ploughed up, 'as if a vast herd of swine had been living on them'. When they went on shore to examine the ground they found 'the wild yam in considerable quantities, but in general very small, not larger than a walnut'. The natives had done the ploughing". G. Burnett Barton, *History of New South Wales from the Records, Vol. 1 Governor Phillip* (Sydney: Charles Potter, 1889).

2 P. Boon, *The Hawkesbury River: A Social and Natural History* (Clayton, Victoria: CSIRO Publishing, 2017), p. 258.
3 R. B. Walker, in the foreword to D. G. Bowd, *Macquarie Country: A History of the Hawkesbury* (Melbourne, Victoria: F. W. Cheshire, 1969), p. ii
4 Boon, *The Hawkesbury River*, p. 221.
5 Ibid., p. 221.
6 R. Parkin, *H. M. Endeavour* (Victoria: The Miegunyah Press, 2003), p. 205.
7 E. Favenc, quoted in Boon, *The Hawkesbury River*, p. 268.
8 S. Ryan, *The Cartographic Eye: How Explorers Saw Australia* (Cambridge: Cambridge University Press, 1996), p. 54.
9 Ibid.
10 This physical act, along with the common symbolic acts of sovereignty, such as erecting cairns, making inscriptions or hoisting flags, could also be viewed as proof of presence in the landscape and as a violent act of colonial possession.
11 B. Field, *Geographical Memoirs of New South Wales* (Lausanne: University of Lausanne, 2009), pp. 422–423.
12 S. Ryan, *The Cartographic Eye: How Explorers Saw Australia* (Cambridge: Cambridge University Press, 1996), p. 56.
13 Ibid.
14 T. Mitchell, *Journal of an Expedition into the Interior of Tropical Australia* in Search of a Route from Sydney to the Gulf of Carpentaria (1848), pp. 135–136.
15 Ibid., p. 222.
16 Ryan has also argued that the picturesque legitimised the absurdity of projecting imaginary 'castles' onto the Australian landscape (e.g., numerous 'Castle Rocks', 'Turrets', 'Towers' and 'ruinous' cliffs) through appealing variously to the aesthetic sensibilities of the reader and the picturesque convention's requirements for a varied middle ground and served to project European culture into a landscape considered to be both 'empty' and 'without history'. Ryan, *The Cartographic Eye*, pp. 77–81.
17 Ryan, *The Cartographic Eye*, p. 74.
18 C. Sturt, *Narrative of an Expedition into Central Australia, Performed under the Authority of Her Majesty's Government, during the Years 1844, 5 and 6 Together with a Notice of the Province of South Australia, in 1847*, 2 vols. (London: T & W Boone, 1849), vol. 1. p. 108.
19 For example, the tendency of some journals to describe Australian flora, fauna and indigenous peoples as peculiar, perverse or odd in relation to the rest of the known world. See J. Oxley, *Journals of Two Expeditions into the Interior of New South Wales, Undertaken by Order of the British Government in the Years 1817–18* (London: Murray, 1820), p. 81; G. Grey, *Journals of Two Expeditions of Discovery in North-West and Western Australia, during the Years 1837, 38, and 39, under the Authority of Her Majesty's Government Describing Many Newly Discovered, Important, and Fertile Districts, with Observations on the Moral and Physical Condition of the Aboriginal Inhabitants*, 2 vols. (London: T & W Boone, 1841), p. 207.
20 Ryan, *The Cartographic Eye*, p. 74.
21 Ibid., p. 57.
22 Mitchell, *Journal of an Expedition into [. . .] Tropical Australia*, p. 309.
23 Bowd, *Macquarie Country*, p. 2.
24 Ibid., p. 2.
25 J. Bach, ed., *John Hunter: An Historical Record of Events at Sydney and at Sea, 1787–1792* (Sydney: Royal Australian Historical Society and Angus & Robertson, 1968), p. 104.

26 G. Burnett Barton, *History of New South Wales from the Records, Vol. 1 Governor Phillip* (Sydney: Charles Potter, 1889), p. 21.
27 Ibid.
28 Because European explorers did not understand indigenous farming and burning practices they viewed Aboriginal peoples as property-less and the landscape before them as a *terra nullius*. This was founded on the belief that "land as property primarily meant agricultural land to the European mind [...] supported by the eighteenth century property theory of John Locke: 'he that in Obedience to this Command of God, subdued, tilled and sowed any part of it, therby [sic] annexed to it something that was his *Property*, which another had no Title to, nor could without injury take from him'". J. Locke, quoted in Ryan, *The Cartographic Eye*, p. 156.
29 Bowd, *Macquarie Country*, pp. 3–4.
30 Burnett Barton, *History of New South Wales from the Records*.
31 Ibid.
32 Ibid.
33 L. Groom, *A Steady Hand: Governor Hunter and His First Fleet Sketchbook* (Canberra, ACT: National Library of Australia, 2012), p. 94.
34 Boon, *The Hawkesbury River*, p. 284.
35 Ibid., p. 285.
36 J. Barkley-Jack, *Hawkesbury Settlement Revealed: A New Look at Australia's Third Mainland Settlement 1793–1802* (Dural: Rosenberg Publishing, 2009), p. 10.
37 Ibid., p. 27.
38 W. Tench, *A Complete Account of the Settlement at Port Jackson* (Adelaide: University of Adelaide Press, 2014).
39 L. Macquarie, *Journals of His Tours in New South Wales and Van Diemen's Land 1810–1822* (Sydney: Trustees of the Public Library of New South Wales, 1956), pp. 31–32.
40 J. M. Freeland, *Architecture in Australia: A History* (Ringwood: Penguin, 1968), p. 31.
41 Boon, *The Hawkesbury River*, p. 221.
42 S. Webb, *Palaeopathology of Aboriginal Australians: Health and Disease across a Hunter-Gatherer Continent* (Cambridge: Cambridge University Press, 1995), p. 286.
43 Boon, *The Hawkesbury River*, p. 301.
44 J. Kohen, *The Darug and Their Neighbours: The Traditional Aboriginal Owners of the Sydney Region* (Blacktown, NSW: Blacktown and District Historical Society, 1993).
45 Boon, *The Hawkesbury River*, p. 302.
46 Ibid., p. 303.
47 L. Stewart, *Blood Revenge: Murder on the Hawkesbury 1799* (Dural: Rosenberg Publishing, 2015).
48 Boon, *The Hawkesbury River*, p. 304.
49 Ibid., p. 302.
50 For more on the Aboriginal cost of colonial expansion see K. Willey, *When the Sky Fell Down: The Destruction of the Tribes of the Sydney Region 1788–1850s* (Sydney & London: HarperCollins Pty Ltd, 1979); J. Kohen, *The Dharug and Their Neighbours*, 1993; I. Clendinnen, *Dancing with Strangers* (Cambridge: Cambridge University Press, 2003); P. Turbet, *The First Frontier: The Occupation of the Sydney Region 1788–1816* (Dural: Rosenberg Publishing, 2011); Stewart, *Blood Revenge*; J. Connor, *The Australian Frontier Wars 1788–1838* (Sydney,

51 Turbet, The First Frontier, p. 230.
52 Connor, The Australian Frontier Wars.
53 John Hirst, *Sense & Nonsense in Australian History* (Melbourne, VIC: Black Inc. Agenda, 2009), p. 211.
54 J. D. Lang, Volume 2 of An Historical and Statistical Account of New South Wales, Both as a Penal Settlement and as a British Colony (Cambridge: Cambridge University Press, 2011), p. 103.
55 For example, Martens's *Regentville, Near Penrith* (1835), *Invermien* (c. 1862), *Tempe, Seat of A. B. Spark Esq.* (1838) and *Salisbury Court, New England*.
56 Boon, *The Hawkesbury River*, p. 476.
57 J. Cato, *The Story of the Camera in Australia* (Melbourne: Institute of Australian Photography, 1977), p. 31.
58 T. Bonyhady, *The Colonial Earth* (Melbourne: Miegunyah Press, 2000) p. 144.
59 *The Picturesque Atlas of Australasia* (1886), quoted in Boon, *The Hawkesbury River*, p. 480.
60 Even depicting it in *Traveller's Rest*, also known as *The Old Inn, Richmond, Hawkesbury River* (1896).
61 A. Streeton, quoted in J. Doherty, "Conder and Streeton Were No Strangers to the Hawkesbury", *Hawkesbury Gazette* (19 February 2016).
62 Including *The Australian Road* (1896), *A Road to Kurrajong* (1896), *A Surveyor's Camp, Upper Hawkesbury* (1896), *Summer Noon, Hawkesbury River* (1896), *Grey Day on the Hawkesbury* (1896), *The River* (1896) and two versions of *The Hawkesbury River* (1896).
63 E. Johns, A. Sayers, E. M. Kornhauser and A. Ellis, *New Worlds from Old: 19th Century Australian and American Landscapes* (Canberra: National Gallery of Australia, 1998), p. 187.
64 Among Sydney Long's paintings of the Hawkesbury are *In the Spring* (c. 1895), *Feeding Time* (c. 1895), *Midday* (1896), *The River* (c. 1896), *The Valley* (1898) and *Hawkesbury at Wisemans Ferry* (1925–26).
65 B. Smith and R. Shaw, *The Windsor Group, 1935–1945: An Account of Nine Young Sydney Artists Who Painted in [. . .] Richmond and Especially Windsor* (Collaroy, NSW: Edwards & Shaw, 1989).
66 B. La Cioppa, "Bridge Action Group Opens Windsor 'War Office' ", *Hawkesbury Gazette* (1 August 2012).
67 www.cawb.com.au [accessed 17/04/2018].
68 La Cioppa, "Bridge Action Group Opens Windsor 'War Office' ".
69 A composite of themes including national heroes (e.g., Ned Kelly, a member of the 'Wild Colonial Boys'), the Eureka Riots (the beginning of the labour movement in Australia, sparked by protests against government controls during Victoria's gold rush) and more general stereotypes of the hard-working, no-nonsense Australian.
70 N. Butler, quoted in B. James, "How a Pop-Up Rally Became Australia's Longest Running Protest (. . .) and It's Still Going", *The Daily Telegraph* (10 March 2018).
71 H. Terry, quoted in James, "How a Pop-Up Rally Became Australia's Longest Running Protest (. . .) and It's Still Going".
72 www.cawb.com.au [accessed 17/04/2018].

5 Richmond Hill, Port Elizabeth, South Africa

In the previous chapters of this book I have suggested that the projection of an acculturated view of 'Richmond Hill' – itself emblematic of broader conventions of vision, including the panoramic and the picturesque – upon North American and Australian landscapes coincided with the displacement of indigenous understandings of the land and the violent processes of colonial possession. If this is so, might the same be observed in other colonies of the British Empire, or did the overlaying of 'Richmond Hills' serve different purposes and embody different values in other social, cultural and temporal contexts? In this chapter I follow the example of Richmond Hill, Port Elizabeth, South Africa, with the aim of further unpicking the values at work in the projection of this particular view.

Located on the south-eastern coast of South Africa, around 700 kilometres from Cape Town, the region of Port Elizabeth (today widely known as 'PE') had been explored by Portuguese explorers from 1488 onwards. Settled by the Dutch East India Company from 1652, and subsequently occupied by the British during the Napoleonic Wars, the region became part of Britain's Cape Colony. Although an informal European settlement had existed around Port Elizabeth's historic Fort Frederick (constructed by the British in 1799 and named after Frederick, Duke of York), the town, commonly viewed as the nation's second oldest settlement, was officially established by the Cape Colony government only in 1820. By encouraging the settlement of the colony's borderlands[1] with 4,000 white settlers, the founding of Port Elizabeth was part of a broader colonial strategy to strengthen British possession of the land against indigenous Xhosa occupation.

Nine successive 'Frontier Wars' erupted between the Xhosa and colonists from 1779 to 1879.[2] Bolstering the population of white settlers in the Eastern Cape was viewed as a means to reinforce colonial control over the land, but expulsion of native peoples altogether was not the goal. Rather, governor of Cape Colony Sir George Grey, who had gained first-hand experience of colonial governance by serving first as governor of South Australia (1841–45) and second as governor of New Zealand (1845–53), viewed the integration of native peoples as critical to (colonists') peace and prosperity. Grey was quoted as saying, "We should try to make them (the Xhosas) a part of ourselves, with a common faith and common interests, useful servants, consumers of our goods, contributors to our revenue".[3] It may be abhorrent today, but to Grey, the integration of the Xhosa into colonial society as a subordinate labouring class was both good governance and commercially astute. Under his leadership the colonial government introduced European, Christian mission–style education and wage labour, encouraging an influx of native migrants to Port Elizabeth in search of education and work.

An insight into the motives of the town's early development is given by the composition of its first Municipal Board, formed in 1848, of which six of the eight elected commissioners had commercial interests in shipping and a burgeoning wool farming industry. Although many of these industries were reliant upon the availability of low-paid indigenous labourers, a rising merchant middle class also increasingly lobbied for the regulation and control of native settlements, and even for their removal to make way for expanding farms, factories and middle-class suburbs. As such, indigenous homes were liable to be removed and destroyed without notice wherever they were not expressly granted permission, leading to the establishment of permitted native settlement sites, to be known as 'Locations'.[4]

Strangers' Location

It is within this context that the settlement which would later become 'Richmond Hill' first formed. Port Elizabeth's 'Central' district, laid out in typical colonial fashion on a grid plan and around a central square, was home to the majority of white European settlers, while migrants, farm workers, domestic servants and the unemployed were compelled to live on the edge of the town, on the adjacent hill across Hyman's Kloof.[5] As Martin Hall has described, the segregation of people in this way into 'civilised' and 'uncivilised' groups reflects the contrast between the geometric regularity of the urban grid "imposed on the troubling disorder of the colonised landscape" as constructed through colonial-era accounts of the Cape Colony.[6] For example, Francois Valentyn described Table Mountain above Cape Town as "barren and rocky", "everything that is horrid and frightening", in contrast to the "very fine and delightful arbours roofed with foliage, where one can long sit hidden from everyone" and where "Nature and Art seem to have brought together in unity all that can give pleasure".[7] The separation of indigenous African populations into 'reservations' or townships known as 'Locations' reflects the notion that 'civilised' and 'uncivilised' populations required differing forms of governance. Theophilus Shepstone, secretary for native affairs in the South African province of Natal, wrote that

> Whilst humanity, and especially the injunctions of our religion compel us to recognise in the native the capability of being elevated to perfect equality, social and political, with the white man, yet it is as untrue as it would be unwise to say, that the native is now in this position, or that

he is in his present state capable of enjoying or even understanding the civil and political rights of the white man. Her Majesty's government has most wisely recognised and acted upon this principle by providing a form of government for the natives [. . .] which [. . .] is capable of being modified as to advance their progress towards a higher and better civilisation.[8]

According to Gail Ching-Liang Low, Shepstone's belief that indigenous peoples were not yet 'capable' of regular governance segregates native reality and time from colonial reality and time – "Segregation and 'reservations' ", Low argues, "pretend to a pristine, frozen native time".[9] In the colonial conception of time as linear, the colonised are *prehistoric*, and might expect to achieve 'civilisation' if they accept governance and follow guidance from colonisers.[10] Shepstone's implementation of controlled native settlement, the establishment of 'Locations', displaced indigenous populations from both South Africa's urban centres and natural landscapes, separating them into a different space and time. Just as the native was prehistoric, history begins with the coloniser; the presence of the white settler in the 'empty' landscape was often depicted as the domestication of "wild country into a safe and pastoral one; here a man may live and work like an original Adam, creating and refashioning an Eden".[11]

Appearing on a detailed map of 1849,[12] the hilltop settlement above Port Elizabeth's Hyman's Kloof was partially legitimised via a colonial government land grant of 1855, which allowed for the temporary abode of "foreign natives" or "strangers" visiting or working in Port Elizabeth.[13] Known as 'Strangers' Location' (or 'Fingo City', after the many Mfengu people, along with Xhosa, Basotho, Zulu and Khoi, who resided there), the use of the word 'Location' for these settlements[14] seems to demand their temporary nature, denying them the dignity of a proper name, or even the permanency of a descriptive title, like 'settlement' or 'township', limiting them to geographical coordinates incapable of possessing a real sense of place or cultural life of their own. By 1884, however, 'Strangers' Location', a 'temporary' settlement of simple cottages and round, grass-thatched 'beehive' huts, had become very much a permanent home for as many as 1,700 people.[15]

This had been largely the result of rapid population growth,[16] firstly because of the development of the railway in 1873, which enabled the town's port to service a wide area of the Cape Colony, secondly because indigenous migrants were forced into Locations or risked the destruction of their homes and property at the hands of the municipal government[17] and thirdly due to the displacement of both settler and indigenous communities by the Boer Wars (1880–81; 1899–1902). While strict Calvinist Boer farmers had earlier in the century viewed native peoples virtually as slaves to their God-given right over the land, in the urban Locations displaced natives were granted the relative liberty of the government's permission to erect homes in exchange for the payment of ground rent.[18] The London Missionary Society also took a land grant at Strangers' Location, erecting a fine missionary church to serve its thriving community (Figure 5.1).

The increasing permanency of the Locations was a concern to some white settlers, not least the lack of sanitation, building control and planning which totally differentiated them from the colonial city in terms of architectural and urban form. Although a 'model cottage' was erected at Strangers' Location with the intention of compelling migrants to adopt attributes of European domesticity, many continued to construct the traditional round, grass-thatched dwellings with which they were comfortable and familiar. Following an epidemic in 1901, widely blamed on overcrowding and the poor sanitary conditions of Strangers' Location,[19] the government presented its view that the settlement was a "health hazard that needed to be destroyed".[20] While sanitation, propriety and decorum are typical of Victorian value systems, a 1901 article in African newspaper *The Spectator* entitled 'Let Us Be Clean' presented the state of the Locations as the failure of its residents to be respectable citizens of the empire. The editor railed against "the picturesque filth which is permitted to strut about the streets to the delight of the enemies of the race, and the advocates for the inferior treatment of the race but to the disgust of the decent and respectable citizen".[21] The editor's description of the "picturesque filth" of the Locations, a "delight" to the "enemies of the race", reveals the tension between the editor's own sense of imperial citizenship, his ability to both recognise and sympathise with the white colonisers' gaze, and the sense of shame the gaze (both applied and received) induces within himself. The ability of the colonisers' gaze to objectify and racialise is central to Frantz Fanon's seminal *Black Skin, White Masks* (1952).[22] Although the context in this case was francophone Martinique, Fanon's work has broader relevance to other postcolonial states where structures of racial discrimination remain. Fanon viewed colonisation as a violent act, and linked structural racism to the visual sense (the 'scopic drive'), in particular via the gaze's ability to impose

Figure 5.1 View of traditional grass huts and the London Missionary Church, Strangers' Location on Richmond Hill, 1836.

"a sense of blackness which objectifies and alienates the colonised man",[23] rendering "*human beings as matter*".[24] Two years after *The Spectator*'s appeal to clean up the Locations, most of the population of Strangers' Location had been evicted and its buildings razed to the ground or torched, leaving, on a map of 1905, the 'Native Burial Ground' as the only indicator of its prior existence (Figure 5.2). The violence of the white colonisers' gaze,

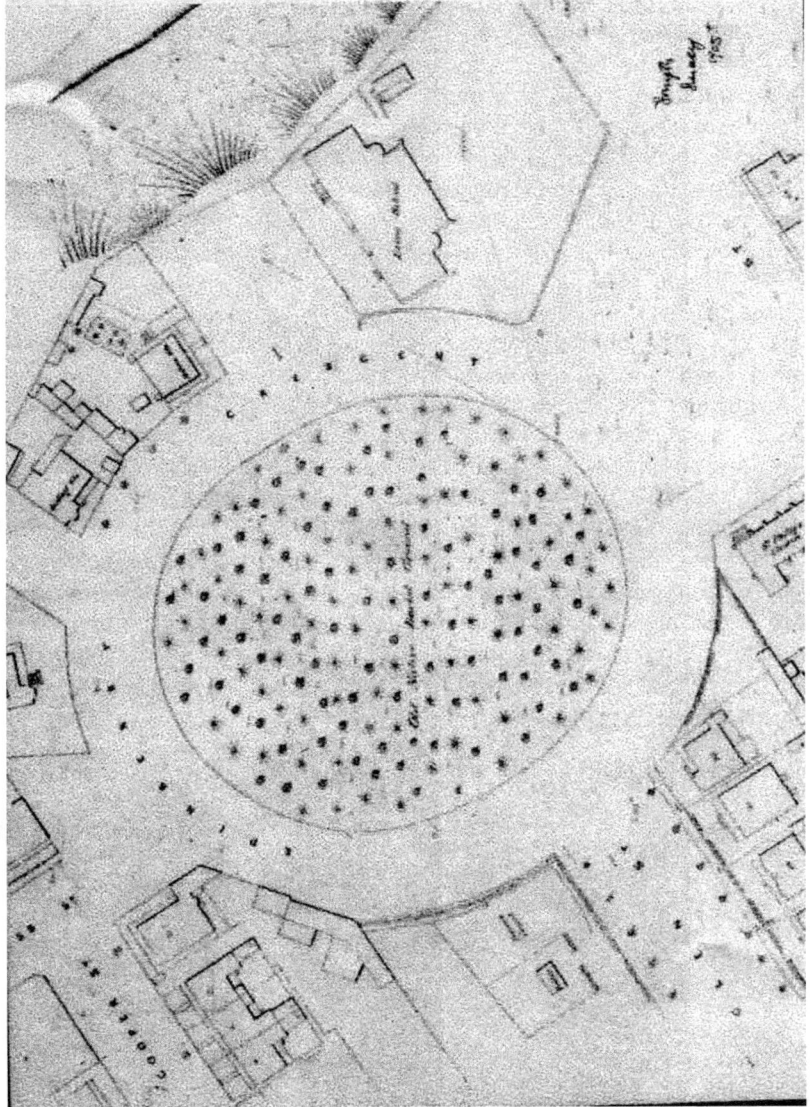

Figure 5.2 Historic plan showing the indigenous burial ground, Richmond Hill.

as described by Fanon some 50 years later, is all too apparent in a 1903 photograph showing timber buildings at Strangers' Location ablaze, under the gaze of white settlers clearly entranced by the spectacle of raging fires and human tragedy (Figure 5.3).

Although the Plague Board did pay compensation to those individuals it evicted from Strangers' Location, compensation was not equal to the value of the land, which, close to Port Elizabeth's Central district and port, ought to have been considerable. According to Vuyisile Msila, many of those evicted used their limited compensation to lease or purchase land (held in freehold) in the neighbouring district of Korsten. However, when later forced to give up freehold property, under the Native Land Act of 1913, no compensation was given and refugees were forced into government tenancies in New Brighton (later to become infamous as 'Red Location', a political stronghold in the struggle against apartheid).[25]

The Native Land Act split opinion among many, but was broadly consistent with the burgeoning nationalism which characterised the period after the Union of South Africa in 1910. To John Merriman, last prime minister of the Cape Colony, racial segregation was the only means by which an 'intelligent' race could be protected from the 'barbarism' of another,[26] while for many white settlers, resentful of their dependence on native farmers, the Native Land Act offered a mechanism by which native sharecroppers would be displaced from the land.[27] Such a displacement of indigenous populations is also apparent in architect Herbert Baker's design for the Union Buildings to house the new South African government (1910), a neoclassical complex placed conspicuously on a hill overlooking a pastoral landscape outside Pretoria. Describing its symmetrical plan, Baker wrote of the "[bringing together] of the two races in South Africa, Boer and Brit", which Nick Shepherd and Noëleen Murray view as an embodiment of the "growing blindness and arrogance of white South Africans to the majority

Figure 5.3 The burning of Strangers' Location, 1903.

black population" which would later characterise the apartheid period.[28] Although a delegation, later to be known as the African National Congress (ANC), was sent to London to express opposition to the Native Land Act, the British government declined to involve itself in the Union of South Africa's internal affairs, setting in motion the foundations of apartheid.[29]

Richmond Hill

The indigenous population of Strangers' Location was forcibly removed less than 50 years after the same municipal government had established, and enforced, its development in 1855. Justified by those in charge on grounds of health, it cannot be overlooked that the municipality stood to benefit financially from the redevelopment of the land, which, located on high ground at the edge of Port Elizabeth and enjoying fine views over the harbour, was likely to become a preferred address for a wealthy, white middle class. That such an outcome could already have been foreseen is suggested by the municipal government's subdivision of land neighbouring Strangers' Location as early as 1866 to pay for the construction of Albany Road through Cooper's Kloof. In a section of the new subdivision a circular road named 'Edinberry Crescent' was constructed around the 'Old Native Burial Ground' in a curious juxtaposition of European urbanism and indigenous memory.[30] Surrounded by comfortable Victorian and Edwardian bungalows, a gothic church and cape Dutch colonial schoolhouse, and commanding wide-ranging views east over the ocean and west over former farmland, this vision of turn-of-the-century colonial comfort eclipsed the site's indigenous history, surviving today as 'Richmond Park, Richmond Hill' (Figure 5.4).

It is somewhat ironic that from the burial ground at Richmond Hill, the observer may look towards 'Red Location', a lone connection between the site of Strangers' Location and the final destination of its displaced peoples. Such a separation demonstrates the force of the privileged white, middle-class gaze, implicit in the processes which drove native people from the frame of view, omitting them from the colonised landscape.

It is also somewhat ironic, given the themes of this book, that it should be a 'Richmond Hill' which becomes the mechanism of displacement and obliteration of indigenous memory. According to the applicant for the Port Elizabeth suburb's official name (it was officially named 'Richmond Hill' only in 1991, though had been unofficially so since at least the late nineteenth century), the area was known as such due to a large number of the 1820s British settlers having been from the Thames-side town in Surrey, England. However, the idea that many were English, let alone from Richmond, seems fictitious. C. V. Reed writes that "funded by a £50,000 grant from parliament, 4,000 British (mostly Scottish) settlers arrived in [Port Elizabeth] to farm the land with free labour and consolidate the frontier in 1820".[31] The mythology of 1820, celebrated today with its own ritual ceremonies and fictions, has nurtured unique local narratives of belonging.

Figure 5.4 The view from Richmond Hill, Port Elizabeth, today.

According to Saul Solomon, Graham's Town "pride[d] itself, and not quite unreasonably, [as] the most thoroughly English town in Southern Africa".³² Other place names, such as Caversham Glen, Featherbrooke Estate, Walmer Downs, Wibsey Dip, Croquet Lawn and Faerie Glen, intentionally recalled British landscapes in a manner which Elwyn Jenkins has described as "excruciating examples of the chocolate-box variety".³³ This is consistent with much research on the subject of toponymy in postcolonial studies. For example, in "Changing Place Names in Post-Apartheid South Africa" author Mcebisi Ndletyana writes that place names are "an outward manifestation of how people perceive themselves, both their history and value system",³⁴ drawing upon Cohen and Kliot's argument that toponyms are part of a "process of attaching meaning to one's surrounding through mutual sharing of symbols" as "part of human comprehension and socialization".³⁵ In a study of colonial Singapore, Yeoh interpreted the use of dislocation in names such as 'Devonshire Road' or 'Chatsworth Road' as indicative of settlers who sought to "escape the impress of the tropics and native culture and symbolically to exist in British settings",³⁶ although, as Clifton Crais has argued, settlers who came to build "England in miniature", complete with a "manor house on the hill", required "growing markets, plentiful land, docile labourers and a cooperative colonial state".³⁷ Naming practices were thus complicit with the processes which drove social, cultural and political conflicts between white masters and native servants, those in possession of the land and those dispossessed.

The dispossession of indigenous peoples was legitimised in the political statements of numerous authors to local journals. For example, in describing Prince Alfred's visit to the Eastern Cape in 1867, a correspondent of the *Graham's Town Journal* noted Alfred's interest in a number of paintings of the 1820s settlers, elaborating that

> At that time [. . .] the land was peopled with barbarians, who revelled in heathenish customs and rights [. . .]. But England sent forth from her shores the pioneers of civilisation [. . .] as [Alfred] visits town after town, [. . .] [he] will see how well England has done her duty – how well British ideas and habits are spreading amongst the population.³⁸

Such views were seemingly common among the various authors of local journals, and hint at the motivations behind the commissioning of such 'historical' paintings; as Reed notes, in the pages of the *Graham's Town Journal*

> political and cultural discourses appropriated the languages of Britishness and imperial citizenship, particularly through the mythology of 1820, to justify a particular political and social order in the Eastern Cape, which transcended ethnicity and class, legitimised and empowered social elites, and justified the subjugation of local peoples.³⁹

Such feelings of legitimacy revived a fleeting separatist movement to secure the independence of the Eastern Cape from the 'corruption' of the colonial government in the west (which was actually more 'liberal' in outlook). As Reed points out, Albany's 1820s 'radicals' "sought larger land grants, greater control of labour, public offices, and official patronage, to replicate the privileges and patronage of English rural society" in direct conflict with the policies of the British colonial government.[40]

Of course, to suggest that all white South Africans shared oppressive views, or that all non-whites were opposed to empire, would be a gross oversimplification. Contemporary newspapers show that there were those among the white British middle class that advocated strongly for the inclusion of native populations as a matter of principle: that no citizen of the empire should be denied education (if not full-blown equality) on the basis of race.[41] Likewise, among the non-white population there were those – dubbed, somewhat contemptuously, by white commentators the 'respectables'[42] – that viewed support for the empire as "an investment in a just and more equitable future that lived up to the promises of Britishness".[43] However, the usage of the place name 'Richmond Hill' from the late nineteenth century onwards, in its displacement of the uncomfortable realities of Strangers' Location – and the city's Dutch and Afrikaner history alike – seems to parallel the journals' languages of Britishness, imperial citizenship and progress, replicating – and legitimising – a privileged white British landowning class via its connotations of an idealised Thames landscape.

Richmond Hill as emblematic gentrification

If the languages of Britishness and imperial citizenship played a part in the nineteenth-century origins of the name 'Richmond Hill', were there other motives for granting the suburb its official name in 1991? According to one observer, "It was named Richmond Hill in 1991 to better enable easier identification of the historic parts of Port Elizabeth",[44] allowing a number of discrete enclaves of heritage buildings and streets to be grouped together as a coherent 'heritage district'. Interest in 'heritage' had developed as a national project around South Africa's Union in 1910, with the declaration of monuments by the Commission for the Preservation of Natural and Historical Monuments, Relics and Antiques. Although both European and indigenous sites were initially recognised, subsequent amendments had, by 1972, shaped an inventory of mainly European colonial-era buildings as representative of this nationalist history.[45] At the same time, a group of enthusiasts under James Walton came together to form the Vernacular Architecture Society of South Africa in 1964, promoting the appreciation and archaeological recording of 'vanishing' settler or 'folk' architecture from the eighteenth century onwards,[46] an architecture which was increasingly associated with understandings of South African national heritage.[47] The official naming of Richmond Hill in 1991 and its designation as a 'heritage district' reflect the broader themes of this nationalist history promoted during South Africa's apartheid era. Such a practice may be thought of as a form of rebranding exercise, which tended to ignore the area's run-down nature, numerous twentieth-century apartment blocks, social ills and crime problems, promoting only the nostalgic connotations of a genteel colonial past.

In this sense, the district's rebranding tied into the contemporary turn towards heritage conservation as a regenerative force. For example, Port Elizabeth's famous Donkin row houses (Figure 5.5), a terrace of elegant colonial homes descending to the harbour, were heavily 'restored' just a few years prior (1988), under the amateur guidance of – woefully underqualified – medical professional Dr Nic Woolff. Woolff's description of the works, much to the distress of heritage professionals today, argued that the value of Donkin Terrace lay almost solely in its aesthetic (by which Woolff intended to mean a romantic vision of colonial order and uniformity, rather than the characterful jumble which had been the result of numerous phases of building and upgrade), as the quaint backdrop to an open space "where [a] considerable number of [. . .] visitors pass every day".[48] Woolff's approach had been to remove the various brick additions and later cast-iron verandas, evidence of the changing fortunes of individual owners, replacing them with a singular timber veranda design and a unifying paint scheme, in

Figure 5.5 The 'tidied up' colonial vision of the Donkin Street row houses, Port Elizabeth.

an effort "to make them appear largely the same at least at first glance".⁴⁹ Such comments reveal the power of a vision which viewed the colonial past with a degree of romanticism, but whose value lay only in providing an aesthetic experience for the tourist.

The fate of Woolff's sanitised Donkin Street houses, like many other 'heritage restoration' projects in Port Elizabeth from the mid-twentieth century onwards, in many ways reflects a broader movement in the presentation of South African history, which turned away from discourses of colonial 'conquest' towards apparently more benign discourses of 'settlement'. Far from benign, however, Leslie Witz has argued that the dominant historiography of the 1820s settlers in the Eastern Cape, and particularly in Port Elizabeth, had its origins in the apartheid government of 1948. Where previously the discourse of colonial contact had emphasised violent conquest – for example, in the presentation of the then British governor, Harry Smith, as the "great [British] Chief" who ordered the Xhosa chief Makoma "to kneel and set his foot on the Chief's neck",⁵⁰ Witz argues that post-1948 historiography (in line with the policies of the apartheid state) established a sense of legitimacy among those who racially designated themselves as white (inclusive of those of both European and Afrikaner decent), founded upon a unified white identity backed up by a shared heritage of European settlement.⁵¹

Such a turn in the presentation of South African history is evident in the promotion of settler culture throughout the mid-twentieth century – for example, in historically themed festivities, including the three-hundredth anniversary of Jan van Riebeeck's landing. Staged in Port Elizabeth in 1952, the aim of this festival was to present "South Africa after 300 Years – The Building of a Nation", and it centred around themes of Dutch colonial 'discovery' and British colonial 'settlement'. At the festival's close, a bizarre torchlit tableau simultaneously illustrated the historically discrete events of Riebeeck's landing and the landing of the 1820s settlers,⁵² followed by the naming of 'Settlers Park' and the municipality's adoption of a semi-historical coat of arms,⁵³ both contributions to the city's dominant identification with white settler history.⁵⁴ Likewise, institutions such as the Port Elizabeth Historical Society and the Port Elizabeth Ratepayers Association appropriated this historiography, playing down uncomfortable aspects of colonisation, such as the Frontier Wars, in preference for narratives of 'civilisation' and 'settlement'.⁵⁵

Significantly, Palesa Kadi has viewed the promotion of places of selective and sanitised white European heritage, such as the Donkin Street row houses, as symptomatic of this mid-twentieth-century turn in South African historiography.⁵⁶ Conceived by the Port Elizabeth Historical Society, the Donkin Heritage Trail and Richmond Hill Heritage Trail, a 5-kilometre self-guided walking trail linking more than 50 places of Port Elizabeth's European colonial heritage, promote a neatly packaged history of colonial settlement. Along the route, selective examples of Victorian (British) cultural and architectural achievements are presented to heritage tourists, set out in a guidebook available from tourist information centres. Among the prominent landmarks presented are the Donkin Street row houses (symbolic of an idealised colonial domestic life), City Hall and the marble statue of Queen Victoria in Market Square (symbols of imperial governance), the Public Library, Opera Theatre and Cricket Grounds (symbols of 'civilised' colonial culture), the Campanile (symbolic landing place of the 1820s settlers) and the mausoleum to the Cape Colony's governor Sir Rufane Donkin's wife, Elizabeth, after whom Port Elizabeth was named in 1820. It is significant that the trail should end here, on high open ground offering extensive views over the city, landscape and coast beyond, at a monument described by local historian Margaret Herradine as "a pyramid [. . .] not at all unusual for the time" based upon "the memorial to Gaius Cestius in Rome and the British architect Hawksmoor's pyramid in the grounds of Castle Howard in Yorkshire";[57] yet again, it seems that the overlay of a picturesque landscape and its continued promotion via practices of heritage tourism serve to reinforce narratives of the legitimacy of white dominance over the landscape founded upon a shared heritage of European settlement. As Kadi writes, "[I]t is not a history of colonial conquest but a history of settlement that is prominent. [T]he point of the trail is to depict the 'virtues' of settlement and entrench the activities of settlers as 'civilized' ".[58]

Similarly, the naming of Richmond Hill in 1991 acted as a force for gentrification of the district through repackaging it as a suitably picturesque heritage destination for tourists completing South Africa's famous 'Garden Route' from Cape Town to Port Elizabeth. Here, the tourist would find a comfortable, safe district of B&Bs, cafes and 'boutique' shops in adapted heritage buildings (Figure 5.6). That this was the intention of the rebranding exercise is highlighted by the policies put in place by the municipal authorities over the following years: the establishment of the Mandela Bay Development Agency (MBDA) in 2003, with the mandate to "renew, revive and inspire" the city,[59] the promotion of Richmond Hill as a 'gastronomic' destination, and in 2014, the district's designation as a Special Rating Area (SRA). Following the model of Cape Town's 16+ SRAs[60] established from 1994 onwards, property owners pay a supplementary levy to contribute to the costs of private security patrols and targeted gentrification projects within the district.

To some, such moves have successfully encouraged an influx of private sector development in the regeneration of Richmond Hill, marketed by real estate agents as Port Elizabeth's 'most historic' residential area "oozing with colonial charm and bohemian chic";[61] to others, gentrification has priced out local residents and destroyed its character through attracting "a not-so-diverse demographic of patrons [. . .]: the haunt of those privileged enough to enjoy an occasional gourmet dinner [. . .], or those who prefer their beer micro-brewed while discussing the best beard moisturizer".[62] When asked to submit suggestions at a public meeting of the MBDA, one resident wrote,

Figure 5.6 Street scene in gentrified Richmond Hill Special Ratings Area, Port Elizabeth.

"I know what I don't want to see in Central . . . I don't want another Richmond Hill".[63]

The gentrification of Port Elizabeth's Richmond Hill district has been accused of excluding numerous demographics, not least those of modest incomes, residents of social housing and others who do not 'fit' with the district's new identity. In this way there are parallels with colonial naming practices described by Ndletyana, such as the use of place names to indicate the permitted districts of certain racial groups (e.g., 'Arab Street' or 'Chin Chew Street'), justified at the time by colonial administrators for their prevention of "confusion and disputes".[64] This could explain the origins and use of the 'Richmond Hill' name for a district of middle-class white housing from the nineteenth century onwards, as well as calls for its official formalisation in 1991, a time of significant racial tension and rising violent crime rates across South Africa. In effect, the naming of Richmond Hill was more than a benign exercise in rebranding, with knock-on effects which have determined the social and racial fabric of the district. Just as colonial toponymy had acted as a mechanism for racial segregation, so too apartheid-era toponymy may be viewed alongside forced removals, the migrant labour system and the Immorality Act as a means by which the apartheid state controlled the population via spatial segregation.[65] Shepherd and Murray have written, " 'White spaces' and 'black spaces' remained separate through devices such as empty tracts of land – 'buffer zones' between areas declared for different racial groups – [. . .] and spaces of resistance and racial coexistence [. . .] were systematically destroyed".[66] Viewed in this light, the 1991 naming of Richmond Hill could be interpreted as a mechanism by which to officially delineate the neighbourhood as a 'white space', and to displace both its indigenous past and people.

Since the end of the apartheid era in 1994 efforts have been made across South Africa to amend misspelled and contentious colonial place names with respect to indigenous African history, culture and memory, including the renaming of Port Elizabeth's Main Street to Govan Mbeki Street in 2000 and the renaming of the King George VI Art Gallery to the Nelson Mandela Metropolitan Art Museum in 2002. In the process, South Africa was being reframed as the 'Rainbow Nation', characterised by diversity and multiculturalism, under the governance of Mandela's African National Congress.[67] According to Ciraj Rassool, these narratives

> were emerging and taking shape in almost every sphere of heritage construction and public culture in South Africa, from television histories and cultural projects in the press, to the TRC [Truth and Reconciliation Commission] and claims for land, for museums and legacy projects, to new memorials and cultural tourism.[68]

Packaged as the triumphant emergence of a multicultural South Africa, Rassool instead argues that post-apartheid heritage practices created a "kaleidoscope of frozen ethic stereotypes".[69] 'Community tourism', from township tours to the creation of "ethnically packaged cultural villages", including 'Shakaland' in KwaZulu-Natal and 'Xhosaville' in the Eastern Cape,[70] played to these narratives of diversity, while at the same time such 'Disneyfication' of South Africa's heritage also justified the establishment of colonial heritage–themed attractions.

Theorists of postmodernism, such as Edward Soja, have understood such 'historical' attractions as a demonstration of the "intrusion and growing power of an urban hyperreality, of simulations and simulacra [. . .] into the material reality and ideological imagery of urban life".[71] Roy Coleman adds to this analysis, suggesting that "hegemonic images, the preferred connotation and marketing of cities", have become integral to "systems of social control [. . .] normalised into the contemporary urban landscape".[72] Soja's and Coleman's argument may help to explain why, despite such a transformation in understandings of 'heritage' in South Africa at this time, Richmond Hill was not affected by post-apartheid renaming practices: the romantic ideal of colonial Richmond Hill, as symbolised by the neat, ordered elevations of heavy-handed 'restorations' and postmodern new builds, was upheld over the true complexity of the district's history. Certainly, any renaming of Richmond Hill in respect of its indigenous past would have attracted public criticism from local residents and business owners: writing in *The Herald* newspaper, G. E. Turley of Walmer, Port Elizabeth, argued that

> [I]f it is necessary to rid this province of every last vestige of colonial rule why not demolish all the cities, towns, roads, and factories built by colonialists and start afresh?
>
> The bald truth is, of course, that the colonists brought civilization and creature com-forts [. . .] and without their efforts [. . .] the current elite who govern this country would not now be enjoying the good life with all the trappings of luxury they feel they deserve.[73]

Such a sentiment was repeated by another Port Elizabeth contributor to *The Herald*, who stated in incendiary terms that

> [t]o carry this name changing frenzy to its ridiculous conclusion and get rid of everything colonial, we should also throw out the English language, isolate ourselves from the rest of the developed world and go back to living in the trees.[74]

Where toponymical amendments led, calls for more drastic physical interventions followed. In Port Elizabeth in particular, historical statues became the focus of contested viewpoints. Regional deputy chair of the African National Congress Mike Xego argued in a series of newspaper articles (2004) for the replacement of all colonial statues with those reflecting the African struggle. Of particular offence to Xego was the marble statue of Queen Victoria, which now found itself standing in the recently renamed Govan Mbeki Avenue. Xego argued that "It must be dug out, the more I pass it, the more I feel like pulling it down as the American and British soldiers did to the Saddam Hussein statue in Iraq", adding that it should be replaced with "one representing African kings and queens".[75] Of course, Xego's comments divided observers between those in support and those in vehement disagreement. One resident argued that "if Xego was offended by the colonial past, why stop at statues? Why do you wear a suit, ties and shoes and why not wear some African king's attire? [. . .] For that matter switch off the electricity and pull down the telephone lines",[76] while another noted that "seeing all these things as evil, the library, the railway line and St Georges Park Cricket grounds should be destroyed as well".[77]

One could argue that such activities in the manipulation of heritage have in effect served to strengthen and embed the identity of Richmond Hill despite its relatively recent definition from 1991 onwards: the district's predominantly white middle-class residents, charging the authorities with a desecration of colonial heritage through post-apartheid renaming practices and the threat of physical destruction, have reacted by clinging on to vestiges of the colonial past, conceiving Richmond Hill as a distinct and sanitised heritage compound protected from the 'outside' by special security patrols. In the process Richmond Hill perpetuates the promotion of a sanitised version of its historical past to a predominantly white middle class and international tourist demographic.

Policing Richmond Hill: vision, surveillance and the SRA

It is important here to stress the role of the visual sense in contested interpretations of Port Elizabeth's heritage. The Port Elizabeth Historical Society's Donkin and Richmond Hill Heritage Trails are predominantly visual itineraries, with a particular focus on celebrating the architectural and aesthetic achievements of European colonists. In drawing attention to Port Elizabeth's restored and sanitised heritage buildings, such as the Donkin Street row houses, Elizabeth Donkin's mausoleum and Richmond Hill's picturesque colonial bungalows, the trails promote an idealised vision of the colonial past centred around 'civilised' domestic life. At the same time, it is the *sight* of Queen Victoria's statue and the *gaze* of the statue over the city's spaces of civic governance which so offended Xego. In each case distinct interpretations of heritage are cast by the gaze, determined by what is seen, what is unseen, by whom and from which vantage points.

If the visual sense plays an important part in the construction of distinct heritage narratives, it is also implicit in forging exclusive interpretations of heritage, identity and belonging (and likewise, un-belonging). This has its most literal manifestation in the Special Ratings Area administration of Richmond Hill, policed by private security patrols who provide 24-hour surveillance across the district, and whose logo, emblazoned across patrol cars, rubbish bins and social networking websites, is an ever-watching eye (Figures 5.7 and 5.8).

Figure 5.7 Waste bin emblazoned with the all-seeing eye, logo of the Richmond Hill Special Ratings Area.

First director of the Richmond Hill SRA Kevin Slattery has stated, "Maintaining the historic value and [. . .] character of our suburb is one of our core values",[78] values which the SRA authority urged would drive up property values within the district.[79] To achieve this, from April 2015 Richmond Hill residents have been charged an additional levy,[80] covering

Figure 5.8 Richmond Hill Special Ratings Area patrol car.

the costs of security patrol officers, branded vehicles and uniforms, and a cleaning service over and above standard municipal services. The almost absurd sense of Richmond Hill's constant surveillance is given by statements in the local press: for example, Slattery stated that "We have a 24 hour visible patrolling service [. . .]. Our patrollers are in constant contact with the SA Police Service and the private security companies",[81] while another correspondent writes that "SRA members make use of two-way radios to communicate with each other during neighbourhood patrols. [. . .] [helping to] keep the suburb looking lovely and litter free".[82] The organisation also constantly monitors its social media pages, with one reviewer noting that "In August someone tried to break into my house but I notified the SRA through WhatsApp and within seconds they arrived at my house".[83] Such anecdotes, along with conspicuous branding in the form of special uniforms, branded patrol cars, signs, bins and lamp posts, serve to heighten the sense of constant surveillance over the community.

Evident in the Richmond Hill SRA's branding is an almost violent sense of penetration into people's private lives – following Edward Said's understanding of the 'Other' in *Orientalism*,[84] the surveillance gaze distances the self from the unwanted 'Other', be it a gang of youths, homeless person, suspicious individual or simply someone who doesn't 'fit'. At the same time, such a sense of 'otherness' defines the self and feeds into the delineation of boundaries and processes of inclusion and exclusion. Mike Davis has argued that "The universal and ineluctable consequence of this crusade" in private urban surveillance will be "the destruction of accessible public space", adding that the "privatisation of the architectural public realm [. . .] is shadowed by parallel restructuring of electronic space, as heavily policed, pay-access information orders; elite data-bases and subscription cable services appropriate parts of the invisible agora".[85] To Davis, private surveillance is part of an exclusionary force, which will ultimately forge "fortress cities, brutally divided between fortified cells of affluent society and places of terror where the police battle the criminalized poor":[86] a place where "the market provision of security generates its own paranoid demand".[87]

In the example of Richmond Hill, Port Elizabeth, surveillance moves beyond the prevention of crime, affecting the actions of residents through a psychological power imbalance – a sense not unlike that experienced by the inmate in Foucault's description of nineteenth-century prison design, the *Panopticon*;[88] residents take more care to prevent litter, and to maintain outwardly visible aspects of their properties and gardens. In this sense, the establishment of an SRA is not unlike the development rules applied to urban developments of the 'New Urbanism', including Seaside, Florida, or, in the UK, HRH Prince Charles's Poundbury, Dorset, which may regulate everything from refuse schedules to acceptable paint colours. In her discussion of New Urbanism, Amanda Rees describes it as a form of postmodernism influenced by traditional senses of community and neighbourhood interaction. According to Rees, practitioners of New Urbanism believed that "physical design can promote and discourage behaviours and attitudes".[89] Observing the relationship made between neighbourhood surveillance and a broader, controlling society in *The Truman Show* (1998), Rees notes the film's setting of Seaside, Florida, as a means to "signify controlled perfection as part of a larger, damning critique of the vacuity of contemporary life".[90] Similarly, Martin Hall has painted a bleak picture of contemporary South Africa, which he sees as being "particularly susceptible to [a] combination of nostalgia, desire and consumerism, which provide new senses of home in a burgeoning, but markedly unequal, economy".[91] To Hall, South Africa's heritage-themed retail destinations (of which the Richmond Hill SRA is arguably one example), featuring secure parking, perimeter controls, surveillance and security, are defined by exclusivity and exclusion, and their packaging of entertainment "seek[s] to legitimate [. . .] new grids of control and authority".[92] The prevalence of enclosed luxury malls (Figure 5.9) and Special Ratings Areas within South Africa is considered by some to be a sad indictment of the nation's pursuit of surveillance, private security and private finance as remedies for continuing social ills, while others have lauded the scheme for regenerating once neglected inner-city neighbourhoods, boosting safety and service provision within areas marketed to an elite as 'boutique', 'safe' and brimming with 'heritage character'.

Figure 5.9 The ultimate expression of a safe, secure, picturesque environment: Port Elizabeth's Disneyesque 1990s Boardwalk Mall, Summerstrand.

Concluding observations

Through a detailed study of Richmond Hill, Port Elizabeth, South Africa, this chapter has argued that connotations of 'Richmond', loosely based upon the model of the Thames-side British town of the same name, have been used from the late nineteenth century as a means to displace indigenous Africans from the landscape. Surely, this chapter argues, there must have been a relationship between the connotations of an affluent, white, English middle class projected by descriptions and depictions of Richmond-upon-Thames and the transformation of 'Strangers' Location' into 'Richmond Hill' that commenced from the middle of the nineteenth century. What may first appear as an apparently innocent change of place name may be reinterpreted, in the light of South Africa's more recent experiments in toponymical change, as intensely political. The immense power of such place names to convey associations, values and expectations is apparent in the phenomenon of Richmond Hill's Special Ratings Area designation, and the sense of constant surveillance which has shaped not only the aesthetic appearance of the neighbourhood but also the very composition of its social fabric.

Notes

1. The establishment of official colonial borders might be viewed as the origins of racial segregation in South Africa. In the 1770s, Baron Joachim van Plettenberg, governor of the Cape of Good Hope (1771–1785), had declared the Bushman's River Mountains and the Fish River as official borders, with the intention to separate whites and non-whites in the prevention of violence.
2. The first three between Dutch colonists and the Xhosa, the remainder between British colonists and the Xhosa.
3. Quoted in V. Msila, *A Place to Live: Red Location and Its History from 1903 to 2013* (Port Elizabeth, South Africa: Sun Press, 2014), p. 18.
4. In fact, as early as 1847, the Cape Colony government had encouraged the Municipality of Port Elizabeth to set aside distinct 'Native Locations' some distance from the centre of towns, demonstrating that official colonial government policy was always inclined towards segregation, and indigenous populations as 'temporary'. Msila, *A Place to Live*, p. 29.
5. A 'kloof' is a Cape Dutch word for a kind of gulley or ravine.
6. M. Hall, N. Murray and N. Shepherd, *Desire Lines: Space, Memory and Identity in the Post-Apartheid City* (London: Routledge, 2007), p. 287.
7. F. Valentyn, *Description of the Cape of Good Hope with the Matters concerning It 1726* (Cape Town: Van Riebeeck Society, 1971), p. 107. Quoted in N. Murray, N. Shepherd and M. Hall, eds., *Desire Lines: Space, Memory and Identity in the Post-Apartheid City* (London: Routledge, 2007), p. 287.
8. T. Shepstone, quoted in G. Ching-Liang Low, *White Skins, Black Masks: Representation and Colonialism* (London: Routledge, 1996), p. 72.
9. Ching-Liang Low, *White Skins, Black Masks*, p. 72.
10. M. Silverman, ed., *Black Skin, White Masks: New Interdisciplinary Essays* (Manchester: Manchester University Press, 2005), p. 35.
11. Ching-Liang Low, *White Skins, Black Masks*, p. 38.
12. J. J. Redgrave, *Port Elizabeth in Bygone Days* (Port Elizabeth, South Africa: Rustica Press, 1947).
13. Msila, *A Place to Live*, p. 49.
14. For example, also Kooper's Kloof Location and Gubbs Location.
15. J. Kirk, *The African Middle Class, Cape Liberalism and Resistance to Residential Segregation at Port Elizabeth, South Africa, 1880–1910* (Ann Arbor: University Microfilms International, 1987).
16. The population of Port Elizabeth increased by 83% between 1891 and 1904. Msila, *A Place to Live*, p. 29.
17. Gary Baines notes that "the removal of Port Elizabeth's African population to the site of the Native Strangers' Location was eventually achieved with a measure of coercion". G. Baines, *The Control and Administration of Port Elizabeth's African Population c. 1834–1923* (Port Elizabeth, South Africa: Department of History, Vista University, Port Elizabeth Campus, n.d.).
18. Msila, *A Place to Live*, p. 49.
19. It was claimed that as many as 25 people lived in one hut. Msila argues that overcrowding and poor sanitation were the result of: the expense entailed in building even a rudimentary hut; the ground rent demanded by the erection of a dwelling and the unwillingness of the municipality to provide sanitation or housing in this district. Msila, *A Place to Live*, p. 56.
20. Msila, *A Place to Live*, p. 49.
21. *South African Spectator* (9 February 1901).
22. F. Fanon, *Peau Noire, Masques Blancs* (Paris: Seuil/Points, 1952); C. L. Markmann, trans., *Black Skin, White Masks* (London: Pluto Press, 1986).
23. Silverman, ed., *Black Skin, White Masks*, p. 119.

24 Ibid., p. 41.
25 Msila, *A Place to Live*, p. 50.
26 J. Merriman, quoted in Msila, *A Place to Live*, p. 29.
27 *New Nation, New History* (Johannesburg: New Nation, 1989).
28 Murray, Shepherd and Hall, eds., *Desire Lines* (Routledge, 2007) p. 4.
29 Numerous historians have pointed to the origins of Apartheid's racial segregation in nineteenth-century British colonial rule of South Africa—for example, T. Keegan, *Colonial South Africa and the Origins of the Racial Order* (Charlottesville: University of Virginia Press, 1996); N. Penn, *The Forgotten Frontier: Colonist and Khoisan on the Cape's Northern Frontier in the Eighteenth Century* (Athens, OH: Ohio University Press, 2006).
30 Appearing on an early map dated 1905.
31 C. V. Reed, *Royal Tourists, Colonial Subjects and the Making of a British World 1860–1911* (Manchester: Manchester University Press, 2016), p. 95.
32 S. Solomon, quoted in E. Jenkins, *Falling into Place: The Story of Modern South African Place Names* (Cape Town, South Africa: David Philip, 2007), p. 95.
33 Jenkins, *Falling into Place*, p. 16.
34 M. Ndletyana, "Changing Place Names in Post-Apartheid South Africa: Accounting for the Unevenness", *Social Dynamics: A Journal of African Studies*, 38(1) (2012), p. 89.
35 S. Cohen and K. Nurit, "Place Names in Israel's Ideological Struggles over Administered Territories", *Annals of the Association of American Geographers*, 82(4) (1992), p. 655.
36 B. Yeoh, "Street Names in Colonial Singapore", *Geographical Review*, 82(3) (1992), p. 316.
37 C. Crais, quoted in E. Jenkins, *Falling into Place*, p. 95.
38 *Graham's Town Journal* (15 August 1860). Quoted in *Reed, Royal Tourists, Colonial Subjects and the Making of a British World 1860–1911*, p. 96.
39 Reed, *Royal Tourists, Colonial Subjects and the Making of a British World 1860–1911*, p. 95.
40 Ibid., p. 97.
41 Ibid., p. 148.
42 Ibid.
43 Ibid., p. 149.
44 www.travelground.com/accommodation/loft-on-lansdowne/location [accessed 02/05/2018].
45 Murray, Shepherd and Hall, eds., *Desire Lines*, p. 4.
46 Studies include those by Ronald Lewcock, Hans Fransen, Mary Cook and John Rennie.
47 Murray, Shepherd and Hall, eds., *Desire Lines*, p. 56.
48 www.theheritageportal.co.za/article/looking-back-woolff-restoration-donkin-row-houses [accessed 02/05/2018].
49 Ibid.
50 L. Witz, *Apartheid's Festival: Contesting South Africa's National Pasts* (Bloomington: Indiana University Press, 2003), p. 227.
51 Ibid.
52 *Evening Post*, 8 April 1952, in Witz, *Apartheid's Festival*, p. 238.
53 Based upon the heraldic arms of Sir Rufane Donkin, and granted by Letters Patent from the College of Arms in August 1958.
54 *Evening Post*, 6 March 1952, in Witz, *Apartheid's Festival*, p. 238.
55 Witz, *Apartheid's Festival*, p. 227.
56 P. Kadi, "The Group Areas Act and Port Elizabeth's Heritage: A Study of Memorial Recollection in the South End Museum", MA Dissertation (2007), p. 57.

57 M. Herradine, quoted in Kadi, "The Group Areas Act and Port Elizabeth's Heritage", p. 67.
58 Kadi, "The Group Areas Act and Port Elizabeth's Heritage", p. 68.
59 "Special Rating Area Revives Richmond Hill", *Port Elizabeth Express* (23 September 2015).
60 Formerly known as City Improvement Districts (CIDs).
61 www.myguideeasterncape.com/regionalinfo/richmond-hill-port-elizabeth [accessed 03/05/2018].
62 L. Coetzee, "Young People Building a New Vision for Port Elizabeth: Young Urbanists Meet in Nelson Mandela Bay" (12 December 2016), http://future capetown.com/2016/12/young-people-building-a-new-vision-for-port-elizabeth-young-urbanists-meet-in-nelson-mandela-bay [accessed 03/05/2018].
63 Ibid.
64 Ndletyana, "Changing Place Names in Post-Apartheid South Africa", p. 10.
65 Murray, Shepherd and Hall, eds., *Desire Lines*, p. 6.
66 Ibid.
67 C. Rassool, "Memory and the Politics of History in the District Six Museum", in N. Murray, N. Shepherd and M. Hall, eds., *Desire Lines: Space, Memory and Identity in the Post-Apartheid City* (London: Routledge, 2007), p. 114.
68 Ibid.
69 Ibid., p. 115.
70 Ibid.
71 E. W. Soja, "Postmodern Urbanization: The Six Restructurings of Los Angeles", in S. Watson and K. Gibson, eds., *Postmodern Cities and Spaces* (Oxford: Blackwell, 1995), p. 135.
72 R. Coleman, *Reclaiming the Streets: Surveillance, Social Control and the City* (Cullompton, UK: Willan Publishing, 2004), p. 73.
73 G. E. Turley, quoted in "Name Changes Distort History", *The Herald* (23 July 2002), p. 6.
74 'Sinbad', quoted in "Name Changes Distort History", p. 6.
75 "Pull Down All Colonial Statues in the Metro Demands Mike Xego", *Eastern Province Herald* (19 April 2004).
76 *Eastern Province Herald* (23 April 2004).
77 Ibid.
78 K. Slattery, "SRA Making Difference in Richmond Hill", *The Herald* (16 February 2016).
79 "Special Rating Area Revives Richmond Hill".
80 An extra R50 to R70 depending on the value of individual properties.
81 Slattery, "SRA Making Difference in Richmond Hill".
82 "Special Rating Area Revives Richmond Hill".
83 Ibid.
84 E. Said, *Orientalism* (London: Pantheon Books, 1978).
85 M. Davis, *City of Quartz: Excavating the Future in Los Angeles* (London: Verso, 1990), p. 226. Quoted in Coleman, *Reclaiming the Streets*, p. 65.
86 Davis, *City of Quartz*, p. 224, quoted in Coleman, *Reclaiming the Streets*, p. 65.
87 Ibid.
88 M. Foucault, *Discipline and Punish*. See also J. Bannister, N. R. Fyfe and A. Kearns, "Closed Circuit Television and the City", in C. Norris, ed., *Surveillance, Closed Circuit Television and Social Control* (Aldershot: Ashgate, 1998); C. Norris, "From Personal to Digital: CCTV, the Panopticon, and the Technical Mediation of Suspicion and Social Control", in D. Lyon, ed., *Surveillance as Social Sorting: Privacy, Risk and Digital Discrimination* (London: Routledge, 2003).

89 A. Rees, "New Urbanism: Visionary Landscapes in the Twenty-First Century", in M. J. Lindstrom and H. Bartling, eds., *Suburban Sprawl: Culture, Theory and Politics* (Lanham: Rowman & Littlefield Publishers, Inc., 2003), p. 97.
90 Ibid., p. 104, quoted in P. Marks, *Imagining Surveillance: Utopian and Dystopian Literature and Film* (Edinburgh: Edinburgh University Press, 2015), p. 104.
91 Murray, Shepherd and Hall, eds., *Desire Lines*, p. 290.
92 Ibid.

Conclusion

The two intersecting aims of this book were to investigate the intellectual and cultural histories of the idea of the 'protected vista' in architecture, landscape architecture and urbanism and to examine the values inherent within London's original protected vista – the view from Richmond Hill. I argue that these values have subsequently come to inform, and are reinforced by, contemporary policies of view protection, which have become increasingly global phenomena. The intellectual histories of each Richmond given here have been necessarily detailed, as it is only through tracing the recurring details of imagery and language that the recycling, absorption and development of a set of values may be highlighted.

Beginning with an intellectual and cultural history of Britain's first protected vista, the view from Richmond Hill, Part 1 of this book has demonstrated that the values at work in the idea of the view, and the idea of view protection, derive in no small part from a highly particular physical and intellectual landscape: not just Western, not just British, but from a few miles of the Thames's river banks to the West of London, and the values associated with it. While these values may originate from a particular place, they are not of a particular time. They have been subtly reformulated with multiple re-inscriptions over time, shifting with each iteration yet remaining remarkably consistent.

The examples of worldwide Richmonds presented here are at once exceptional and typical: unusual examples of places named in direct reference to an 'original' historic view – and not just any view but an important progenitor of the picturesque – and yet, also typical of the protected vista's absorption of picturesque values more generally. The idea of the picturesque vista seems to contain within itself a sense of its own authenticity, attributing authority to the gaze and its subject, rendering the object a sense of completeness and finitude. Yet the picturesque view to be protected is not a view from a particular period in time but an idealised, supposedly timeless, view composed of those elements of its imagined history which have been deemed most desirable. Its supposed authenticity, regularly reinvented anew, produces – and is produced by – claims to individual, cultural, regional and/ or national identities. In this way, the idea of the picturesque view has always demanded its own reproduction – in painting, literature, photography, postcards, film, in the view from the windscreen, in architecture, in landscape and in the continual remaking of itself. The authentic view is so recognisable, so familiar, that it also reproduces itself away from itself; seen, read, posted and played in representations but also, most powerfully, reproducing itself in physical form in export and in translation to radically different contexts, exerting power to make the new context conform with the values of the old. It is so pervasive that it demands its own conservation. So effective have been these processes of reproduction and conservation that they now go largely unnoticed. Yet the very idea of the view – legislated for in protected view policy – has served to universalise the picturesque landscape seen from Richmond Hill in law, so that all protected views have become, to some extent, the view from Richmond Hill.

The chapters of this book have identified five broad themes underlying the values of the protected view: an understanding of the gaze – the vista as manifestation of surveillance and panoptic power; the aesthetic, and pictorial, convention of the picturesque; a sense of nostalgia for a perceived 'golden age', whether melancholic mourning for a lost past or aspiration for an imagined present or future; the question of authenticity in relation to romanticism; and the view as expressive of identity, whether personal, regional, national or cultural. These five themes, which should by no means be thought of as exhaustive or exclusive, have been shown to converge in a single vista whose extensive reproduction has made it almost universal: the view from Richmond Hill and its reflected 'mirror images' across the world.

Intriguingly, the river view preserved by the 1902 *Richmond, Petersham and Ham Open Spaces Act* forms one half of the panoramic view observed from 'King Henry's Mound' in Richmond Park, while, turning through 180 degrees, the observer takes in a vista protected by the contemporary London View Management Framework. The apparent opposition of these views – one rural, one urban; one expansive, one narrow; one defined by the protection of lands, one by a series of view-shed lines – is undermined by the coincidence of their values, their viewing positions and common conservation goals. In fact, this coincidence of position, geographical and ideological, offers a tantalising link between the two, apparently opposing, systems of protection. This book demonstrates that the contemporary London View Management Framework owes a great deal to the Act which saved the view from Richmond Hill and all that the view stands for. Thus, an understanding of the arguments behind the 'Indignation' campaign, which brought about the 1902 Act, underpins an understanding of the values and narratives attached to London's contemporary protected vistas.

A sense of nostalgia

It would seem that a pervasive sense of nostalgia has permeated the view from Richmond Hill for centuries, from its symbolic reference to Henry

VII's favourite earldom of Richmond, North Yorkshire, and its mysterious French predecessor to the 'Indignation' campaigns of the twentieth century. Campaigners have attached value to the landscape not only for its visual and natural beauty, or its witness to historical events, but also for its familiar and repeated representation in the works of highly regarded national and international artists, poets and authors. They have argued that it was on this spot that artists sketched Henry VII's fantastical chivalric palace of Richmond, and painted the genteel riverside estates of an eighteenth-century nobility.

Already well known by the late seventeenth century, the hill was embellished with grand townhouses, the 'Terrace Walk', medicinal mineral springs, pleasure garden and theatre. The later 'Indignation' campaigns focused on this evidence to claim that the Richmond landscape enjoyed a refined and elegant 'golden age' in the past, and that subsequent developments have somehow cheapened and vandalised a pastoral landscape whose authority derived from classical models. However, research has demonstrated that a plethora of drinking establishments, and the somewhat infamous reputation of the Richmond Hill pleasure gardens, catered to every type of social behaviour. A contrary picture thus develops of the hill as a raucous leisure resort within easy reach of the city. As such, the view of the Thames from Richmond Hill was not only geographically opposed to the vista of the city but also set up symbolically in opposition to it; here was a romanticised and nostalgic vision of the 'country', albeit an urbanised landscape, where leisure time and playing at 'country' pursuits were encouraged and celebrated. This is not to say that Richmond in the eighteenth century was a rural or agricultural community, tied to the land and little affected by the city. On the contrary, Richmond's symbolic opposition to the city highlights their fundamental reliance upon one another. This was where George, Prince of Wales, retreated away from the politics of the city to try his hand at experimental 'farming', though this was more accurately an exercise in landscape gardening than agricultural production, his gardens the venue of 'rustic' fêtes galantes where the city's aristocracy played at being rustic peasants. Likewise, the poets and painters that flocked to the Richmond and Twickenham resorts throughout the eighteenth century did so to infiltrate the city's fashionable set, and to sell their pastoral works among the city merchants. As such, though it might be said the works of eighteenth-century artists, architects, landscape architects and writers have done much to sustain the two conceptual poles of Raymond Williams's *Country and the City*, a much more complex interrelationship emerges from the proto-suburban communities encircling eighteenth-century London, and even from the former British colonies, which to a significant degree were also perceived as satellites of the city.

No doubt the notoriety of the Richmond Hill prospect had much to do with the increasing popularity of the leisure resort among the artists, architects, their patrons and the general public who flocked to the banks of the Thames at Richmond at this time. This pastoral view was seen as a living image of an Arcadian landscape, drawing up nostalgic associations from popular classical literature – the gentleman that 'retired' to country estates here compared to the classical retirement of Cicero, Horace and Pliny to comfortable suburban villa estates. Classical retirement was seen as a return to an 'authentic', noble and rustic simplicity, where one could reconnect with nature through experimental husbandry, and spend one's time expanding the mind through scholarly pursuits. It could even be argued that the natural view of the river, frequently compared to the paintings of Claude Lorrain, Nicholas Poussin and Gaspar Dughet, acted as inspiration to local retirees Alexander Pope's and Lord Burlington's pioneering forays in naturalistic landscape architecture.

The Richmond Hill view's eighteenth-century transposition onto the landscapes of colonies all over the world, with all its connotations of classical authority, pastoral innocence and picturesque beauty, is another consequence of pervasive nostalgia, in its original sense as a physiological yearning for the colonist's distant homeland. In the example of Virginia, the overlaying of the Richmond Hill view both represented and helped to produce the values of that youthful colony: a mirror of the apparently already past 'golden age' of genteel, civilised, learned Richmond-upon-Thames. Later, in the build-up to the American Revolution, this sense of nostalgia would shift poles from the 'golden age' of England to classical Rome, reflecting a wave of optimism in the fledgling nation's future. While the values attached to the view have remained largely consistent, perceptions of those values have been in constant flux. For example, a familiar nostalgia arose during the escalation of the American Civil War, as a means to separate out the American South as the 'real' America of elegance and tradition. At this time, familiar narratives of the 'authentic' rural farmer came to symbolise the struggle of a romanticised age-old southern plantation economy against the dark forces of an industrial North. This nostalgic sensibility would continue to be felt in the aftermath of the Civil War, as the defeated Confederacy was presented as a fallen civilisation, on a par with the fall of Rome or of Carthage, and commemorated through the erection of classical monuments to the South's Lost Cause.

The aesthetic convention of the picturesque

One cannot discuss the view from Richmond Hill, the progenitor of all protected views, without coming back repeatedly to the picturesque movement in art, architecture, landscape architecture and literature. As this book has argued, it was in the Richmond landscape that the influential pioneers of the picturesque movement, including Pope, Burlington, Henrietta Howard and Queen Caroline, first set themselves up in opposition to the 'outmoded' formal styles of landscapes, such as those at Hampton Court, Ham House and Petersham's New Park. It was in this landscape too that the picturesque received, arguably, its first physical manifestation in the gardens of Pope, as well as its first manifestation in literature, in the words and poetry of Pope, James Thompson, Jonathan Swift and John Gay, among others. Finally, it was in this landscape that the picturesque movement reached its climax, in the landscape work of Humphrey Repton and 'Capability' Brown; in the fanciful architecture of Horace Walpole at Strawberry Hill and William Chambers at Kew Gardens; and in the pattern books of Twickenham's Batty Langley and others. In art too, the view from Richmond Hill was captured on canvas by numerous canonical figures, from the Royal Academy of Art's first president, Sir Joshua Reynolds, and Jasper Francis Cropsey, key figure of the American 'Hudson River School', to Joseph Mallord William Turner. The romance of Turner's views, replete with a sense of nostalgia for the past, is echoed in the poetry of William Wordsworth and the romantic novels of Sir Walter Scott, both of whom set elements of their literary works in the familiar Richmond landscape.

Having identified Richmond as decisive to the birth of the picturesque movement, this book has demonstrated that the legacies of that movement survived in the 'Indignation' campaigns of the early twentieth century, transposed through a series of technological innovations – from the mass production of inexpensive prints to the transport, advertising and photographic revolutions. Picturesque modes of vision may be detected in the railway engineering and advertising of the nineteenth century and, as London continued to spread outwards into green field sites, in the formation of the Garden City movement and the professionalisation of town planning. Early suburban planning and design were expressed through a picturesque mode of vision – even modernists cultivated a curiously pictorial design convention in the 'townscape' movement of the 1950s, a language instantly legible to a society with generations of training in the viewing of mass-produced picturesque images.

Regional, cultural or national identity

Encoded within the Richmond Hill vista lies a complex narrative of 'Englishness', associated with the idea of an 'English landscape movement' and the nationalist undertones of works by Turner, Wordsworth, Walter Scott and others. The Richmond landscape has been held up as a symbol of a romanticised vision of England, just as Cropsey's American works were championed as symbolic of 'American-ness'. Indeed, one might trace this narrative back through George III and George IV's remodelling of Windsor Castle (which, prior to the construction of Heathrow Airport, formed a backdrop to the Richmond Hill view), in which the glorious 'restoration' of the ancient fortress represented growing introverted, nationalist feeling during the Napoleonic Wars with France. It is interesting also to speculate on the motives behind George III's establishment of an observatory and meridian at Richmond, according to which the royal time was attuned, thus placing George, and his picturesque landscape gardens at Richmond, at the epicentre of the British Empire, a notion highlighted by Queen Caroline's eclectic garden *fabriques*, which notably included a 'Chinese pagoda' and 'Moorish alhambra', mediated via a colonial picturesque mode of vision.

Though it seems likely that the founder of Richmond, Virginia, William Byrd I, named the city after its English counterpart, my research has found that there is in fact no definitive first-hand evidence. Perhaps what is more interesting is that the *assumption* subsequently led many an architect, artist and writer to view the Virginian landscape through the lens of Richmond-upon-Thames's already pervasive picturesque reproductions. This was despite the site's own fascinating indigenous history, as the site of Emperor Powhatan's encampment and the birthplace of his infamous daughter, Pocahontas. Thus, the James River landscape, its pre-colonial history and its indigenous identity were soon overlaid with the imagery and borrowed sense of fictive classical history according to which depictions of Richmond-upon-Thames were reproduced. In this way, whole landscapes, histories and cultures, alien to waves of incoming settlers, were erased by the imposition of the British colonial scopic regime. For example, in Richmond, Virginia, William Byrd's explicit nostalgic connection to the Richmond Hill view simultaneously dissociated a millennium of indigenous history, paralleled by Princess Pocahontas's absorption into the English aristocracy (and her symbolic renaming as Rebecca Rolfe). The wealthy plantation owners of the Tidewater region of Virginia, William Byrd I included, soon began to build ambitious mansions on the banks of the James River, in a self-conscious echo of the villa landscape of the Thames Valley at Richmond, visually appropriating the American continent for the British Empire.

In the years immediately preceding the American Revolution, the Richmond landscape, once inseparably associated with the old colonial motherland, was the backdrop to the revolution-inciting Virginia Conventions. At this time, Richmond, Virginia's ties to Richmond-upon-Thames were either forgotten or, more likely, suppressed. Rather, America's picturesque landscapes were championed as at least equal to, if not surpassing, those of her colonial master.

Towards the end of the eighteenth century, optimism over the future of a young, independent America was high. Amateur architects such as Thomas Jefferson, English-educated architect Benjamin Henry Latrobe and America's 'first architect' Robert Mills identified America with the youthful Roman Republic and soon began to embellish the Virginian landscape with classical villas, understood once more through reproductions of contemporary English picturesque landscape gardens made famous in Richmond-upon-Thames. Far from a nostalgic reference to England, however, at this time the picturesque was promoted as a symbol of a refined, modern America, every bit the equal of the former colonial power. In capturing and recapturing these landscape views, Richmond's public buildings, villas, gardens, parks and cemeteries have consistently reinforced a particular set of visual and compositional forms. The strength of Richmond's visual identity contributed to the city's praise throughout the nineteenth century as one of America's most beautiful cities. Chapter 3 goes further, to suggest that Richmond's strong visual identity played a certain role in the cultivation of a southern cultural identity during its time as capital of the Confederacy. Either way, the destruction of Richmond's picturesque cityscape at the close of the American Civil War served as a bitter reminder to the southern plantation gentry, and a symbol to the Unionist North, of the abolition of an archaic hierarchical society built on the immoral foundations of slavery.

Post–Civil War Richmond reminisced with rose-tinted nostalgia for its once infamous, if not glorious, past. Monuments were erected all over the city, but the most interesting, for the purposes of this book, are those that were deliberately juxtaposed with landscape views. On Libby Hill, the Confederate Soldiers and Sailors Monument drew from classical models to inscribe a romantic historical narrative into the city's landscape setting; thus, Richmond's views were historicised, and in doing so, converted into monuments in their own right. In each of the examples outlined earlier it is clear that specific readings of landscape views have been promoted as symbolic of shared cultural and national identities. In many ways, the preservation of these views, and their legislative protection, can be understood as just the latest contribution to these shifting narratives of identity.

The power of the gaze

Inseparably linked to the notion of the picturesque mode of vision is an underlying conception of the power of the gaze: of the image and of surveillance. For example, in the aforementioned example of George III's gardens at Richmond-upon-Thames the royal observatory was positioned symbolically at the centre of the monarchy, the centre of the empire, the exotic lands beyond, the observable universe, even at the epicentre of time itself. Even then, Richmond was imagined as universal, long before its view became a near universal template for the very idea of the view, and protected view. The visual sense is critical to this understanding. George's conceptual meridian is conspicuously marked by a series of garden obelisks, surrounded by fanciful *fabriques* representing every exotic corner of the earth, and the state-of-the-art optical instruments of his observatory sit at the heart of it all, surveying the whole landscape, as well as the distant reaches of the universe, from its hilltop position.

Equally, many of Richmond, Virginia's earliest public buildings, from Jefferson's Capitol to Latrobe's Penitentiary – both symbols of civic power – were themselves also viewing machines, carefully positioned and configured to enhance surveillance, whether of the landscape, city or individuals themselves. To echo Michel Foucault's description of Jeremy Bentham's Panopticon, it might be argued that from the seventeenth century, discourses of power in society shifted towards surveillance. This shift may be demonstrated in contemporary movements in landscape architecture, a growing interest in scientific and astronomical observation and the overwhelming importance placed on the visual sense at a time of rapidly increasing mass production of images. This preoccupation with the visual sense was heightened by the proliferation of new visual experiences, from the high-velocity panorama of the railway carriage window to the invention of the photographic camera, and the global reach of the photographic postcard. If Richmond's eighteenth-century buildings had acted as huge, static viewing machines, the camera, film camera and the automobile now rendered visual experiences of urban and natural landscapes mobile and convenient.

Chapter 4 argued that the tendency to view the Richmond, New South Wales, landscape with the same painterly and nostalgic vision by which Richmond-upon-Thames and Richmond, Virginia, have been observed should not be understood as a simple coincidence. Even before colonists had ventured into the Hawkesbury landscape they had projected a vision of Richmond Hill upon it – visual 'proof' that prosperous agricultural land awaited settlers prepared to commit to the significant hardships of a pioneer's life. Colonial administration of the Hawkesbury settlements also ensured that they evolved in line with this predetermined colonial gaze; land grants and regulations determining building construction set the parameters for the future development of Richmond's and Windsor's handsome townscapes.

Throughout the course of the region's development, comparisons made between the visual characteristics of the Hawkesbury and Thames landscapes were routinely made, with the effect of writing out the aboriginal history and contribution to the landscape. This was perpetuated by the work of travelling artists who tended to depict – at first – 'empty' natural wildernesses and later quaint colonial farmsteads, both streams of which contributed to national movements in landscape art. This is the Hawkesbury vision which persisted in the late twentieth-century craze for 'restoring' heritage buildings and in the pseudo-historical forms adopted for new buildings, and which continues to persist in the cultural products of landscape art, literature, television and cinematography today. Yet, although views of the Hawkesbury are presented as *benign* amenities with aesthetic and heritage value to *all*, obvious questions remain about to *whom* these landscape views have been and are valuable, and what are the *values* embedded within such perceptions – perceptions which ultimately displaced traditional indigenous understanding of the landscape and continue to wield a controlling power over its architectural and urban development.

The question of authenticity

One might have expected the picturesque, and its nostalgic connotations, to disappear from Richmond, Virginia, after the Civil War, but in fact their resurgence became a counterpart to the rapid modernisation of American cities in the early twentieth century. As Richmond's centre of trade moved away from the river towards improved road and rail links, and the city began to develop as a densely packed cluster of ever-taller and more massive buildings, the river landscape became a valued visual amenity.

The increasing speed of travel, coupled with the increasing speed of camera mechanisms and exposure times, led to an appreciation of the moving image of cities and landscapes. Taking physical form in the curious American invention of the scenic parkway, an initial appreciation of scenic landscapes quickly turned to the protection, and then the staging, of views. The National Park Service's Colonial Parkway, Virginia, took an untouched natural site of inaccessible marshland and drove a road through it, enabling the motorist to drive through 23 miles of 'authentic' eighteenth-century landscapes. Modern intrusions were cleared away or disguised, an approach also utilised in Rockefeller's reconstruction of Colonial Williamsburg. The idea of the view's authenticity itself became paramount, as interpreted through historical imagination, in preference to the often less perfected, more complex and suspect awkwardness of historical veracity.

The increased staging of the view, demonstrated by the Colonial Parkway project, is evident in the unsightly stretches of Richmond's highways, now designated as 'interstate image corridors', where projects intended to enhance the motorist's image and perception of the city are actively pursued. Rather than imposing a strictly 'classical' or 'colonial' narrative upon the viewer, views are cultivated which exude a tourist-friendly general sense of Richmond as an 'authentic' 'historical' city; the city is composed as a series of 'historic' 'snapshots' laced with a generalised nostalgia.

Likewise, Chapter 5 argued that in Richmond Hill, Port Elizabeth, South Africa, connotations of 'Richmond', loosely based upon the model of the Thames-side British town of the same name, have been used from the late nineteenth century as a means to displace indigenous Africans from the landscape. Surely, this chapter argues, there must have been a relationship between the connotations of an affluent, white, English middle class projected by descriptions and depictions of Richmond-upon-Thames and the transformation of 'Strangers' Location' into 'Richmond Hill' that commenced from the middle of the nineteenth century. What may first appear as an apparently innocent change of place name may be reinterpreted, in the light of South Africa's more recent experiments in toponymical change, as intensely political. The immense power of such place names to convey associations, values and expectations is apparent in the phenomenon of Richmond Hill's Special Ratings Area designation, and the sense of constant surveillance which has shaped not only the aesthetic appearance of the neighbourhood but also the very composition of its social fabric.

The set of values inherent in the Richmond vista – the gaze, the picturesque, nostalgia, authenticity and identity – is presented here as decisive to the idea of the protected vista. The theoretical understanding of the view and its application in landscape art, architecture and the linked discourses of aesthetics, political and cultural identity, all formulated between the eighteenth and nineteenth centuries, just so happened to coincide with, arguably, the apogee of Britain's imperial power and influence. As a result, one could argue that the values promoted by a vision of 'English landscape' were left indelibly upon the reading of landscapes in many parts of the world. Modelled upon London's contemporary policies, each diverse policy of view protection therefore has a relationship to the seemingly universal values inherent within London's original protected vista: the view from Richmond Hill.

'The Great Indignation'

This book has argued that the values inherent within the vista from Richmond Hill inevitably demanded its protection. In Richmond, Virginia, too, the continued re-inscription of the same set of values has led to a contemporary conservation movement calling for the protection of this view, this time bringing together the two Richmonds in the most explicit of ways yet. This may be viewed as another kind of fictive history – the imagination of a definitive link between the two Richmonds which has always been much less explicit in the past. This fictive history may be interpreted as both produced by and producing the idea of the protected vista.

In contemporary Richmond, Virginia, the ongoing campaign for the protection of the Libby Hill vista, dubbed the 'Great Indignation', is a direct, and self-conscious, reference to the 1902 'Indignation' campaign that saved the view from London's Richmond Hill. The protection of the James River view can thus be located in a nostalgic desire for rural imagery and a deep sense of heritage stretching back to eighteenth-century Richmond-upon-Thames, imagined as an authentic, authoritative past which seems all the more vivid when juxtaposed against the perceived failings of industrial modernity. These historical associations were legitimised and reinforced by the transatlantic twinning of the two Richmonds in May 1981 "in order to afford official recognition to their resemblance to one another, sharing of name, and to promoting and continuing the spirit of goodwill and cooperation existing between [them]".[1] One Richmond newspaper has stated that

> As the global community continues to grow closer together, these ties will have more and more influence on all our lives. The view from Libby Hill is a living tribute to the commonwealth's direct tie to the United Kingdom – past, present, and future – to be shared by all Virginians.[2]

In the spirit of these ties, in 2002, director of the Great Indignation campaign Rick Tatnall was among the Virginian representatives invited to Richmond-upon-Thames in celebration of the hundredth anniversary of the 1902 *Richmond, Petersham and Ham Open Spaces Act*. The visit coincided with controversy in Virginia, as land fronting the James River was re-zoned to allow for taller buildings. Residents feared that "The council [was] literally authorizing a concrete canyon that would prevent the public from enjoying the river", suggesting instead that it should be left "in a natural state".[3] The controversy spurred one of the first cooperative projects to be undertaken by the two Richmonds: the erection of a memorial sign-board on Libby Hill to commemorate Byrd's supposed naming of Richmond after its Thames-side counterpart, dedicated by Mayor L. Douglas Wilder of Richmond, Virginia, and Councillor Robin Jowit of Richmond-upon-Thames, in 2006.[4] This single act renders the oral tradition as historical 'fact', ensuring that no visitor can be in doubt as to the city's provenance, despite the lack of records that Byrd did indeed compare the two views.

This 'fact' definitively entered the history books for the first time in 2007, when the General Assembly of Virginia approved a resolution celebrating the panoramic view and its role in the naming of Richmond,[5] a copy of which was presented to Queen Elizabeth II during her visit for the four-hundredth anniversary of the settlement of Jamestown.[6] The Assembly's resolution thus promoted Richmond's links with England just at the time of the Jamestown anniversary – an act designed to capitalise on increased historical tourism and investment in the region. These events have served to further historicise the view, fuelling the Great Indignation campaign's aim to preserve and, indeed, 'improve' the view, in order that it lives up to the expectation of its projected image; as Tatnall has stated in his campaign manifesto, "The greatest opportunity for the future of the Richmond Region is to harness the power of our past to positively shape our future".[7]

Though the appropriation of the two Richmond views by differing movements has shifted with time, at their heart lies a series of near-constant narratives: a yearning for a romanticised and orderly past tied to a fear of, or overwhelming dissatisfaction with, the disorder of the present. This attachment of nostalgic sentiment to the two Richmond views is accompanied by the visual construction of the picturesque in their many reproductions. The Virginian Indignation campaign has made extensive use of picturesque representations as a means of communicating its principal message – that the Libby Hill view is of cultural, historical and artistic significance. This utilisation of picturesque representation for political means is perhaps best demonstrated by the exhibition *View: An Exhibition on Richmond Hill*, held at Waterstone's, Piccadilly, Orleans House, Twickenham and a number of Virginian venues in 2003. A key component of this touring exhibition was a series of contemporary landscape paintings, depicting both Richmond Hills through the eyes of local artists, thus strengthening historical and artistic links between the two vistas.

To quote David Lowenthal, the protected vista could be described as providing a sense of "familiarity and recognition; reaffirmation and validation; individual and group identity; guidance; enrichment and escape".[8] In the case of Libby Hill, the vista provides familiarity and recognition via culturally engrained images of 'authentic' pastoral life, learned via mass-produced prints and literature. The view reaffirms and validates the present through a sense of the preserved past, while the historical narratives of the view proclaim the validity of individual and group identities: middle-class, white, southern, American. As Lowenthal clarifies, "remembering the past is crucial for our sense of identity: [. . .] to know what we were confirms that we are".[9] It is fitting that Lowenthal leaves escape to the last, singling it out as a fundamental facet of heritage. The preserved view of an 'authentic' landscape acts as a visual escape from the dense crowding and apparent chaos of modern urbanity. Stephen Spender notes the American longing for the past as an escape from the present "as though [history] were geography", treating themselves "as though they could step out of the present into the past of their choice".[10] One might view the desire to preserve the view from Libby Hill then as a nostalgic escape from the here and now which serves to bolster the values of the present, building upon an established narrative of such romantic vision ultimately stretching back to the imagined 'golden ages' of Pope, Thompson, Burlington, Kent and many others. It is the idea of the protected view itself which has brought about the explicit connection between the two Richmond vistas for the first time, reinforcing and even producing the fictive history in which the two Richmonds seem always to have been inevitably interconnected through the promotion of a shared set of values. Thus, it is the idea of the protected view itself which has created the latest iteration of the Richmond Hill story.

Concluding observations

Returning to Richmond-upon-Thames and Richmond Hill's intriguing King Henry's Mound, it is now possible to close the apparent gap between the preservation of the 1902 Act's naturalistic river view and the London View Management Framework's city vista. The physical coincidence of these two viewpoints, I would argue, tells us something of the common origins of each policy. The viewer, subconsciously trained in an appreciation of picturesque landscapes through the observation of thousands upon thousands of images, casts his or her gaze back upon the city. In this specific vista, the observer views St Paul's Cathedral framed to dramatic effect by the avenue of trees in Richmond Park. The avenue intensifies the observer's gaze, creating a sense of power over the built form of the city. The foreground setting is, however, a naturalistic park of Repton's design. The city is entirely absent apart from the dome of St Paul's; this is an idealised view of a pastoral London, a London 'tidied up' as in Rocque's famous plans of the city. The avenue and cathedral recall elements of Wren's unbuilt vision of the city, an English Baroque reinterpretation of classical Rome, bringing to mind the imagery of a romanticised former 'golden age'. At the same time, the silhouette of the dome could be said to represent a cultivated 'brand image' or identity of the city, familiar to the observer via countless images from Canaletto's paintings to Herbert Mason's iconic photographs of the blitz. These cues convey to the observer that the city and its society are constant, unchanging, an 'authentic' and timeless art object to be gazed upon as in a gallery or museum. As such, the vistas of the London View Management Framework, just as that from Richmond Hill, could be said to be of more value than simple visual amenities; rather they convey multiple and diverse narratives through their identification of landmarks worthy of contemplation. Via our previous exposure to hundreds of thousands of images, vistas have become symbols of themselves, texts that invite us to 'read' and to translate them from one landscape to another.

Thus, I argue that established notions of the *gaze*, the *picturesque*, *nostalgia*, *authenticity* and *identity* are inevitably, and unwittingly, absorbed into London's contemporary policy, as views of our cities have become integral to notions of historical and cultural identity and important factors in the touristic potential of cities. As Boym has written, "In the nineteenth century the nostalgic was an urban dweller who dreamed of escape from the city into the unspoiled landscape. At the end of the twentieth century the urban dweller feels that the city itself is an endangered landscape".[11] It is no wonder then that we seek to engineer historic views of our cities, designating landmarks, settings and vistas as historical monuments to be protected from change.

At the same time, technical and scientific advancements, from travel to photography, industrial processes of mass production, the moving image and the Internet, have contributed to the continued acceleration and proliferation of images. Online software, such as Google Street View, Google Earth and Bing Maps, allows users to travel through famed landscapes and vistas at the touch of a button. The viewer is thus able to 'travel' through the landscape vista on-screen, and to search a freely accessible online database of vistas 'constructed' by other users worldwide. One might speculate on the consequences of an ever-increasing 'simulation' of the vista, perhaps removing the necessity and desire for seeking out 'real' visual experiences. These technical advances in the modelling, mapping and simulation of vistas may be reflected by the increasing technical precision with which vistas are now defined. Today, planning policies seek to protect vistas with series of lines, angles and GPS coordinates inscribed onto the city plan and modelled using complex computer simulation, as in the London View Management Framework. While these policies are largely successful in securing designated vistas, I would argue that the technical precision advocated by contemporary view protection policy misses – or at least underestimates – the importance of the *values* promoted by such vistas.

This book has argued that values of the picturesque, nostalgia and authenticity continue to play powerful roles in the protection of urban and natural landscapes. Intensified by the collective gaze of millions of citizens, tourists, their cameras and the images they make, economic development pressures take a back-seat to the overwhelming power and ubiquity of this nostalgic picturesque gaze. Possessing the knowledge that these values remain at work in our visual environments, we may begin to read their traces etched into the skylines of our cityscapes, cutting through sites of potential development and determining their urban and architectural form. Ultimately, this book has shown that the meanings associated with the view from Richmond Hill have shifted over the centuries with each subjective reading of the vista, as demonstrated by the view's various narratives – from eighteenth-century Britain as a new classical Arcadia to the nineteenth-century American South as backwards and corrupt, to the exclusionary elitism of South Africa's Special Ratings Areas. Therefore, while policies of view protection adopt a scientific approach to preserving vistas through the geometrical designation of sites with coordinates, lines and planes, these policies are unable to influence the shifting meanings attributed to the vista by the subject. I propose that such a renewed understanding has important implications for contemporary architectural and urban design practice. Politicians, developers, architects and urban planners may be better equipped to discuss *what values* are associated with particular vistas, *by whom, how* they are observed and interpreted, and how these values *shift or evolve* with time. This culturally and historically conscious interpretation of visual environments, a sensibility which seems to have been commonplace at periods in the past, could encourage greater creativity and flexibility, and a move away from the rigid technical specificities of existing policy.

Notes

1. R. Tatnall, Campaign Manifesto for "The Great Indignation 2009", *Restoring Our Heritage and Preserving the View That Named Us Richmond*, 30 June 2009.
2. R. Tatnall, "Development with a View: Visions of Richmond's Future: Vista Here Is as Vital as across Pond", *Richmond Times-Dispatch* (18 February 2007).
3. J. Redmon, "The Debate Is Building: Riverfront Zoning Pits Nature", *Richmond Times-Dispatch* (24 April 2002).
4. T. Rice, "Libby Hill Park – The View That Named Richmond, Virginia", *Richmond Examiner* (8 November 2010).
5. Tatnall, "Development with a View", *Richmond Times-Dispatch*.
6. J. Walker, "Resolution Hails James View: Lawyer Fears Proposal Takes Aim at Project Near Libby Hill Park", *Richmond Times-Dispatch* (6 February 2007).
7. Tatnall, Campaign Manifesto, *Restoring Our Heritage and Preserving the View That Named Us Richmond*.
8. D. Lowenthal, *The Past Is a Foreign Country* (Cambridge: Cambridge University Press, 1985), p. 38.
9. Ibid., p. 197.
10. S. Spender, *Love-Hate Relations: A Study of Anglo-American Sensibilities* (London: Hamish Hamilton, 1974), p. 121.
11. S. Boym, *The Future of Nostalgia* (New York: Basic Books, 2001), p. 80.

Bibliography

Abercrombie, P. "Wren's Plan for London After the Great Fire", *The Town Planning Review,* X(2), (May 1923).
Adams, W. H. ed., *Jefferson and the Arts: An Extended View* (Washington, DC: National Gallery of Art, 1976).
Adler, K. *Pissarro in London* (London: National Gallery Company, 2003).
Alberti, L. B. *Ten Books on Architecture* (London: Tiranti, 1955).
Andrews, M. *The Search for the Picturesque: Landscape Aesthetics and Tourism in Britain, 1760–1800* (Aldershot: Scolar, 1989).
Bach, J. ed., *John Hunter: An Historical Record of Events at Sydney and at Sea, 1787–1792* (Sydney: Royal Australian Historical Society and Angus & Robertson, 1968).
Bacon, F. "Of Gardens" in Spedding, Ellis and Heath, eds., *The Works of Francis Bacon* (London, 1890).
Baines, G. *The Control and Administration of Port Elizabeth's African Population c 1834–1923* (Port Elizabeth, South Africa: Department of History, Vista University, Port Elizabeth Campus, n.d.).
Barkley-Jack, J. *Hawkesbury Settlement Revealed: A New Look at Australia's Third Mainland Settlement 1793–1802* (Dural: Rosenberg Publishing, 2009).
Barnard, E. *Capturing Time: Panoramas of Old Australia* (Canberra, ACT: National Library of Australia, 2012).
Batey, M. *Alexander Pope: The Poet and the Landscape* (London: Barn Elms, 1999).
Batey, M., H. Buttery, D. Lambert and K. Wilkie, *Arcadian Thames* (London: Barn Elms, 1994).
Baudrillard, J. *Simulacra and Simulation* (Ann Arbor: University of Michigan Press, 1994).
Berenson, B. *Italian Painters of the Renaissance* (Oxford: Clarendon Press, 1930).
Berger, J. *Ways of Seeing* (London: BBC & Penguin Books, 1972).
Bonehill, J. and S. Daniels, " 'Real Views from Nature in this Country': Paul Sandby, estate Portraiture and British Landscape Art", *British Art Journal*, March 22 (2009).
Bonyhady, T. *The Colonial Earth* (Melbourne: Miegunyah Press, 2000).
Boon, P. *The Hawkesbury River: A Social and Natural History* (Clayton, Victoria: CSIRO Publishing, 2017).
Boorstin, D. J. *The Image, or What Happened to the American Dream* (New York: Atheneum, 1962).

Bowd, D. G. *Macquarie Country: A History of the Hawkesbury* (Melbourne, Victoria: F. W. Cheshire, 1969).
Boym, S. *The Future of Nostalgia* (New York: Basic Books, 2001).
Braun, G. *Civitates Orbis Terrarum* (Cologne, 1572).
Bruce, W. *Travels to Discover the Source of the Nile* (Edinburgh and London, 1790).
Bryant, J. *Finest Prospects: Three Historic Houses: A Study in London Topography* (London: English Heritage, 1986).
Burnett Barton, G. *History of New South Wales from the Records, vol. 1 Governor Phillip* (Sydney: Charles Potter, 1889).
Bussagli, M. *Piero della Francesco* (Rome, Italy: Giunti Editore, 2007).
Caesar, G. J. *The Conquest of Gaul*, trans. S. A. Handford, rev. J. F. Gardner (Harmondsworth and New York: Penguin Books, 1951).
Carr, E. *Mission 66: Modernism and the National Park Dilemma* (Amherst: University of Massachusetts Press, 2007).
Carter II, E. C. *The Virginia Journals of Benjamin Henry Latrobe 1795–1798* (London and New Haven: Yale University Press, 1977).
Carter II, E. C., J. C. Van Horne and C. E. Brownell, eds., *Latrobe's View of America, 1795–1820: Selections from the Watercolours and Sketches* (New Haven, CT: Yale University Press, 1985).
Cato, J. *The Story of the Camera in Australia* (Melbourne: Institute of Australian Photography, 1977).
Chalcraft, A. and J. Viscardi, *Strawberry Hill: Horace Walpole's Gothic Castle* (London: Frances Lincoln Ltd., 2007).
Ching-Liang Low, G. *White Skins, Black Masks: Representation and Colonialism* (London: Routledge, 1996).
Clendinnen, I. *Dancing with Strangers* (Cambridge: Cambridge University Press, 2003).
Clerisseau, C. *Les Antiquités de la France, Monuments de Nîmes* (Paris: Philippe-Denys Pierres, 1778).
Cloake, J. *Richmond Past: A Visual History of Richmond, Kew, Petersham and Ham* (London: Historical Publications, 1991).
Cohen, S. and K. Nurit, "Place Names in Israel's Ideological Struggles over Administered Territories", *Annals of the Association of American Geographers*, 82 (4) (1992).
Coleman, R. *Reclaiming the Streets: Surveillance, Social Control and the City* (Cullompton, UK: Willan Publishing, 2004).
Colomina, B., A. Brennan and J. Kim, eds. *Cold War Hothouses: Inventing Postwar Culture, from Cockpit to Playboy* (New York: Princeton Architectural Press, 2004).
Connor, J. *The Australian Frontier Wars 1788–1838* (Sydney, NSW: University of New South Wales Press, 2002).
Cookson, B. *Crossing the River* (Edinburgh: Mainstream, 2006).
Cooper, J. F. *Notions of the Americans: Picked up by a Travelling Bachelor* (London: Colburn, 1828).
Crandell, G. *Nature Pictorialized: "The View" in Landscape History* (Baltimore and London: John Hopkins University Press, 1993).
Cunliffe, B. *Iron Age Communities in Britain: An Account of England, Scotland and Wales from the Seventh Century BC until the Roman Conquest* (London: Routledge, 2009).

D'Argenville, D. *La Théorie et la Practique du Jardinage* (Paris, 1709).

Darley, G. "Ian Nairn and Jane Jacobs, the Lessons from Britain and America", *The Journal of Architecture*, 17(5) (2012), pp. 733–746.

Desmond, R. *Kew: The History of the Royal Botanic Gardens* (Kew: The Harvill Press with the Royal Botanic Gardens, 1995), p. 18.

Dixon Hunt, J. and P. Willis, eds., *The Genius of the Place: The English Landscape Garden 1620–1820* (Cambridge, MA and London: MIT Press, 1988).

Dorrian, M. "The Aerial View: Notes for a Cultural History", *STRATES*, vol. 13 (Paris: LADYSS, 2007).

Dunbar, J. *A Prospect of Richmond* (London and New York: White Lion Publishers, 1966).

Dyce, A. ed., "Spring, or Damon" in *The Poetical Works of Alexander Pope* (W. Pickering, 1831).

Early, J. *Romanticism and American Architecture* (New York: A.S. Barnes & Co., 1965).

Edgerton, S. *The Mirror, the Window and the Telescope: How Renaissance Linear Perspective Changed Our Vision of the Universe* (Ithaca and London: Cornell University Press, 2009).

Ellis, M. "'Spectacles within Doors': Panoramas of London in the 1790s", *Romanticism*, 14(2) (2008).

Elwall, R. "How to Like Everything': Townscape and Photography", *The Journal of Architecture*, 17(5) (2012), p. 672.

Evans, R. *The Projective Cast* (Cambridge, MA: MIT Press, 1995).

Fanon, F. *Peau Noire, Masques Blancs* (Paris: Seuil/Points, 1952); C. L. Markmann, trans., *Black Skin, White Masks* (London: Pluto Press, 1986).

Fazio, M. W. and P. A. Snadon, *The Domestic Architecture of Benjamin Henry Latrobe* (Baltimore, MD: JHU Press, 2006).

Fortier, J. *Fortress of Louisbourg* (Toronto: Oxford University Press, 1979).

Foster, H. ed., *Vision and Visuality* (Seattle, WA: DIA Art Foundation, 1988).

Foucault, M. *Discipline and Punish: The Birth of the Prison* (London: Penguin Group, 1977).

Foucault, M. "Panopticism" in N. Leach, ed., *Rethinking Architecture: A Reader in Cultural Theory* (London: Routledge, 1997).

Freeland, J. M. *Architecture in Australia: A History* (Ringwood: Penguin, 1968).

Garrick, D. "The Clandestine Marriage" in *The Dramatic Works of David Garrick, Esq: To Which Is Prefixed a Life of the Author* (London: A. Millar, 1798) vol. 3.

Gilpin, W. *Observations on the River Wye, and Several Parts of South Wales, etc., relative Chiefly to Picturesque Beauty: Made in the Summer of 1770* (London: A. Strahan, 1800).

Girouard, M. *Life in the English Country House: A Social and Architectural History* (New Haven, CT: Yale University Press, 1978).

Girouard, M. *Sweetness and Light* (Oxford: Oxford University Press, 1977).

Grey, G. *Journals of Two Expeditions of Discovery in North-West and Western Australia, during the Years 1837, 38, and 39, under the Authority of Her Majesty's Government Describing Many Newly Discovered, Important, and Fertile Districts, with Observations on the Moral and Physical Condition of the Aboriginal Inhabitants.* 2 vols. (London: T & W Boone, 1841).

Groom, L. *A Steady Hand: Governor Hunter and His First Fleet Sketchbook* (Canberra, ACT: National Library of Australia, 2012).

Hale Smith, M. *Sunshine and Shadow in New York* (New York: J. B. Burr, 1869).
Henderson, M. C. *The City and the Theatre: The History of New York Playhouses* (New York: Back Stage Books, 1973, 2004).
Higgins, H. B. *The Grid Book* (Cambridge, MA: MIT Press, 2009).
Hirst, J. *Sense & Nonsense in Australian History* (Melbourne, VIC: Black Inc. Agenda, 2009).
Hoagland, A. K. and K. A. Breisch, eds., *Constructing Image, Identity, and Place: Perspectives in Vernacular Architecture IX* (Knoxville: The University of Tennessee Press, 2003).
Jackson, J. B. *The Necessity for Ruins: and Other Topics* (Amherst: University of Massachusetts Press, 1980).
Jay, M. "Scopic Regimes of Modernity" in H. Foster, ed., *Vision and Visuality* (New York: New Press, 1988).
Jefferson, T. *Notes on the State of Virginia*, ed. William Peden (Chapel Hill, NC: University of North Carolina Press, 1955).
Jenkins, E. *Falling into Place: The Story of Modern South African Place Names* (Cape Town, South Africa: David Philip, 2007).
Johns, E., A. Sayers, E. M. Kornhauser and A. Ellis, *New Worlds from Old: 19th Century Australian and American Landscapes* (Canberra: National Gallery of Australia, 1998).
Karsken, G. *The Colony: A History of Early Sydney* (Sydney, NSW: Allen & Unwin, 2009).
Kaynor, F. C. "Thomas Tileston Waterman: Student of American Colonial Architecture", *Winterthur Portfolio*, 20(2/3) (1985).
Keegan, T. *Colonial South Africa and the Origins of the Racial Order* (Charlottesville: University of Virginia Press, 1996).
Kipp, D. "Alberti's 'Hidden' Theory of Visual Art", *British Journal of Aesthetics*, 24(3) (1984).
Kirk, J. *The African Middle Class, Cape Liberalism and Resistance to Residential Segregation at Port Elizabeth, South Africa, 1880–1910* (Ann Arbor: University Microfilms International, 1987).
Kohen, J. *The Darug and Their Neighbours: The Traditional Aboriginal Owners of the Sydney Region* (Blacktown, NSW: Blacktown and District Historical Society, 1993).
Lang, J. D. Volume 2 of An Historical and Statistical Account of New South Wales, Both as a Penal Settlement and as a British Colony (Cambridge: Cambridge University Press, 2011), p. 103.
Langhorne, J. *The Poetical Works of William Collins* (New York: Trow & Co., 1848).
Lavoie, C. C. "Architectural Plans and Visions: The Early HABS Program and Its Documentation of Vernacular Architecture", *Perspectives in Vernacular Architecture*, 13(2) (Anniversary Issue, 2006/2007).
Lindstrom, M. J. and H. Bartling, eds., *Suburban Sprawl: Culture, Theory and Politics* (Lanham: Rowman & Littlefield Publishers, Inc., 2003).
Longstaffe-Gowan, T. *The London Town Garden, 1700–1840* (New Haven and London: Yale University Press, 2001).
Lounsbury, C. *The Reconstruction of Williamsburg's First Colonial Capitol, 1928–1934: A Critique* (Williamsburg, VA: Colonial Williamsburg Foundation Library, 1989).

Lowenthal, D. *The Past Is a Foreign Country* (Cambridge: Cambridge University Press, 1985).
Macarthur, J. *The Picturesque: Architecture, Disgust and Other Irregularities* (London: Routledge, 2007).
Macarthur, J. "The Revenge of the Picturesque, Redux", *The Journal of Architecture*, 17(5), (2012), pp. 643–653.
MacColl, D. S. "Richmond Hill and Marble Hill", *Architectural Review* X (1901).
Macquarie, L. *Journals of His Tours in New South Wales and Van Diemen's Land 1810–1822* (Sydney: Trustees of the Public Library of New South Wales, 1956).
Malden, H. E. *A History of the County of Surrey Volume 3* (London: Constable & Company Limited, 1911).
Marks, P. *Imagining Surveillance: Utopian and Dystopian Literature and Film* (Edinburgh: Edinburgh University Press, 2015).
Mason, W. *The English Garden: A Poem* (London, 1778).
Maurice, T. *Richmond Hill: A Descriptive and Historical Poem* (London: W. Bulmer, 1807).
McLuhan, M. *Understanding Media: The Extensions of Man* (Cambridge, MA: MIT Press, 1994).
McPhee, G. *The Architecture of the Visible* (London and New York: Continuum, 2002).
Meeker, R. K. ed., *Collected Short Stories of Ellen Glasgow* (Baton Rouge: Louisiana State University Press, 1963).
Metz, C. *The Imaginary Signifier: Psychoanalysis and the Cinema* (Bloomington: Indiana University Press, 1982).
Mitchell, T. *Journal of an Expedition into the Interior of Tropical Australia in Search of a Route from Sydney to the Gulf of Carpentaria* (London: Longman, Brown, Green, and Longmans 1848).
Msila, V. *A Place to Live: Red Location and Its History from 1903 to 2013* (Port Elizabeth, South Africa: Sun Press, 2014).
Murray, N., N. Shepherd and M. Hall, eds., *Desire Lines: Space, Memory and Identity in the Post-Apartheid City* (London: Routledge, 2007).
Ndletyana, M. "Changing Place Names in Post-Apartheid South Africa: Accounting for the Unevenness", *Social Dynamics: A Journal of African Studies*, 38(1) (2012).
Oxley, J. *Journals of Two Expeditions into the Interior of New South Wales, Undertaken by Order of the British Government in the Years 1817–18* (London: Murray, 1820).
Panofsky, E. "Die Perspektive als 'symbolischen Form'", *Vortrage der Bibliothek Warburg* (1924–5).
Parkin, R. *H. M. Endeavour* (Victoria: The Miegunyah Press, 2003).
Parnell, S. "AR's and AD's Post-War Editorial Policies: The Making of Modern Architecture in Britain", *The Journal of Architecture*, 17(5) (2012), pp. 763–775.
Pendleton Gaines, F. *The Southern Plantation: A Study in the Development and the Accuracy of a Tradition* (New York: Columbia University Press, 1925).
Penn, N. *The Forgotten Frontier: Colonist and Khoisan on the Cape's Northern Frontier in the Eighteenth Century* (Athens, OH: Ohio University Press, 2006).
Perez-Gomez, A. *Architecture and the Crisis of Modern Science* (Cambridge, MA: MIT Press, 1983).
Pope, A. *Epistles*, ed. F. W. Bateson (London: Methuen, 1951).

Pope, A. *An Essay on Criticism* (W. Lewis, 1711).
Powell, M., R. Hesline. "Making Tribes?: Constructing Aboriginal tribal entities in Sydney and coastal NSW from the early colonial period to the present", in *Journal of the Royal Australian Historical Society* vol. 96, no. 2 (December 2010) pp. 115–148.
Quitman Moore, J. "Southern Civilisation: Or the Norman in America", *DeBow's Review*, 32 (Jan–Feb 1862).
Redgrave, J. J. *Port Elizabeth in Bygone Days* (Port Elizabeth, South Africa: Rustica Press, 1947).
Reed, C. V. *Royal Tourists, Colonial Subjects and the Making of a British World 1860–1911* (Manchester: Manchester University Press, 2016).
Reed, N. *Pissarro in West London: Kew, Chiswick and Richmond* (Folkestone: Lilburne Press, 1997).
Repton, H. *Sketches and Hints on Landscape Gardening* (1795).
Rice, H. C. ed., *Travels in North America in the Years 1780, 1781 and 1782* (Chapel Hill, NC: University of North Carolina Press, 1963).
Richards, J. "The Second Half Century", *The Architectural Review* (January, 1947).
Rogers, H. A. ed., *Views of Some of the Most Celebrated By-Gone Pleasure Gardens of London* (London: Dodo Press, 1896).
Ryan, S. *The Cartographic Eye: How Explorers Saw Australia* (Cambridge: Cambridge University Press, 1996).
Said, E. *Orientalism* (London: Pantheon Books, 1978).
Scott, W. *The Heart of Mid-Lothian* (Edinburgh and London: Waverley Novels, 1843).
Sheppard, F.H.W. ed., *Survey of London: St James Westminster* (London: English Heritage, 1960).
Silverman, M. ed., *Black Skin, White Masks: New Interdisciplinary Essays* (Manchester: Manchester University Press, 2005).
Smith, B. and R. Shaw, *The Windsor Group, 1935–1945: An Account of Nine Young Sydney Artists Who Painted in [. . .] Richmond and Especially Windsor* (Collaroy, NSW: Edwards & Shaw, 1989).
Sontag, S. *On Photography* (New York: Picador, 1977).
Sorlin, P. *The Film in History: Restaging the Past* (London: John Wiley & Sons, 1980), pp. viii–ix.
Spender, S. *Love-Hate Relations: A Study of Anglo-American Sensibilities* (London: Hamish Hamilton, 1974).
Sprat, T. *The History of The Royal Society of London, for the Improving of Natural Knowledge* (London: The Royal Society, 1667; 1958), p. 113.
Stanard, M. N. *Windsor Farms: Hauntingly Reminiscent of Old England* (Richmond, VA: Windsor Farms, 1926).
Stern, R.A.M. and J. M. Massengale, eds., *The Anglo-American Suburb* (London: Architectural Design, 1981).
Stewart, L. *Blood Revenge: Murder on the Hawkesbury 1799* (Dural: Rosenberg Publishing, 2015).
Stiverson, G. A. and P. H. Butler III, eds., "Virginia in 1732: The Travel Journal of William Hugh Grove", *Virginia Magazine of History and Biography*, 85 (January 1977).
Strong, R. *The Renaissance Garden in England* (London: Thames & Hudson, 1984).
Strong, R. *The Renaissance Garden in England* (London: Thames & Hudson, 1994).

Sturt, C. *Narrative of an Expedition into Central Australia, Performed under the Authority of Her Majesty's Government, during the Years 1844, 5 and 6 Together with a Notice of the Province of South Australia, in 1847*. 2 vols. (London: T & W Boone, 1849) vol. 1.
Summerson, J. *Architecture in Britain 1530–1830* (Harmondsworth: Penguin, 1979).
Tench, W. *A Complete Account of the Settlement at Port Jackson* (Adelaide: University of Adelaide Press, 2014).
Turbet, P. *The First Frontier: The Occupation of the Sydney Region 1788–1816* (Dural: Rosenberg Publishing, 2011).
Turner, T. *English Garden Design: History and Styles since 1650* (Woodbridge, Suffolk: Antique Collectors' Club, 1986).
Venturi, R. *Learning from Las Vegas: The Forgotten Symbolism of Architectural Form* (Cambridge, MA: MIT Press, 1977).
Virilio, P. *The Vision Machine* (Paris: Galilée, 1992).
Walpole, H. *Essay on Modern Gardening* (Canton, PA: Kirgate Press, 1904).
Waterman, T. T. *Dwellings of Colonial America* (Chapel Hill: The University of North Carolina Press, 1950).
Waterman, T. T. *English Antecedents of Virginia Architecture* (Philadelphia, PA: American Philosophical Society, 1939).
Waterman, T. T. *The Mansions of Virginia 1706–1776* (Chapel Hill: The University of North Carolina Press, 1945).
Watkin, D. *The Architect King: George III and the Culture of the Enlightenment* (London: Royal Collection Publications, 2004).
Watson, S. and K. Gibson, eds., *Postmodern Cities and Spaces* (Oxford: Blackwell, 1995).
Watts, A. A. *Lyrics of the Heart* (London: Longman, 1850).
Webb, S. *Palaeopathology of Aboriginal Australians: Health and Disease across a Hunter-Gatherer Continent* (Cambridge: Cambridge University Press, 1995).
Weddell, A. W. *Richmond Virginia in Old Prints* (Richmond: Johnson Publishing Company, 1932).
Wenger, M. R. ed., *The English Travels of Sir John Percival and William Byrd II: The Percival Diary of 1701* (Columbia, MS: University of Missouri Press, 1989).
West, N. M. *Kodak and the Lens of Nostalgia* (Charlottesville and London: University Press of Virginia, 2000).
Wilkie, K., M. Battaggia, M. Batey, D. Lambert, H. Buttery, J. Pearce, D. Goode and D. Bentley, *The Thames Landscape Strategy* (London: Thames Landscape Steering Group, June 1994).
Willey, K. *When the Sky Fell Down: The Destruction of the Tribes of the Sydney Region 1788–1850s* (Sydney & London: HarperCollins Pty Ltd., 1979).
Wilson, R. G., S. Eyring and K. Marotta, eds., *Re-creating the American Past: Essays on the Colonial Revival* (Charlottesville and London: University of Virginia Press, 2006).
Witz, L. *Apartheid's Festival: Contesting South Africa's National Pasts* (Bloomington: Indiana University Press, 2003).
Wordsworth, W. "Lines Written Near Richmond, upon the Thames at Evening 1790" in *Lyrical Ballads* (Washington, DC: Woodstock Books, 1997).
Wright, L. B. and M. Tinling, eds., *The Secret Diary of William Byrd of Westover, 1709–1712* (Richmond, VA: The Dietz Press, 1941).
Yeoh, B. "Street Names in Colonial Singapore", *Geographical Review*, 82(3) (1992).
Young, A. *Tudor and Jacobean Tournaments* (New York: Sheridan House, 1987).

Index

Note: Figures are denoted with *italicized* page numbers; note information is denoted with n and note number following the page number.

Abercrombie, Patrick 68
Adam, Robert 41, 44, 102
Adams, Abigail 89–90
Adams, John 87, 89
Addington, Henry 46
advertising: photography-related 111–12; preservation efforts to avoid land use for 63–5, *64*; Richmond, Virginia, US view in 111–12; suburbia development 115; transportation-related 49, 51, 56–9, *57*, *59*
aerial view, oblique 11–15, 18, 21
African National Congress (ANC) 173, 181, 182
Afterglow, Foulweather Reach, Hawkesbury River, New South Wales, The (Ashton) 155
Alberti, Leon Battista 12, 19
Alfred, Prince 175
Alpers, Svetlana 18
America (Griffith) 126
American Landscape: A Critical View, The (Nairn) 132
American Mutoscope and Biograph Company 126
Amherst, Jeffrey 89
Analysis of Beauty (Hogarth) 39
anamorphosis 20
ANC (African National Congress) 173, 181, 182
Ancaster, Duke of 26
Ancient Architecture, Restored, and Improved [. . .] in the Gothic Mode for the Ornamenting of Buildings and Gardens (Langley) 45–6

Ancient Monuments Consolidation and Amendment Act (1913, UK) 67, 70
Andrews, Malcolm 14
AR (Architectural Review) 132, 133
architectural design: aerial vantage point in 14–15; artistic representations of *31*, *45*, *102–3*; garden design integration with 20–1, 26, 33–4, *35*, 46, 73n32; gothic 44–6; movement in 102, 136n52; oriental 47, *47*, 197; protected views affected by 1–2; protected views effects on 3; in Richmond, NSW, Australia view *150*, 150–1, 157, *158*, 159, *160*, 163; in Richmond, Virginia, US view 95, 98–100, 101–8, *102–3*, 115–26, *118–19*; in Richmond Hill, Manhattan, New York, US view 87, *88*, 88–9; in Richmond Hill, Port Elizabeth, South Africa view 170, *170*, 172, 176–83, *177*, *180*; in Richmond Hill, Surrey, UK 10–11, 14–15, 16–17, 201, 26–8, 30, *31*, 33–4, *34*, 42–8, *43*, *45*, *47*, 56, 196–7; suburban 56, 115–22, *118–19*
Architectural Review (AR) 132, 133
Argyll, Duke of 33, 91
Aristotle 1
artistic representations: of architectural design *31*, *45*, *102–3*; of garden design 22, 34, *35*, 38–41, *40*, 104, *105*; protected views celebrated in 2, 4; railway-related 55; of Richmond, NSW, Australia view *149*, 152–9, *156*, 162, 163; of Richmond,

Virginia, US view 96, *97–8*, 104, *105*, 107, 127; of Richmond Hill, Manhattan, New York, US view *88*; of Richmond Hill, Port Elizabeth, South Africa view 175; of Richmond Hill, Surrey, UK view 10, 14, 16, 20–1, *25*, 26–8, *27*, *31*, 34, *35*, *36*, 38–41, *40*, *45*, 51–6, *52–3*, 194–5, 196; *see also* advertising; photography
Art of Colouring and Painting Landscapes in Water Colours, The (Lucas) 101
Ashton, Julian Rossi 155
Astor, John Jacob 90
Augusta, Princess 40, 47, 84
authenticity: classical retirement as return to 195; oblique aerial view for 11; picturesque conventions and 192–3, 199–200; preservation efforts for 70, 71; Richmond, NSW, Australia colonial ideals *vs.* 159; Richmond, Virginia, US view claims of 87, 106, 113, 121–2, 125–7, 129, 195, 199–200, 203; Richmond Hill, Port Elizabeth, South Africa claims of 200
automobiles: interstate image corridors and 131–4, 200; Richmond, Virginia scenic views and parkways for 115, 119–20, 123, 124–6, 127–34, 139nn136–7, 140n146, 199, 200
Away Down South (Cobb) 109
axial garden design 15, 17, 20–1, 23, 25–6, 32

Bacon, Francis 18
Baker, Herbert 172
Barton, George Burnett 146
Batey, Mavis 29, 31, 33, 41
Bath Road, Bedford Park (C. Pissarro) 55
Bathurst, Lord 153
Beauclerk, Di 28
Bell, Arthur G. 58
Bentham, Jeremy 99–100, 136n33, 198
Bentham, Samuel 99, 136n36
Berenson, Bernard 19
Berger, John 18–19
Betjeman, John 55–6
Bischoff, Joseph 155
Black Skin, White Masks (Fanon) 170
Blake, Peter 132–3
Boer Wars 169

Bonyhady, T. 155
Boon, Peter 141, 147, 155
Boorstin, D. J. 112, 115, 130, 132
Bottomley, William Lawrence 120–2
Boym, S. 134, 204
Braun, Georg 12
Bridgeman, Charles 33–4, *35*, 38, 41
bridges: in Richmond, NSW, Australia view 160–2, *161*; in Richmond Hill, Surrey, UK view 50, 51–2
Brogan, Patrick 126
Brother Rat 126
Brown, Lancelot "Capability" 38–41, *40*, 50, 55, 84, 94, 196
Bruce, Phillip Alexander 110
Bruce, William 101
Brunelleschi, Filippo 18
Bryant, Julius 33
Bryson, Norman 19
Buccleuch, Duchess of 28, 38
Burke, Edmund 45
Burlington, Lord 30, 32, 33–4, 38, 44, 104, 195
Burnaby, Andrew 93
Burr, Aaron 87, 90
Burt, Charles 61, 63, 65
Butler, Nina 161–2
Byrd, William, I 197, 202
Byrd, William, II 91, 93–4, 95

Caesar 9–10
Cambridge, Richard Owen 41
'camera obscura' 20, 30, 75n100
Campbell, Archibald 91
Campbell, Colen 33–4
Canute 9
Cardigan, Earls of 28
Caroline, Princess 32, 33, 34, 51, 54, 84, 194, 197
Carter, E. C., II 101
Cartesian perspectivalism 18–19
Cartographic Eye: How Explorers Saw Australia, The (Ryan) 143–4
cartography 12
cartoons, indignation at view obstruction in 61, *62*
Cary, Henry 122
Cash, Wilbur Joseph 109
Cassivellaunus 9
Castell, Robert 33
CAWB (Community Action for Windsor's Bridge) 160–2, *161*
Chambers, William 27, 40, 44, 47, *47*–8, 196

Index 215

"Changing Place Names in Post-Apartheid South Africa" (Ndletyana) 175
Charles I 10–11
Charles II 11
Charley, Phillip 157, *158*, 163
Ching-Liang Low, Gail 169
Chiswick House (Ross) 58
Cholmondeley Walk (Heckel) 26
Church Hill 95–8, *97–8*, 101–3, *102–3*, 106–10, *107*, 112, 113–15, *114*, 123
Cicero 195
cinematic view 126–7, 133–4
Civil Works Administration 123
Civitates Orbis Terrarum (Braun) 12
Clandestine Marriage, The (Garrick) 41
Clarence, Duke of 28
Cloake, John 16, 24
Cobb, James 109, 113, 121
Cockerell, Pepys 96, 135n23
Cohen, S. 175
Cole, B. 23
Coleman, Roy 182
Collins, Edward 27
Collins, William 37
colonialism: protected view carried through 3–4, 13–14; Richmond, NSW, Australia settlement via 142–3, 145–7, 150, 151–2, 153, 159–60, 162–3, 164n10, 166n28, 199; Richmond, Virginia, US view re-imagining era of 120–31, *130*, *131*, 133, 195, 200; Richmond Hill, Port Elizabeth, South Africa settlement via 167–73, 175–83, 187, 188n1; *see also* imperial identity
Colonial National Monument/Historic Park 124–5
Colonial Parkway 124–6, 127, 131, 139nn136–7, 200
commerce: advertising in (*see* advertising); commodification of Richmond, Virginia, US view 111–12, 129–30; panorama exhibitions as 14; Richmond, Virginia placement for 91; Richmond Hill, Manhattan, New York developed for 90–1; Richmond Hill, Port Elizabeth, South Africa colonisation and 168
Commission for the Preservation of Natural and Historical Monuments, Relics and Antiques 176

Community Action for Windsor's Bridge (CAWB) 160–2, *161*
Conder, Charles 155–6
conservation efforts *see* preservation efforts
control: aerial view affording sense of 13, 14; visual sense ties to 1, 2
Cook, James 142, 146
Cornman, F. 22
Country and the City (R. Williams) 194
Crais, Clifton 175
Cramton, Louis 125–6
Crandell, Gina 33
Cronin Hastings, Hubert de 132
Cropsey, Jasper Francis 196
Cullen, Gordon 69, 132, 133
cultural history: artistic (*see* artistic representations); colonial (*see* colonialism); literary (*see* literary representations); protected views celebrated in 2
Cunard, William 65–6
Cutshaw, Wilfred 114–15

Darwin, Charles 154
da Vinci, Leonardo 18
Davis, Mike 185–6
Davis, Timothy 127, 131
Death and Life of Great American Cities (Jacobs) 132
de Caus, Solomon 11, 20
Defoe, Daniel 26
Demainbray, Stephen 48
Designs of Buildings Erected or Proposed to be Built in Virginia 1795–1799 (Latrobe) 101, 102
de Stael, Madame 46
de Tocqueville, Alexis 105–6
Dickens, Charles 54
Diocletian, Emperor 114
Discipline and Punish (Foucault) 99
Dixon Hunt, John 23, 32
Domestic Colonial Architecture of Tidewater Virginia (Waterman) 122, 123
Du Faur, Frederick Eccleston 142, 155
Dughet, Gaspar 195
Dunbar, Janet 68–9, 70
Dunmore, John 154
D'Urfey, Tom 17
Dwellings of Colonial America (Waterman) 124
Dysart, Earl of 61, 63

216 Index

Early, James 48, 105
Eastman Kodak Company 111, 112, 116–17
Edgerton, Samuel 12
Edison Company 126
Edward I 10
Edward III 10
Edward Ironside 9
Egbert 9
Elizabeth I 10, 94
Elizabeth II 127, 202
Ellis, Whittaker 61, 63
Enclosure Acts (UK) 74n82
England: Richmond Hill, on the Prince Regent's Birthday (Turner) 53, 53–4
English Antecedents of Virginia Architecture (Waterman) 124
English Garden, The (Mason) 42
English Heritage 69, 70
English landscape movement: Richmond, Virginia, US view influenced by 104, 106; Richmond Hill, Surrey, UK view valued in 2, 3, 4, 70, 71, 196, 201
Epistle to Lord Burlington (Pope) 32
Essay on Criticism, An (Pope) 31
Essay on Landscape, An (Latrobe) 100–1, 104
Essay on Modern Gardening, An (Walpole) 42
Essay on the Picturesque (Price) 46
Evans, Robin 21
Exact Plan of the Royal Palace Gardens and Park at Richmond, An (Rocque) 34, 35, 38

Faerie Queene (Spenser) 42
Fanon, Frantz 170–1, 172
Farm, Richmond, New South Wales, The (Conder) 156
Favenc, Ernest 143
Fazio, M. W. 101
Federal Aid Highway Act (1944, US) 132
Felixstowe poster 56
Fenimore Cooper, James 107, 109
Field, Barron 144
Flinders, Matthew 153
Footbridge at Bedford Park, The (C. Pissarro) 55
Forrester, Robert 152
Fortier, John 133
Fortunate Isles and Their Union, The (Johnson) 20
Foucault, Michel 99–100, 186, 198

France, Alfred 58
Francesca, Piero della 19, 21, 73n62
Fraser, John 142
Frontier Wars: Australian 151–2; South African 167, 178, 188n2

Gaines, Francis Pendleton 109
Garden City movement 116, 196
garden design: architectural design integration with 20–1, 26, 33–4, 35, 46, 73n32; artistic representations of 22, 34, 35, 38–41, 40, 104, 105; axial 15, 17, 20–1, 23, 25–6, 32; geometric 14, 26, 31, 34, 38, 41; imperial identity reflected in 47–9, 197; knot 18; naturalistic 29–32, 34, 39, 47; oblique aerial view of 14–15, 18; oriental 47, 47–9, 197; panorama views in lieu of actual 14; planning policy on 69–70; Renaissance 11, 15, 17, 19–21, 22; in Richmond, NSW, Australia view 157; in Richmond, Virginia, US view 94, 104–5, 105, 121; in Richmond Hill, Surrey, UK view 11, 13–16, 17, 18, 19–21, 22, 23–6, 29–32, 33–4, 35, 38–42, 40, 46, 47, 47–9, 84, 194–5, 196, 197; serpentine 39, 40–2; theatre design and 23–6, 32; theatre of human interaction in 23–6; theorising picturesque conventions in 38–42
Garden History Society 69
Garrick, David 41, 50
Gay, John 30, 196
gaze: colonial or imperial 4, 13, 90, 143, 170–2, 173, 183, 199 (*see also* colonialism; imperial identity); composed scenes for 41; Panopticon design and power of 99–100, 198; perspective of (*see* perspective); picturesque conventions and authority of 192; power of 99–100, 192, 198–9; proprietorial 14; psychological effect of 1; of surveillance 95, 185, 198–9; theoretical understanding of 71, 193; tourist 117, 131
geometric garden design 14, 26, 31, 34, 38, 41
George, Prince 194
George I 34
George II 34
George III 39, 44, 45, 46, 48, 84, 196–7, 198

Index   217

George IV 44, 196
Giant 126
Gilpin, William 55, 58, 69, 100, 144, 154
Glasgow, Ellen 109–10, 121
Glover, Joseph 63–5, 64
Glover, Thomas George 155
godlike view 12, 19
God's Own Junkyard (Blake) 133
gothic architectural design 44–6
Govett, William Romaine 155
Govett's Leap and Grose River Valley, Blue Mountains, New South Wales (von Guérard) 155
Grahame, Kenneth 163
Greater London Plan 68
Greek Revival design 107–8
Grenville, Kate 159
Grey, George 167–8
Griffith, D. W. 126
Grimes, James 148
Grose, Governor 148, 151
Grove, William Hugh 89

HABS (Historic American Buildings Survey) 123–4
Hall, Martin 168, 186
Harrison, Henry 140n146
Hawkesbury, at Wisemans Ferry, The (Ashton) 155
Hawkesbury River 141–2
Hawkesbury River, View No. 13 (Westall) 153
Hawkesbury River: A Social and Natural History, The (Boon) 141
Hawkesbury River with Figures in a Boat: On the Nepean (Piguenit) 155
Hawthorne (James) 85
Heart of Mid-Lothian, The (Scott) 51
Heckel, Augustin 26
Heidegger, Martin 19
Henry, Patrick 95, 123
Henry, Prince 11, 20
Henry V 10
Henry VI 10
Henry VII 10, 83, 193–4
Henry VIII 10, 11, 13
Herradine, Margaret 179
Hesline, Rex 142
Hilditch, George 27, 51–2
Hilliard, Nicholas 18
Hirst, John 152
Historic American Buildings Survey (HABS) 123–4

Hoare, Henry 75–6n129
Hogarth, William 39, 41
Hogenberg, Franz 12
Home as Found (Fenimore Cooper) 107
Horace 29, 31–2, 195
Houblon, Susanna 24
House and Town Planning Act (1909, UK) 68
Howard, Henrietta 30, 33, 38, 91, 195
Howard, John 99
human interaction, garden design for 23–6
Hunter, John 147

Ideal City (Francesca) 19, 73n62
idealised city design 21, 203
idealised English landscape 39–40, 70, 192–3
Imaginary Signifier: Psychoanalysis and the Cinema, The (Metz) 17
imperial identity: Richmond Hill, Port Elizabeth, South Africa settlement and 176, 179; Richmond Hill, Surrey, UK view conveying 13–14, 47–9, 83, 197; *see also* colonialism; national identity
indignation at view obstruction: cartoons of 61, 62; planning policy reflecting 68–70; preservation efforts as outgrowth of 61, 63–8, 70, 71, 201–3; of Richmond, NSW, Australia view 160–2, *161*; of Richmond, Virginia, US view 201–3; of Richmond Hill, Surrey, UK view 17, 50, 61–70, 194, 201; suburban sprawl and 132–3
industrial cities: panorama views of travelling exhibits in 14; Richmond, Virginia realities as 100, 103, 107, 110, 112–13, 129, 199–200; Richmond Hill, Manhattan, New York changes into 90
International Garden Cities Federation 68
interstate image corridors 131–4, 200

Jackson, John 21, 23
Jacobs, Jane 132
James, Henry 85
James, John 14–15
James I 10, 94
Jay, Martin 1, 17, 18, 19
Jefferson, Thomas 95, 99, 103–6, 108, 114, 136n46, 197
Jenkins, Elwyn 175

Jenner, C. 24
Johnson, Ben 20
Johnston, James 14
Joinville, Prince of 28
Jones, Inigo 11, 20, 32
Jowit, Robin 202
Jubilee Fête at Bedford Park (C. Pissarro) 55

Kadi, Palesa 178
Kaynor, F. C. 122
Kent, William 30, *31*, 32, 33–4, *35*, *36*, 38–9, 41, 44
Kim, Jeannie 127
Kimball, Fiske 124
King, Governor 152
King, Phillip Parker 144
King, Sidney E. 127
King Henry's Mound 12–13, 193, 203
Kip, Johannes 21, *22*
Kliot, Nurit 175
Knapp, John 16
Knaresborough poster 56
knot garden design 18
Knyff, Leonard 16, 24, 26
Kodak and the Lens of Nostalgia (West) 111
Kohen, James 151
Ku-ring-gai Chase National Park 142

Lacan, Jacques 99
Landscape, The (Payne Knight) 46
landscapes: English landscape movement 2, 3, 4, 70, 71, 104, 106, 196, 201; garden design in (*see* garden design); protected views of (*see* protected view); Richmond Hill as symbol of paradigm for 4
Langley, Batty 45–6, 196
Lansdowne, Earl of 28
'Lass of Richmond Hill, The' 24–5, *25*, 49, *61*, *62*
Latrobe, Benjamin Henry 95, 96–103, *97–8*, *102–3*, 104–5, *105*, 135n23, 136n33, 197
Latrobe, John 101
Learning from Las Vegas (Venturi) 131
Lee, Robert E. 95, 120
Leigh, Samuel 26, 49
Lewin, John William *149*, 153
Libby Hill Park 106–10, *107*, 112, 113–15, *114*, 201–3
literary representations: protected views celebrated in 2, 4; of Richmond, NSW, Australia view 144, 148, 159; of Richmond, Virginia, US view 95, *96*, 100–1, 105, 108–10, 121; of Richmond Hill, Manhattan, New York, US view 89–90; of Richmond Hill, Surrey, UK view 17, 24, 29–32, 35–8, *36*, 42, 48, 49, 50–3, 58, 60–1, 68–9, 148, 194–5, 196
Lloyd, John Henry 56, *57*
Locke, Joseph 51–2
London, UK: aerial view of 12; axial design for rebuilding of 21; origins of protected view of 2, 4, 9–79, 192–205; planning and protected views in 1–2, 68–70, 193, 203–5; railway expansion from 49, 51–2, 54–8; suburbia developments around 49, 54–6; *View Management Framework* for 1, 2, 193, 203–4
London Missionary Society 170
London Town Garden, The (Longstaffe-Gowen) 14
Long, Sydney 157
Longstaffe-Gowen, Todd 14
Lordship Lane Station (C. Pissarro) 55
Lorrain, Claude 33, 42, 50, 85, 101, 195
Lounsbury, Carl 125
Lowenthal, David 85, 116, 202–3
Lucas, Fielding 101
Lucretius 18
Lycett, Joseph 153–4
Lyrics of the Heart (Watts) 48

Macarthur, John 152
Mackay, George 104
Macquarie, Governor 147–8, 150, 151, 152, 153
Mahboub, Dennis 159, *160*
Makoma 178
Mandela, Nelson 181
Mansions of Virginia, The (Waterman) 124
Marlow, William 27
Marot, Daniel 11
Martens, Conrad 154–5
Mason, Herbert 204
Mason, William 42
Maurice, Thomas 50–1
Mayo, William 93
McCubbin, Frederick 155
McLuhan, Marshall 1, 111
McPhee, Gina 20
Merriman, John 172

Metz, Christian 17
military: aerial view in surveys for 13, 72n24; Richmond, Virginia, US engagement with 95, 113–15, *114*, 120, 198; Richmond Hill, Manhattan, New York, US use by 87, 89; sightline 1
Mills, Robert 108, 197
Milton, John 31
Mind of the South, The (Cash) 109
Mitchell, Thomas 144, 145
Mollet, André 11, 21
Mollet, Gabriel 11
Molyneux, Charles William 28
Molyneux, Samuel 21
Montagu, Duke of 28, 38, 40
Mordecai, Samuel 108
Moritz, Charles 23–4
Morris, Roger 33–4, *34*, 44
Morse, Henry G. 117
Mortier, Abraham 88–9
motorcars *see* automobiles
Mr and Mrs Garrick by the Shakespeare Temple at Hampton (Zoffany) 41
Msila, Vuyisile 172
Murray, Noëleen 172, 181
Muthesius, Herman 56
Mylne, Robert 27, 28

Nairn, Ian 132–3
national identity: Australian cultural and 148, 157, 161–2, 163; Richmond, Virginia, US view symbolising 95–8, 197–8; Richmond Hill, Surrey, UK view forging 13, 70, 196–7; South African 172, 176–7, 178; *see also* imperial identity; patriotic symbolism
National Park Service (NPS) 126–7, 200
National Society of the Colonial Dames of America (NSCDA) 119, 122–3
National Trust 67
Native Land Act (1913, South Africa) 172–3
naturalistic garden design 29–32, 34, 39, 47
Ndletyana, Mcebisi 175, 181
newspapers: photography and 137–8n85
New Urbanism 186
New Worlds from Old: 19th Century Australian and American Landscapes (Johns et al.) 157
Nolen, John 116

Northumberland, Duke of 41
nostalgia: for colonial era design 120–31, *130*, *131*, 159–60, 162, 176–8, 183, 195; photography as tool for 111, 113, 116–17; Richmond Hill, Surrey, UK view evoking 37, 53, 71, 83, 84–6, 193–5; for romanticized South 109–10, 113, 114, 119, 120, 122–4, 127, 195, 198, 203; sense of, exploring 193–5
NPS (National Park Service) 126–7, 200
NSCDA (National Society of the Colonial Dames of America) 119, 122–3
Nutting, Wallace 116, 117, 123, 127

oblique aerial view 11–15, 18, 21
Observations on the River Wye [. . .] 1770 (Gilpin) 154
obstruction of view indignation *see* indignation at view obstruction
Ode Occasion'd by the Death of Mr. Thomson (Collins) 37
Ode to Cynthia Walking on Richmond Hill (D'Urfey) 17
'Of Gardens' (Bacon) 18
Old South: What Made It, What Destroyed It, What Has Replaced It, The (Rutherford) 110
Olmsted, Frederick Law 139n137
origins of protected view: advertising in 49, 51, 56–9, *57*, *59*; architectural design in 10–11, 14–15, 16–17, 20–1, 26–8, 30, *31*, 33–4, *34*, 42–8, *43*, *45*, *47*, 56, 196–7; bridges in 50, 51–2; Cartesian perspectivalism in 18–19; colonial expansion in 3–4, 13–14; early history of 9–10; garden design in 11, 13–16, 17, 18, 19–21, 22, 23–6, 29–32, 33–4, *35*, 38–42, *40*, 46, *47*, 47–9, 84, 194–5, 196, 197; idealised vision in 21, 40, 70, 192–3, 203; imperial identity in 13–14, 47–9, 83, 197; indignation at obstruction of view 17, 50, 61–70, 194, 201; Italian influence on 33–4, *34*, *35*; literary representations of 17, 24, 29–32, 35–8, *36*, 42, 48, 49, 50–3, 58, 60–1, 68–9, 148, 194–5, 196; national identity in 13, 70, 196–7; oblique aerial view in 11–15, 18, 21; overview of 2, 9, 70–1; patriotic symbolism in 44–6, *47*, *53*, 53–4; picturesque

220 *Index*

conventions in, persistence of 49–61; picturesque conventions in, theorising 2, 4, 38–44, 192–3, 195–6; planning policy in 68–70, 193; pleasure gardens in 23–6, 27, 54–5, 194; postcards in 58, 60, *60*; preservation efforts for 61, 63–8, 70, 71, 201; railway expansion and 49, 51–2, 54–8; Richmond Hill, Surrey, UK view 2, 4, 9–79, 192–205; royal retreat influencing 10–11; scopic regimes in 17–19; suburbia developments and 49, 54–6; Terrace Walk in 15–17, 22, 24–7, 31, 40–1, 194; theatre design in 20, 22–3, 32
Orkney, Earl of 91

Page, Thomas Nelson 109
Paine, James 50, 51
Palladio, Andrea 33
Palmer, Fyshe 151–2
Panofsky, Erwin 19
Panopticon designs 99–100, 186, 198
Panorama of the Thames from London to Richmond (Leigh) 26, 49
panoramas: commercial potential of 14; in Richmond, NSW, Australia view 143–4; in Richmond, Virginia, US view *107*
Pass above Wisemans Ferry, Hawkesbury River (Martens) 154
Pastoral Dialogue between Richmond Lodge and Marble Hill (Swift) 60
patriotic symbolism 44–6, 47, *53*, 53–4; *see also* national identity
Payne Knight, Richard 38, 46, 133
Percival, John 94
perspective: axial 15, 17, 20–1, 23, 25–6, 32; Cartesian 18–19; illusion and 20, 32; oblique aerial 11–15, 18, 21; theatre and 20, 22–3
Petersham and Ham Lands and Footpath Bill (1896, UK) 61, 63
Peterson, Charles E. 124–5
Pevsner, Nikolaus 132
Pew, Michael 16–17
Phillip, Governor 142–3, 145–6
photography: newspapers and 137–8n85; planning influenced by 133; for railway poster art 56; of Richmond, NSW, Australia view 155, 162; of Richmond, Virginia, US view 111–14, *114*, 116–17, 199; of Richmond Hill, Surrey, UK view 58, *60*

Piano, Renzo 2
Picturesque Atlas of Australasia, The 155
picturesque conventions: gothic's absorption of 44–6; history and evolution of 11, 32, 34, 71, 84, 192–3; Latrobe and 100–1, 103; movement in 134; oblique aerial view characterising 15; persistence of 49–61, 159–60; planning policies based on 3, 4, 193, 196; in Richmond, NSW, Australia view 143–5, 159–60, 164n16; in Richmond, Virginia, US view 100–1, 103, 104, 113, 116–17, 119–21, 124–6, 134, 136n46, 197–8, 199–200, 202; theorising 2, 4, 38–44, 192–3, 195–6; *see also specific representations (e.g. artistic representations)*
Piguenit, William Charles 155
Piper, John 133
Pissaro, Ludovic Rodo 77n202
Pissarro, Camille 55–6
Pissarro, Lucien 55–6
planning policy: establishment of, in Britain 68; interstate parkways and 131–4; picturesque vision influencing 3, 4, 193, 196; protected views in 1–2, 3, 4, 68–70, 193, 203–5; suburbia developments and 49
Plan of Mr. Pope's Garden as It Was Left at His Death, A (Serle) 31
Plan of the City of New York (Ratzer) 88
Plans, Elevations, and Sections of Noblemen and Gentlemen's Houses (Paine) 50
Plato 1
pleasure gardens 23–6, 27, 54–5, 194
Plettenberg, Joachim van 188n1
Pliny 33, 195
Pocahontas, Princess 197
poetic representation *see* literary representations
political power *see* power
'Pompey Pillar' 114
Pope, Alexander: Bathurst influenced by 153–4; Richmond, Virginia, US influence of 91, 94; Richmond Hill, Surrey, UK influence of 28–32, *31*, 33, 34, 37–8, 42, 45, 52, 195–6
Port Elizabeth Historical Society 178, 183
Port Elizabeth Ratepayers Association 178

Index 221

postcards: of motor courts/motels 130, *131*; of Richmond, Virginia, US view 111–12, 115, 116, 199; of Richmond Hill, Surrey, UK view 58, 60, *60*
Poussin, Gaspar 33
Poussin, Nicholas 195
Powell, Michael 142
power: aerial view affording sense of 12, 13, 14, 21; Panopticon designs and 99–100; Richmond Hill, Manhattan, New York, US symbolizing 90; visual sense ties to 1 (*see also* gaze)
Poynter, Edward 65, 67
preservation efforts: for Richmond, NSW, Australia view 142; for Richmond, Virginia, US view 119, 122–4, 201–3; for Richmond Hill, Port Elizabeth, South Africa view 176–83, *177*, *180*; for Richmond Hill, Surrey, UK view 61, 63–8, 70, 71, 201
Price, Uvedale 38, 46, 133
Prior, T. A. 28
prison design 1, 99–100, 136n33, 186, 198
Private Mailing Card Act (1898, US) 111
Progressive Drawing Book, The (J. Latrobe) 101
Prospect Mount 143, 145, 146
Prospect of Richmond, A (Dunbar) 68–9
protected views: cultural history of (*see* cultural history); development affected by 3; development effects on 1–2; origins of 2, 3–4, 9–79, 192–5; Richmond views as (*see* Richmond entries)
protests *see* indignation at view obstruction
Purcell, Henry 17
Purple Noon's Transparent Might, The (Streeton) *156*, 156–7

Queensberry, Duchess of 30

railway: Richmond, Virginia tourism tied to 112, 199; Richmond Hill, Port Elizabeth, South Africa growth with 169; Richmond Hill, Surrey, UK view and expansion of 49, 51–2, 54–8
Rain, Steam and Speed (Turner) 55
Randolph, William, III 122
Rassool, Ciraj 181
Ratzer, Bernard 88

Raworth, William 155
'Red Books' (Repton) 46
Reed, C. V. 173, 175–6
Rees, Amanda 186
Reflections of the Revolution in France (Burke) 45
regional identity: Richmond, Virginia, US view symbolising 113–14, 198
Renaissance garden design 11, 15, 17, 19–21, *22*
Renaissance Garden in England, The (Strong) 15
Repton, Humphrey 46, 100, 196, 203
Repton, John 'Jack' 100, 133
Reynolds, Joshua 26–7, *27*, *43*, 44, 196
Rhododendron Dell at Kew (C. Pissarro) 55
Richards, J. I. 27
Richmond (France) 58
Richmond, Brunswick, Germany 40, 84
Richmond, Charles Lennox, Duke of 134n1
Richmond, New South Wales, Australia view: architectural design in *150*, 150–1, 157, *158*, 159, *160*, 163; artistic representations of *149*, 152–9, *156*, 162, 163; colonialism and 142–3, 145–7, 150, 151–2, 153, 159–60, 162–3, 164n10, 166n28, 199; development of landscape in 147–51; 'discovery' of 142–3; Frontier Wars and 151–2; garden design in 157; gaze on 143, 199; Hawkesbury River in 141–2; history of 3, 141–66; indignation at obstruction of 160–2, *161*; literary representations of 144, 148, 159; national identity and 148, 157, 161–2, 163; overview of 141, 162–3; panoramas in 143–4; photographs of 155, 162; picturesque conventions in 143–5, 159–60, 164n16; preservation efforts for 142; Prospect Mount in 143, 145, 146; The Terrace in 148, *149*, 157; three Richmond Hills in 145–7; topography of 143
Richmond, North Yorkshire, UK 83, 194
Richmond, Petersham and Ham Open Spaces Act (1902, UK) 49, 67, 68, 70, 71, 193, 201
Richmond, Virginia, US view: architectural design in 95, 98–100, 101–8, *102–3*, 115–26, *118–19*;

222 Index

artistic representations of 96, 97–8, 104, *105*, 107, 127; automobiles and 115, 119–20, 123, 124–6, 127–34, 139nn136–7, 140n146, 199, 200; Church Hill in 95–8, 97–8, 101–3, *102–3*, 106–10, *107*, 112, 113–15, *114*, 123; cinema capturing 126–7, 133–4; civic beautification of 111, 120, 129; colonial era re-imagined in 120–31, *130*, *131*, 133, 195, 200; Colonial Parkway and 124–6, 127, 131, 139nn136–7, 200; commodification of 111–12, 129–30; Confederate memorial in 113–15, *114*, 120, 198; 'Flush Time' period influence on 107; Gamble Hill Park in 112–13; Garden City movement in 116, 196; garden design in 94, 104–5, *105*, 121; gaze on 95, 99–100, 117, 131, 198–9; history of 3, 91–140; indignation at obstruction of 201–3; interstate image corridors and 131–4, 200; Jefferson's influence on 95, 99, 103–6, 108, 114, 136n46, 197; Latrobe on 95, 96–103, *97–8*, *102–3*, 104–5, *105*, 197; Libby Hill Park in 106–10, *107*, 112, 113–15, *114*, 201–3; literary representations of 95, 96, 100–1, 105, 108–10, 121; monumentalising of 113–15, *114*, 120, 198; national identity/nationalism symbolised by 95–8, 197–8; overview of 87–8, 134; photographs of 111–14, *114*, 116–17, 199; picturesque conventions and 100–1, 103, 104, 113, 116–17, 119–21, 124–6, 134, 136n46, 197–8, 199–200, 202; planning policies for 131–4; plans for 91, *92–3*, *97*; postcards of 111–12, 115, 116, 199; preservation efforts for 119, 122–4, 201–3; prison design in 99–100, 136n33, 198; regional identity symbolised in 113–14, 198; romanticized South and 109–10, 113, 114, 119, 120, 122–4, 127, 195, 198, 203; scenic byways as staged representation of 127–31, *128*, *130*, *131*, 140n146, 200; suburbia developments in 91, *92–3*, 106, 115–22, *118–19*, 133–4; topography of 91; Windsor Farms in 115–20, *118–19*
Richmond, William Blake 67

Richmond Bridge, View from My Window at Richmond (L. Pissarro) 55
Richmond Bridge Act (1772, UK) 50
Richmond for Walking . . . and Other Jollities poster 58, *59*
Richmond from beneath the Railway Bridge (Hilditch) 51–2
Richmond Hill, Manhattan, New York, US view: architectural design in 87, 88, 88–9; artistic representations of *88*; history of 3, 88–91; literary representations of 89–90; overview of 87–8; subdivision and development of 90–1; topography of 89, *90*
Richmond Hill, Port Elizabeth, South Africa view: architectural design in 170, *170*, 172, 176–83, *177*, *180*; artistic representations of 175; colonialism and 167–73, 175–83, 187, 188n1; gentrification of 176–83, *177*, *180*; heritage projects and historical attractions in 176–83, *177*, *180*, 186; history of 4, 167–91; national identity/nationalism and 172, 176–7, *178*; overview of 167–8, 187; place names or toponyms in 173, 175, 176, 179, 181, 182, 187, 200; policing and surveillance of 4, 183–6, *184*, *185*, 187, *187*, 200; preservation efforts for 176–83, *177*, *180*; racial segregation and 168–73, *170–2*, 181, 188n1, 188n4; redevelopment and subdivision in 173–6, *174*; Richmond Park in 173, *174*; Special Ratings Area administration of 183–6, *184*, *185*, 187, 200; Strangers' Location in 168–73, *170–2*, 188n17, 188n19
Richmond Hill, Surrey, UK view: advertising including 49, 51, 56–9, *57*, *59*; architectural design in 10–11, 14–15, 16–17, 20–1, 26–8, 30, *31*, 33–4, *34*, 42–8, *43*, *45*, *47*, 56, 196–7; artistic representations of 10, 14, 16, 20–1, *25*, 26–8, *27*, *31*, 34, *35*, *36*, 38–41, *40*, *45*, 51–6, *52–3*, 194–5, 196; bridges in 50, 51–2; Cartesian perspectivalism in 18–19; colonial expansion of ideals of 3–4, 13–14; early history of 9–10; English landscape movement on 2, 3, 70, 71, 196, 201; garden design in 11, 13–16, 17, 18, 19–21, 22,

23–6, 29–32, 33–4, *35*, 38–42, *40*, 46, *47*, 47–9, 84, 194–5, 196, 197; gaze on 11–15, 17–23, 25–6, 32, 41, 71, 198; idealised vision of 21, 40, 70, 192–3, 203; imperial identity in 13–14, 47–9, 83, 197; indignation at obstruction of 17, 50, 61–70, 194, 201; Italian influence on 33–4, *34*, *35*; King Henry's Mound in 12–13, 193, 203; literary representations of 17, 24, 29–32, 35–8, *36*, 42, 48, 49, 50–3, 58, 60–1, 68–9, 148, 194–5, 196; name of, prevalence of use 84, *85*, 134n1; national identity tied to 13, 70, 196–7; nostalgia about 37, 53, 71, 83, 84–6, 193–95; oblique aerial view 11–15, 18, 21; origins of protected status of 2, 4, 9–79, 192–205; overview of 70–1; patriotic symbolism of 44–6, 47, *53*, 53–4; picturesque conventions in, persistence of 49–61; picturesque conventions in, theorising 2, 4, 38–44, 192–3, 195–6; planning policy on 68–70, 193; pleasure garden of 23–6, 27, 54–5, 194; postcards of 58, 60, *60*; preservation efforts for 61, 63–8, 70, 71, 201; railway expansion and 49, 51–2, 54–8; royal retreat to 10–11; scopic regimes in 17–19; suburbia developments and 49, 54–6; Terrace Walk in 15–17, 22, 24–7, 31, 40–1, 194; theatre design in 20, 22–3, 32; topography of 84, 89, 143; translating images of (*see* translation of Richmond images)
Richmond Hill: A Descriptive and Historical Poem (Maurice) 50–1
Richmond Hill View Executive Committee 67
Richmond Park (Bell) 58
Richmond Past (Cloake) 16
Richmond-upon-Thames view *see* Richmond Hill, Surrey, UK view
Richmond Virginia in Old Prints (Weddell) 118–19
Riebeeck, Jan van 178
Rise of the New South, The (Bruce) 110
Roberts, Tom 155
Rockefeller, John, Jr. 125, 200
Rocque, John 34, *35*, 38, 203
Rolfe, Rebecca 197
Romance of a Plain Man (Glasgow) 109–10
Rosa, Salvator 144

Ross, Vera 58
Royal Fine Art Commission 69
Royal National Park (Sydney) 142
Ruse, James 147
Rutherford, Mildred 110
Ryan, Simon 143–4, 145

Said, Edward 185
Sandby, Paul 13, 42, 72n24
Sandby, Thomas 72n24
Sarah Thornhill (Grenville) 159
Scenic Roads Study 129
scopic regimes 17–19
Scott, Walter 51, 196
Searle, E. W. 155
Seaside, Florida, US 186
Seasons, The (Thompson) 35–7, *36*, 58, 148
Secret River, The (Grenville) 159
Sefton, Earl of 28
Sentry-Box Reach, Hawkesbury River, New South Wales (Ashton) 155
Serle, John 31
Servi, Constantino dei 20
'Shard' 2
Sharland, Charles 56
Shaw, Richard Norman 56
Shepherd, Nick 172, 181
Shepstone, Theophilus 168–9
Silver Thames, The (Way) 58
Sketches and Hints on Landscape Gardening (Repton) 46
Slade, George Penkivil 155
Slattery, Kevin 184–5
Smith, Harry 178
Smythson, Robert 13, 20
Snadon, P. A. 101
Soane, John 54
Society for the Protection of Ancient Buildings 67
Soja, Edward 182
Solomon, Saul 175
Sontag, Susan 113
Sorrell, Alan 58
Southcote, Philip 42
Southern Historical Society 113
Southern Mystique, The (Zinn) 109
Southwell, Robert 91
Special Ratings Area (SRA) administration 183–6, *184*, *185*, 187, 200
Spence, Joseph 32
Spender, Stephen 203
Spenser, Edmund 42

Spotswood, Susanna 100
'Spring' (Pope) 29
'Spring' (Thompson) 36
Springtime 1888, Pugh's Lagoon, Richmond (Conder) 156
SRA (Special Ratings Area) administration 183–6, *184*, *185*, 187, 200
Stafford, Marquess of 28
States Beautiful (Nutting) 116
St. Aubyn, Lady 27
steamboat travel 49–51
Streeton, Arthur 155, *156*, 156–7
Strickland, William 101
Strong, Roy 13, 15, 17–18, 20, 26
Sturt, Charles 145
suburbia developments: indignation for sprawl of 132–3; in Richmond, Virginia, US 91, *92–3*, 106, 115–22, *118–19*, 133–4; Richmond Hill, Surrey, UK view and 49, 54–6
'Summer' (Pope) 29
Summerson, John 33
surveillance: digital 1; gaze of 95, 185, 198–9; prison design for 99–100; in Richmond Hill, Port Elizabeth, South Africa 4, 183–6, *184*, *185*, 187, *187*, 200
Swift, Jonathan 30, 37, 60–1, 153–4, 196
Switzer, Stephen 14

Talman, William 11
Tatnall, Rick 201–2
Taylor, Jacqueline 118
Taylor, Robert 26, 48, 96, 99, 135n23
Temple, John 89
Tench, Watkin 148
Terrace, Richmond Hill, The (Hilditch) 27
Terrace Walk 15–17, 22, 24–7, 31, 40–1, 194
Terry, Harry 162
Thames at Richmond, The (L. Pissarro) 55
Thames at Syon, The (Wilson) 39, *40*
Thames Connections (Wilkie) 69
Thames Landscape Strategy 69–70
theatre design: garden design and 23–6, 32; perspective and 20, 22–3; scenery in 22–3, 32
Theatrum Orbis Terrarum 12
The Theory and Practice of Gardening, The (James) 14–15
Thompson, James 35–7, *36*, 38, 58, 148, 196

Thomson's Aeolian Harp (Turner) 52, *52*
Three Essays on Picturesque Beauty (Gilpin) 69
Tiebout, Cornelius *88*
Too Much of a Good Thing (Lloyd) 56, 57
Town Eclogues (Jenner) 24
Town Planning Association 68
Townscape (Cullen) 69, 133
Townshend, George 28
Train, Bedford Park, Train (C. Pissarro) 55
translation of Richmond images: overview of 83–6, 192–205; in Richmond, NSW, Australia view 3, 141–66, 199; in Richmond, Virginia, US view 3, 87–8, 91–140, 195–203; in Richmond Hill, Manhattan, New York, US view 3, 87–91; in Richmond Hill, Port Elizabeth, South Africa view 4, 167–91, 200
Travels to Discover the Source of the Nile (Bruce) 101
Trimming the Pie Crust (Nutting) 117
trompe-l'oeil 20
Truman Show, The 186
Turley, G. E. 182
Turner, J.M.W. *52–3*, *52–4*, 55–6, 196
Tusculum (Pliny) 33
Tyler, John 110, 140n146

UNESCO World Heritage Sites 1
universal man, Renaissance 18, 19, 20
Upper Nepean, New South Wales, The (Piguenit) 155
Urry, J. 117

Valentyn, Francois 168
Valley of the Grose, The (Bischoff) 155
Valley of the Thomas (Sharland) 56
vanishing point 18
Vaux, Calvert 139n137
Venturi, Robert 131
Vernacular Architecture Society of South Africa 176
View: An Exhibition on Richmond Hill 202
View from Richmond, Looking towards Twickenham, A (Marlow) 27
View from the Road, The (Lynch, Appleyard & Myers) 133
View from the Terrace, Richmond postcard 58, 60, *60*

View in Hampton Garden with Mr and Mrs Garrick Taking Tea, A (Zoffany) 41
View of Nepean River, at the Cow Pastures, New South Wales (Lycett) 154
View of Pope's Villa during Its Dilapidation, A (Turner) 53
View of the Banks of the River Hawkesbury (after Lewin) *149*
'View of the Present Seat of his Excel. the Vice President of the United States, A' (Tiebout) *88*
View of the River Hawkesbury N.S. Wales, A (Lewin) 153
View of the Seat of the Late David Garrick, Esq., A 41
View of the Wilderness with the Alhambra, the Pagoda and the Mosque, A (Chambers) 47
View of Wilberforce, on the Banks of the River Hawkesbury New South Wales (Lycett) 154
View of Windsor upon the Hawkesbury River (Lycett) 154
View on the Terrace, Richmond postcard 60
Views in Australia (Lycett) 153
Villas of the Ancients Illustrated (Castell) 33
Vint, Thomas 124
Virgil 29, 85
Virginia Historical Society 117–18, 119
Virginia Journals (Latrobe) 96
Virilio, Paul 20
visual sense: gaze as (*see* gaze); Panopticon revolution of 99; picturesque (*see* picturesque conventions); planning-based protection of 1–2, 3, 4 (*see also* protected views); privileged status of 1, 2, 4
Vitruvius Britannicus (Campbell) 33–4
von Guérard, Eugene 155

Waechter, Max 65, 67
Walpole, Horace 28, 39, 41–4, *43*, 45, 46, 50, 196
Walton, James 176

Washington, George 87, 89, 95
Waterhole on the Hawkesbury River, A (Ashton) 155
Waterman, Thomas Tileston 122, 123, 124–5
Watkin, David 40, 45, 47, 84
Watts, Alaric 48
Way, Thomas Robert 58
Weddell, Alexander and Virginia 117–20, 123
Wellesley, Marquess 28
West, Nancy Martha 111–12
Westall, William 153
Wilder, L. Douglas 202
Wilkie, Kim 69
William III 11
Williams, Raymond 194
Williams, T. C. 116, 117
Williams, Trerick John 58
Wilson, Alexander 152
Wilson, Richard 39, 40
Wilson, Richard Guy 123
Wind in the Willows (Grahame) 163
Windsor Farms 115–20, *118–19*
Wisemans Ferry (Martens) 154
Witz, Leslie 178
Wolfe, Thomas 110
Wolsey, Cardinal 11
Woolff, Nic 177–8
Wordsworth, William 37–8, 196
Work of William Lawrence Bottomley in Richmond, The (O'Neal & Weeks) 120
Works in Architecture (Adam) 102
Wren, Christopher 11, 21, 203
written representations *see* literary representations
Wyatt, James 44, *45*
Wyatville, Jeffry 44–5
Wyngaerde, Anton van den 10, 14, 21, 83

Xego, Mike 182–3

Yeoh, B. 175
Young, Arthur 39

Zinn, Howard 109
Zoffany, Johann 41